city baby
new york

The Ultimate Parenting Guide for New York Parents from Pregnancy Through Preschool

By Pamela Weinberg and Kelly Ashton

Universe Publishing

For our City Babies:
Rebecca, Benjamin, Alexander, and Angela

First published in the United States of America in 2010
by UNIVERSE PUBLISHING,
A Division of Rizzoli International Publications, Inc.
300 Park Avenue South
New York, NY 10010
www.rizzoliusa.com

© 2010, 2005, 2003, 2001, 1997 by Pamela Weinberg and Kelly Ashton
First Universe edition published in 2003
Previously published by City and Company
Design by Headcase Design
Cover Illustrations by Mary Lynn Blasutta

2010 2011 2012 2013 / 10 9 8 7 6 5 4 3 2 1
Fourth Edition
Printed in the United States

ISBN-13: 978-0-7893-2030-8
Library of Congress Catalog Control Number: 2010924306

Publisher's Note: Neither Universe Publishing nor the authors have any interest, financial or personal,
in the locations listed in this book. No fees were paid or services rendered in exchange for inclusion in these pages.
Please also note that while every effort was made to ensure accuracy at the time of publication, it is always best to call ahead
to confirm that the information is still up-to-date.

contents

part one

Preparing for Your Baby: Everything You Need to Know!

part two
Shopping for Your Baby: Everything You Need

Acknowledgments

We would like to thank the following people for their encouragement, support, and expert advice in the writing of this book: Matthew Weinberg, Carlo Sant Albano, Susan and Joel Kastin, Sander and Mechele Flaum, Harris and Angela Ashton, Ronni Soled, Laura Deutsch, Tara Mandy Frischling, Tolulope Edionwe, and Marci Blinderman. We would also like to thank Peter at Albee's, Leslie at West Side Kids, and Beth Puffer of Bank Street Bookstore, who sat with us for hours going over every new toy, stroller, and book on the market.

With great appreciation to Cara Scherker for assistance in updating each and every entry and with special thanks and gratitude to Claire L. Gierczak and Elizabeth Smith at Universe, whose invaluable help and advice made this book possible.

Preface to the Fourth Edition

And the babies keep on coming!

Since the first edition of *City Baby* was published more than thirteen years ago in 1997, we've witnessed a baby boom here in New York. More and more couples are opting to raise their children in the Big Apple. It is hard not to notice that many families are having as many as three and four children and still deciding that New York City can't be beat for raising a family. There are indeed (single and double) strollers everywhere—uptown, downtown, and Brooklyn, too. Amazingly, New York continues to be a kindler, gentler, kid-friendly town, no longer just a stop on the way to the suburbs. Dare we say we told you so?

We knew we were on to something when the first edition of *City Baby* quickly went into second and third printings. The book filled a niche. There was nothing like it, and we were delighted to find parents virtually lining up to buy a copy. We caught the attention of television news shows, newspapers, and parenting magazines. The local weekly *Midtown Resident* called *City Baby* "the Fodor's of baby guides," while news anchor Carol Jenkins on Fox News at Noon exclaimed, "Everybody should have a book like this. It's great! What a wonderful idea!" We were hailed as authorities on the awesome experience of childbirth and child care, as well as on children's shopping and activities in Manhattan. For two years, we wrote a column on kid-friendly restaurants in the city. We spoke at the New York Junior League and at several Jewish centers, and Pamela launched a luncheon series for new mothers.

Thirteen years later, our connection to new and expectant moms continues to be strong. Despite the fact that her city babies are now city teens, Pamela speaks regularly at various events all over New York City on topics including traveling with your baby, ten great things to do with your baby in New York, and shopping for your new baby. She is a featured blogger on www.nycmomsblog.com, writing about issues pertaining to raising children in New York City. Kelly has a teen and a preteen and keeps up with all the city baby news from her home in Italy. Do we see a *City Baby Italia* in our future?

We are pleased to present the fourth edition of *City Baby New York* with all new and updated entries. We have added a wealth of new stores, equipment, and even a handy survey on what current new parents think is the best of the best of everything. So pack us into your baby bag, load up the stroller, and take us along for the incredible ride called parenthood. Whether you're an experienced mother or a new mother, we know that *City Baby New York* will remain your New York baby "bible."

—— PAMELA WEINBERG AND KELLY ASHTON

introduction

Unfortunately, when I had my first child sixteen years ago, *City Baby New York* hadn't been published yet. I was twenty-eight years old, had never changed a diaper, and none of my friends had kids. Even though I'd lived in New York City my entire life, I had no idea where to find a Lamaze class, get help with breastfeeding, buy a crib, or meet other new moms. Motherhood was a brand-new adventure, and I eventually managed to figure out everything I needed to know. A few years later, my good friend Kelly Ashton teamed up with Pamela Weinberg when they realized that smart, savvy New Yorkers needed a go-to guide about parenthood—and *City Baby New York* quickly became a must-read for new moms and dads.

Just as I was learning how to parent a preteen, my new husband and I decided to have another child. Despite the fact that I'd been an editor at Parents magazine for more than a decade, having a baby is still daunting—and I've been incredibly grateful to have the latest edition of *City Baby New York* as a resource this time around. How things have changed! You can now find great maternity clothes in black, and there's so much new gear. The stroller choices alone are mind boggling. Although my friends wondered how I could go back to diapers and sleep deprivation, I think that being an older mom has helped me relax and relish every day. I've also discovered that New York City is more baby friendly than ever.

Without a doubt, being a parent is the most challenging and rewarding job you'll ever have. Your time is precious, and Pamela and Kelly have done all the research so you don't have to. Having their updated insider information at your fingertips will make motherhood much less stressful; instead of making phone calls to hunt down what you need, you can take a shower or a nap—or just sit on a park bench with your baby. My best advice: Be good to yourself and get all the help you can—from your spouse, parents, friends, lactation consultants, magazines, websites, and other new moms—and don't feel guilty that you're not perfect. What's really important is having patience, perspective, and a sense of humor.

—*Diane Debrovner*
Deputy Editor, *Parents* magazine

from obstetric care to childbirth

Congratulations! The pregnancy test is positive! Tell the prospective grandparents, aunts, and uncles about the new addition to the clan, then start making the decisions that will keep you busy for the next nine months. First, you will have to consider:

* Who will provide you with prenatal care throughout your pregnancy?
* Who will deliver your baby?
* Where will your baby be born?

Who will look after you and your baby during your pregnancy? Basically, you have two choices: a doctor (who may be the obstetrician/gynecologist you saw in your pre-pregnancy days or another doctor you select at this time) or a midwife. Both of these professionals will essentially perform the same service—meet with you during your pregnancy to monitor your progression and help deliver your baby on the big day.

Where your baby will be born is easy: a hospital, a birthing center, or at home. Yes, the occasional New York City baby has made his or her way into the world via taxi cab in the middle of the Triboro Bridge, but that is a remote possibility. Chances are, you'll make it to the right place at the right time.

You have had the good sense (or blind luck) to be having a baby in a city that seems to have an obstetrician on every other block and some of the best hospitals in the world. Finding excellent care won't be a problem.

This chapter provides everything you need to know about the birthing business in New York—doctors, midwives, hospitals, birthing centers, childbirth preparation classes, labor coaches, lactation consultants, and more.

Looking back on our own birthing experiences with all four of our children, we know that being comfortable with and having confidence in your doctor is the most important part of a positive birth experience. All of the hospitals and birthing centers we list have the qualifications to provide an excellent birthing experience, whether you choose to deliver with an obstetrician or a midwife.

the birth attendant

Whether it's an obstetrician or midwife, you should choose this person as soon as you discover you're pregnant.

Obstetricians

Most women in New York deliver their babies in a hospital under the care of an obstetrician. You probably already have an obstetrician/gynecologist whom you've been seeing for annual checkups, and you may be perfectly happy to continue together throughout your pregnancy. But you may want to find a new doctor for one of several reasons: your current ob/gyn is fine for the routine checkups, but friends have told you about a wonderful new doctor; your ob/gyn is farther away from your apartment than you'd like; your ob/gyn is affiliated with a hospital that doesn't appeal to you; or you may be over thirty-five years old, considered high risk, and want an ob/gyn who specializes in high-risk pregnancies.

If you're a high-maintenance mom, especially a first-timer, you may want an ob/gyn that is very good at hand-holding, one who gets on the phone to comfort you every time you call, or tells you to come into the office. If you are more laid back, you might want an ob/gyn more in keeping with that style. If you're comfortable and happy with your current ob/gyn, stick with her. If you would like to find someone else, do so. With the large number of good obstetricians in New York, you can afford to pick and choose.

To find an obstetrician:

⁘ Ask friends who have had babies or the mother down the hall in your apartment building.

⁘ A recommendation based on the personal experience of a woman who's already been through what you're just beginning is a good way to go.

⁘ Ask your internist or general practitioner to recommend an obstetrician.

⁘ Call the hospital where you would like to deliver, and ask for a referral from the obstetrical department. (After you check out the hospital chart starting on page 20, you may find a hospital that is especially suited to your needs.)

⁘ Go to the library and look up New York magazine's most recent "The Best Doctors in New York" issue.

⁘ Call or visit the website of the New York County Medical Society (212-684-4670; www.nycms.org) for a listing of obstetricians who practice in the city.

Once you have a candidate or two, call for a consultation. Any doctor should be willing to sit down with you and discuss what you can expect over the next nine months and during the birth. Come for your appointment armed with a list of questions, a pen and pad, and your husband or partner—two listeners are better than one.

After this initial consultation, you should be able to decide whether this is the doctor for you. He or she should listen to you carefully, answer your questions thoroughly, and inspire your trust. You need to feel confident that this doctor will be there for you any time night or day during your pregnancy. Feeling confident and comfortable with your ob/gyn is the most important thing.

Here are some questions that you should ask:

⁘ Are you part of a group practice? If so, will I see the other doctors in the practice? What is the likelihood that you will deliver my baby, rather than one of your colleagues? (Ask when the doctor typically takes vacation. You will be able to figure out what month you are delivering, so inquire early on. Many doctors take off two weeks in March and also during the Christmas and New Year holidays, when the private schools are on break.) Do you have school-age children?

⁘ How often will I need to have an office visit?

⁘ What tests should I expect to have and when?

⁘ What is the fee for a vaginal birth? Cesarean birth? What extra charges should I expect? (Many good doctors now charge the same fee for a vaginal or a cesarean delivery, because they do not want to be accused of performing unnecessary cesareans.)

⁘ What are your thoughts on natural childbirth, anesthesia, episiotomy, cesarean section, induced labor? (Ask these and other questions about the doctor's birthing philosophy that are of concern to you.)

⁘ With which hospital are you affiliated? Does the

hospital have birthing rooms; labor, delivery, and recovery rooms; rooming-in for baby and husband; a neonatal intensive care unit?

❋ What do you consider "high risk" birth factors?

❋ How do I get answers to my questions between visits? If you are busy, is there another doctor in the office who will take my call?

❋ Do you have nurses trained to answer basic prenatal questions? (Obstetricians spend half their day doing hospital deliveries or patient check-ins, so it is important to know that if your doctor is not there, someone will be available to answer your questions in a timely manner.)

While you're at the doctor's office for your consultation, check out the waiting room. If you can, ask one or two of the pregnant women leafing through the latest *Parents* magazine how long they usually wait to see the doctor. Routine visits should take about ten minutes, and there is nothing more frustrating than waiting an hour for a ten-minute visit. Also, ask whether the doctor works in a collaborative way with patients, making joint decisions, or whether he likes to call the shots. Again, the doctor's personality must jibe with yours.

The usual schedule for visiting your ob/gyn in a low-risk, normal pregnancy is every three weeks for the first seven months, every two weeks in the eighth month, and every week in the ninth month. Of course, this may vary with different practices, and if your pregnancy is high risk you may see your doctor more often.

Some common tests to expect in the course of your pregnancy are:

❋ *Sonogram.* Typically, a woman has two or three sonograms (ultrasounds) during her pregnancy. The first will be done in the second month (about nine weeks) to date her pregnancy; the second more extensive sonogram will be done in the fifth month (about twenty weeks), sometimes at the hospital, to check the growth and internal organs of the fetus; a third may be done in the ninth month (about thirty-six weeks) to get an idea of the baby's size and position.

❋ *MSAFP* (Maternal Serum Alpha-Fetoprotein Screening) The MSAFP screening is performed in the fourth month (sixteen to eighteen weeks). This simple blood test determines the levels of alpha-fetoprotein (blood protein) present in the mother's blood. High or low levels may indicate serious problems in the development of the fetus. If the MSAFP level comes back either too high or too low, the doctor will probably recommend a second test to confirm the results of the first.

❋ *Amniocentesis.* Known to moms as an amnio, this procedure is performed in the fourth month (sixteen to eighteen weeks) of pregnancy. The technician, guided by an ultrasound image of the uterus, inserts a long hollow needle through the woman's abdominal wall and withdraws a small amount of amniotic fluid. Amniocentesis is recommended for women over thirty-five (although many women over thirty choose to have it performed as well) and in cases in which genetic disorders or chromosomal abnormalities might be suspected.

These tests and procedures are routine, and the obstetrician you choose will have conducted, ordered, or overseen them on hundreds of pregnant women before you. But remember: this is your pregnancy. You should feel perfectly comfortable asking what you think are "dumb questions" about the need for tests and what the results mean. If you are thirty-five or older, you are considered high risk in New York City. Statistics show that women over thirty-five have a slightly greater risk of problems during pregnancy. Other circumstances can also determine a high-risk pregnancy—a previous period of infertility, multiple miscarriages, high blood pressure, diabetes, obesity, and other serious health problems. Make sure your doctor knows your full medical history.

A number of obstetricians specialize in high-risk pregnancies. New York magazine's "The Best Doctors in New York" issue lists many of them. Your own ob/gyn can also refer you to such a specialist. Or call the obstetrical department of any of the hospitals (starting on page 20), and ask for a referral based upon your specific needs.

Midwives

A growing number of New York women opt for a midwife, rather than an obstetrician, to guide them through pregnancy and delivery. A midwife may be a good fit for you if you're low risk, and if you like the idea of working one-on-one. A midwife will likely be more available than an obstetrician to talk with you about the emotional aspects of what you're experiencing, and will probably be more oriented toward natural childbirth.

If this sounds good to you, you will want to find a Certified Nurse Midwife (CNM), a registered nurse

who has undergone extensive formal training through an accredited nurse-midwifery program. The American College of Nurse Midwives (ACNM), based in Washington, D.C., provides midwife certification nationally and sets the standards for the practice of nurse-midwifery. Only ACNM-certified midwives are able to practice in hospitals. Midwives can prescribe pain medications for women in labor and they can call an anesthesiologist when in a hospital.

Two other categories of midwives are Direct Entry Midwives, often referred to as Lay Midwives, and Physician-Assistant Midwives. The latter may also be certified through the ACNM and therefore can practice in hospitals. Direct Entry Midwives, trained through a combination of coursework and apprenticeship, are not permitted to practice in hospitals but do perform or assist at many home births in the New York City area. Home births have been in the news lately, sparked by the documentary *The Business of Being Born* (2008), which was produced by the '90s talk-show host Ricki Lake. This film has become a cult favorite among moms considering home births, but it has also come under scrutiny because it highlights all of the positives but few of the risks associated with home births.

When you choose a CNM, find out about her hospital affiliation. You may prefer to deliver in a birthing center or at home, but in the event of a medical complication, it is critical that your practitioner has access to a hospital nearby. Many CNMs in New York do practice in hospitals and will deliver your baby in the same birthing rooms that the obstetricians use.

With a CNM, you can expect the same schedule you would have with an obstetrician: a visit every three or four weeks at the beginning of your pregnancy, every three weeks in the seventh month, every two weeks in the eighth month, and every week in the ninth month. Like an obstetrician, the midwife will ask how you are feeling and if you have any questions. She will give you an external exam, take your blood pressure and weight, and listen to the baby's heartbeat.

If you would like to check out midwifery, call any of the names listed here, and set up an appointment for a consultation, just as you would for an obstetrician. Use the list of questions we have provided for choosing an obstetrician (see page 12). In addition, you may be especially interested in learning how the midwife will help you through the stages of labor and delivery, the point at which the practices of CNMs and obstetricians usually differ. Many CNMs are skilled at relaxing and preparing the perineum so that anesthesia and episiotomies are rarely necessary.

The following is a list of the hospital-based independent Certified Nurse Midwife practices in New York City:

CBS Midwifery, Inc.

Barbara Sellars (affiliated with St. Luke's-Roosevelt Hospital Center)
103 Fifth Avenue at 17th Street
212-366-4699
www.nycmidwives.com

Risa Lynn Klein, CNM

360 First Avenue at 21st Street, Suite MH
212-477-1325
917-806-4992
email: rlkbirth@aol.com

Risa Lynn Klein is a certified Bradley childbirth educator who has been teaching group and private classes, as well as refresher classes, for over twenty years. Risa is a certified nurse and midwife, and offers gynecological and contraceptive care, in addition to being a breastfeeding consultant. Risa herself took Bradley classes and gave birth to her daughter (now twenty) naturally. The experience changed her life; she left a career in television production for one in birth production. Risa is also licensed in New Jersey where she maintains another office (110 Clifton Avenue, Clifton, NJ; 973-614-1171).

Midwifery of Manhattan

(affiliated with St. Luke's-Roosevelt Hospital Center)
330 West 58th Street at Ninth Avenue, #505
212-957-3006
www.midwiferyofmanhattan.com

Cara Muhlhahn, CNM

646 East 11th Street at Avenue C, #3C
212-388-1837
email: info@cmmidwifery.com
www.cmmidwifery.com

Cara is a graduate of Columbia University School of Nursing, and has practiced as a midwife since 1991. Prior to opening her private practice in 1996, she practiced midwifery at Beth Israel Medical Center and Maternity Center, Inc. Cara has recently published her memoir entitled *Labor of Love: A Midwife's Memoir*, and was the midwife featured in the Ricki Lake documentary, *The Business of Being Born*.

❋ *Martine Jean-Baptiste, CNM, CCE*
212-769-4578; 718-230-4789
email: midwife@classicsoul.com
A certified nurse midwife, registered nurse, and certified childbirth educator, Martine has worked in women's health since 1986. She has served on the Childbirth Education Association of Metropolitan New York (CEA/MNY) board since 1993. In June 2000, she and Karen Jefferson, CM, established a homebirth practice, JJB Midwifery. They provide pre-conceptual counseling, prenatal care, homebirth, well-woman gynecology, and family planning and contraception.

Note: You and your doctor or midwife should decide jointly, based on your wishes and her expertise, on a birthing plan for the big day. Sometime after you begin your visits, but well before your due date, decide what will happen regarding anesthesia, IVs, and episiotomies. Your ideal birthing plan (barring any unexpected surprises) should be in writing, in your doctor's file, and on hand at the hospital when you arrive.

the birth place

Hospitals

All obstetricians are affiliated with a hospital, or maybe two, so once you have selected your obstetrician you will deliver at her hospital.

If you are still in the process of choosing an obstetrician, you may want to work backward—find the hospital you prefer, and then find an agreeable

Top Ten Hospital Tips

1. Decide whether you want a private room before you go into labor.
2. Bring a pillow with a colored pillowcase from home.
3. Bring your robe and slippers.
4. Bring a bath towel and washcloth. (Hospital towels are tiny!)
5. Bring sanitary napkins.
6. Have a friend or family member present as much as possible to go for drinks, run errands, and get the nurse.
7. Have key phone numbers with you—baby nurse, furniture delivery, mohel, etc.
8. Call your insurance company as soon as possible after the baby is born.
9. Rest as much as possible: you are not going to get much rest for the next ten years.
10. Let the nurse feed the baby at 2 or 3 a.m. if you are not exclusively breastfeeding.

You need your sleep!

obstetrician who practices there. Knowing as much as you can about the place your baby will be born is very helpful and comforting.

Here's what's important to know about the hospital: the number of birthing rooms, cesarean rate, level of care provided in the neonatal unit, policies on husbands in the delivery room, rooming-in band

and baby staying overnight in your room), and sibling and family visitors. New York has many hospitals, but some are newer and more comfortable than others. Mount Sinai and Roosevelt hospitals have decorated their labor, delivery, and recovery rooms with Laura Ashley–style touches, so they feel more like a bedroom than a hospital room. While it may be tempting to choose a hospital based upon decor, trust us when we tell you that once you are in labor, the color of the wallpaper in the labor room will be the last thing on your mind.

New York Presbyterian Hospital was one of the last to renovate. When Kelly delivered Alexander it looked like a war zone, but the new wing that was built is state-of-the-art and beautiful, and it continues to provide outstanding care.

We toured all of the private hospitals in New York City where babies are delivered and found them to be similar in many ways. They provide birthing beds, showers, or squatting bars to help your labor and delivery. And in most, if not all, cases, it is your own doctor or midwife—not the hospital or staff—who makes the important decisions concerning your labor.

Other general points to keep in mind:

❖ All the hospitals allow you to preregister. This is a good idea, because once you are in labor, you won't want to fill out forms—registering in advance can keep the paperwork to a minimum upon your arrival.

❖ Be sure to check your insurance company's policy on length of hospital stay permitted for childbirth. Most insurance companies cover either a twenty-four or forty-eight-hour stay for a vaginal delivery and three to four days for a cesarean delivery.

❖ Contact your insurance company when you become pregnant so that later there won't be any problems with the forms you submit. Some insurance companies require notification before you check into the hospital.

❖ Private rooms are available at these hospitals. But keep in mind that the cost of a private room is not covered by insurance—your out-of-pocket expenses will cost you at least $300 per night. Rooming-in for husbands and newborns is permitted in all hospitals in a private room. (In some hospitals it is also permitted in a semi-private room so long as your roommate doesn't object.)

❖ All the hospitals have twenty-four-hour parking lots nearby and will provide you with a list. Find out which hospital entrance to use in case you arrive in the middle of the night.

❖ All hospitals offer weekly classes for new mothers: bathing the baby, breastfeeding, and basic child care. If you cannot make it to a class, ask the nurses, who are trained to help. From our own experience, you must ask to have these lessons. You are in charge, so speak up about your needs.

❖ Many of the hospitals have extremely generous visiting hours. The nurse conducting our tour at New York Hospital gave excellent advice in this regard: She said to be selfish and careful about your visitors for your own health and well-being and for that of the baby. Use your hospital stay to get some rest, if possible, and to bond with your baby. There will be plenty of time for visitors when you and your baby get home.

❖ Bring two pillows from home for your postpartum room. You will be a lot more comfortable sleeping on your own pillows, as most hospital pillows are flat as a board. Make sure your pillowcases are any color but white so they don't get mixed in with the hospital laundry.

❊ You should also consider bringing towels from home. If you plan to shower at the hospital, the bath towels are the size of face towels, and can barely fit around a postpartum woman's body!

After touring ten hospitals, we became experts at predicting the questions we'd most often hear from fellow expectant parents:

❊ Can we bring music into the delivery room?
❊ Can the baby be wrapped in a receiving blanket that we bring from home instead of a regulation hospital blanket?
❊ Can we dim the lights in the labor room?
❊ Can my husband/partner cut the umbilical cord?

The answer to all these questions is yes, but we can tell you that once labor begins your only concern is delivering that baby any way you can, music or no music.

The chart on the following pages provides information to consider while evaluating the hospital in which you will deliver your baby. It includes:

Hospital: The name, address, key phone numbers, and visiting hours.

Labor rooms: The number and type of delivery rooms. In a labor, delivery, and recovery room, known as an LDR room, you will do just that before you are transferred to a postpartum

room. An operating room is where cesareans and complicated vaginal births take place. A labor room is for labor only. A delivery room is where you will be taken when you are ten centimeters dilated and ready to deliver. From delivery you go to a recovery room for one to two hours before going to your own room, where you will stay until you leave the hospital.

Midwives: Hospitals with midwives on staff, and those which allow midwives to deliver babies.

Cesarean birthrate: Numbers indicate the percentage of births by cesarean section each year. The percentages listed are the most recent figures available from each hospital. Generally, hospitals with midwives have the lowest rates; hospitals with a large infertility/high-risk patient base (very New York City) have the highest. The New York cesarean rate for 2006 (the most recent statistics available) is over 31 percent.

Nursery level: Neonatal intensive care units are classified in Levels I through IV, with Level IV being the most advanced. Choosing a hospital with a Level III or Level IV nursery is recommended, especially for high-risk pregnancies.

Classes: Prenatal classes for women and their husbands or partners, including Lamaze, breastfeeding, and preparation for cesarean birth. These classes are given at the hospital (unless otherwise noted), and you must sign up in advance. For second-time moms, many hospitals offer sibling classes. Pamela took Rebecca to

Hospital

Beth Israel Medical Center
16th Street and
First Avenue
212-420-2000 (General)
212-420-2999 (Classes)
212-420-2935 (Patient Care)
www.wehealny.org
visiting hours:
General: 11 a.m.–8 p.m.
Fathers: 10 a.m.–10 p.m.
24 hrs. in private rooms

Labor Rms/other

LDR Rooms: 13
Recovery Rooms: 4
Operating Rooms: 2
Midwives: Yes. Midwives deliver in LDR and birthing rooms at the Birthing Center.
Cesarean rate: 35%
Nursery level: III
Has mother/baby nursing (family centered—the same nurse takes care of you and your baby). One of the largest midwifery programs in the state—over 10 percent of births are delivered by a midwife. All birthing rooms are private and beautifully decorated, and furnished with an easy chair that can be converted into a bed.

Classes

Childbirth Preparation (Lamaze); Baby Care Basics; Preparation for Parenthood Series (Strategies the First Three Months After Delivery); Breastfeeding; Labor Review/Refresher; Meet the Doulas (Free Monthly Information Session); Babysaver CPR and Child Safety; Sibling Preparation

---

Lenox Hill Hospital
100 East 77th Street
between Lexington and
Park avenues
212-434-2000 (General)
212-434-2273 (Parents Education)
212-434-3152 (Babies' Club)
www.lenoxhillhospital.org
visiting hours
General: 12–1:30 p.m.,
7–8 p.m.
Fathers: 24 hrsx
Family: 3–8 p.m.

11 LDR/3 Operating
1 Recovery Suite (holds 8)
Midwives: No
Cesarean rate: 25.7%
Nursery level: III
Many of our friends have delivered here over the years. Some of the best child/birth preparation classes are offered here. Also, we hear great praise for the outstanding nurses in the maternity ward.

Patients are referred to the 92nd Street Y (212-996-1100; www.92y.org) for classes discussing childbirth preparation, infant care, CPR, and physical fitness. Nurses offer natural childbirth classes on location.

Hospital	Labor Rms/other	Classes
The Mount Sinai Medical Center One Gustave L. Levy Place, Klingenstein Pavilion The Jo Carole and Ronald S. Lauder Center for Maternity Care 1176 Fifth Avenue at 98th Street 212-241-6500 (General) 212-241-7491 (Women's & Children's Office) 212-241-6578 (Breastfeeding Warm Line) www.mountsinai.org **visiting hours** General: 11 a.m.–9 p.m. Fathers: 11 a.m.–9 p.m.	14 LDR/ 1 Recovery (holds 4 women) 3 Operating Midwives: Yes Cesarean rate: 32.7% Nursery level IV LDR rooms are decorated with Laura Ashley in mind and resemble hotel rooms more than hospital rooms. Pamela had both her children at Mount Sinai and was thrilled with the care she received. Pamela's daughter Rebecca was in intensive care for seven days, and Pamela credits Mount Sinai with saving her life.	Lamaze Techniques; Cesarean Education; Breastfeeding; Infant Care
New York-Presbyterian Hospital / Columbia University Medical Center / Sloane Hospital for Women* 3959 Broadway at 166th Street www.nyp.org 212-305-2500 (General) 212-305-2040 (Consultants) 212-342-1759 (Admitting) **visiting hours:** General: 12–8:30 p.m. Fathers/Siblings: flexible hours	LDR Rooms: 10 (6 beds are dedicated exclusively to patients requiring high-risk monitoring) Operating Rooms: 3 Midwives: No. Cesarean rate: 35.4% Nursery level: III Aesthetically, the most impressive. Spacious postpartum rooms (both private and semi-private) are beautifully decorated with a bathroom and shower. Moms bring baby to postpartum floor by themselves which provides for nice bonding time. There is also an on-staff post-natal masseuse available. You may have up to two people with you during labor and photography and video are permitted with prior permission. *The Allen Pavilion (5141 Broadway at 220th Street, 212-932-4142) is available for low-risk patients, and offers a full serv-	ice labor and deliver suite including nine newly decorated LDRs, and two surgical suites for Cesarean sections as well as a Level II nursery. Preparation for Childbirth; Breastfeeding; Cesarean Birth; Sibling Tours

Hospital	Labor Rms/other	Classes
New York Presbyterian Hospital at the New York Weill Cornell Center 525 East 68th Street between York Avenue and East River 212-746-5454 (General) 212-746-3215 (Parenthood Prep.) www.nyp.org **visiting hours:** General: 11 a.m.–8 p.m. Partners: 24 hrs.	LDR Rooms: 12 Operating Rooms: 2 Recover: 1 (holds 4) Midwives: No Cesarean rate: 28% Nursery Level: IV Private rooms are lovely and roomy. Kelly delivered Angela and Alexander here and although she was very happy the first time, the new renovations have made this first-class hospital even better.	Lamaze; Breastfeeding; Multiples Class; E-learning (online Childbirth Education Program); Sibling Classes; Discharge/ Baby care; Breastfeeding; Mother's Support Group; Walk-In Breastfeeding Support Group
New York University Medical Center / Langone Medical Center 550 First Avenue at 32nd Street 212-263-7300 (General) 212-263-7201 (Classes) www.nyubaby.org **visiting hours:** General: 12–8 p.m. Fathers/Family: before 10 p.m.	LDR Rooms: 10 Operating rooms: 3 (recovery area with 3 beds) Private Mother-Baby Units: 4 Midwives: Yes Cesarean rate: 32% Nursery Level: III/ Neonatal ICU One of the first NYC hospitals to renovate in style, NYU is pristine. It has very modern facilities with a TV/VCR/CD player, refrigerator, and shower in each room. Spacious birthing rooms (LDR) with rockers and wood floors.	Preparing for Childbirth; Sibling Class; Breastfeeding Class; Breastfeeding Support Group; American Heart Association Infant: Child and Adult CPR Course; Heartsaver Pediatric First Aid CPR Course; Neonatal Intensive Care Unit (NICU); CPR Course

Hospital

St. Luke's Roosevelt Hospital
1000 Tenth Avenue at
59th Street
212-523-4000 (General)
212-523-6222 (Classes)
nywomenshealth.org
visiting hours:
General: 11a.m.–8:30
p.m.
Fathers: 24 hours

Labor Rms/other

LDR Rooms: 10
Birthing Center beds: 12
Operating Rooms: 3
Midwives: Yes.
Cesarean rate: 25.7%
Nursery Level: III
New York City's only in-hospital birthing center is located one floor away from their new, state-of-the-art complete labor and delivery facilities. Center has Jacuzzis, kitchen, special meals, fancy decor, and allows siblings to observe birth. Private birthing rooms are furnished with a rocking chair and an easy chair, which converts to a bed. Both facilities provide the option of a private room, and allow for a midwife, anesthesia, and labor-inducing drugs.

Classes

Preconception; Choices in Childbirth; Lamaze classes (multiple types), Film, Reunion; Prepared Parenthood Film and Discussion; Introduction to the Birthing Center; Early Discharge from the Birthing Center; Hypnobirthing Workshop; Baby Care and Feeding; Baby Care/Feeding (in Japanese); Dad Day; Infant CPR: Birth to 12 Months; Infant/Child CPR: Birth to 8 years; Child CPR and First Aid: One to 8 Years; Prenatal Yoga; Pets and Babies; Breastfeeding; Breastfeeding for Multiples; Vaginal Birth After Cesarean Section (VBAC) Refresher; Sibling Preparation: Mommy and Me Yoga; New Parent Breastfeeding Support Group; Parenting of Toddlers one at Mt. Sinai before Benjamin was born, and it was an excellent way to prepare her for having a new baby at home.

In addition we've included any unique features about the hospital.

Birthing Centers

If you choose a midwife, she may deliver at one of the hospitals listed above or at a birthing center. Many women find the nonhospital-like atmosphere and amenities of the birthing center enormously appealing.

Not only your husband or coach, but your mother, father, best friend, and your new baby's older brother or sister can be with you throughout your birth experience. During your labor you can usually walk around, sip tea, or relax in a Jacuzzi or tub, all of which many women find more labor-enhancing and less alarming than being in a hospital bed hooked up to a monitor. At a birthing center, you can choose to labor and even deliver your baby in a special tub of soothing warm water!

One caveat to delivering at a birthing center: You must be committed to a natural childbirth. No pain relief, such as Demerol or an epidural block, can be administered.

One birthing center exists in Manhattan:

❖ *The Birthing Center*
(affiliated with to St. Luke's-Roosevelt Hospital Center)
1000 Tenth Avenue bet. 58th and 59th streets
212-523-BABY

www.nywomenshealth.com

If the idea of a birthing center appeals to you, call to schedule a tour and an interview with the director. You also can ask for a CNM referral. Or, call a midwife who is affiliated with it (see page 15) and schedule a consultation.

Note: Ask detailed questions about what procedures the center follows should a medical emergency arise at the time of delivery.

childbirth methods

Once the who and the where of your pregnancy and delivery have been settled, you will start to focus—more and more as you grow and grow—on the how of it all. What are the best, easiest, and most pain-free ways to get that baby out?

As you talk with other pregnant women and new mothers, you will hear about the relative merits of one birthing technique over another. Here is a very short course on the three best-known and popular.

The Lamaze Method

This method, named after its developer, Dr. Fernand Lamaze, head of an obstetrical clinic in Paris in 1950, is popularly, if not entirely accurately, known as childbirth without pain. The method combines learned breathing techniques (the "hoo-hoo-hoo, hee-hee-hee") used during contractions, with relaxation exercises designed to help a woman get through labor comfortably.

Most hospitals offer Lamaze classes. Call to sign up. (Also, most of the obstetrical nurses are trained in Lamaze and can assist your coach in the labor room if needed.) Couples usually begin Lamaze in the seventh month.

Some large obstetrical practices also offer Lamaze or will make referrals to private instructors, so ask your obstetrician or midwife. Kelly took Lamaze with Fritzi Kallop (212-906-9255) and was very happy with her. Kallop, formerly an R.N. at New York Presbyterian Hospital, is very funny and down to earth, answers questions day and night, and is there for you long after the birth of your little one.

❋ *Lamaze International*
800-368-4404
email: info@lamaze.org
www.lamaze.org
The Lamaze International website offers an extensive list of qualified instructors and classes that are offered in your particular area. They also have a link to their *Lamaze* magazine, where you can gain very insightful parenting tips and suggestions.

The Bradley Method Husband-Coached Childbirth

This method was developed by Dr. Robert A. Bradley, a Toronto-based obstetrician. The Bradley Method is based on a calming pattern of relaxation, deep abdominal breathing, and close teamwork between husband (or partner) and wife. Bradley's goal is a completely unmedicated pregnancy (no aspirin or cold remedies) and labor and birth (no epidural block or Pitocin).

With Bradley, the pregnant woman learns vari-

ous positions for first-, second-, and third-stage labor. She is encouraged to approach her entire pregnancy as training for labor and to prepare her muscles for birth and her breasts for nursing.

Few New York City hospitals offer Bradley instruction for childbirth. To find the name of a certified Bradley instructor in your area, write to:

❋ *The American Academy of Husband-Coached Childbirth*
P.O. Box 5224
Sherman Oaks, CA 91413
800-4-ABIRTH
www.bradleybirth.com

❋ *Mindful Birth NY*
Mary Esther Malloy-Hopwood, MA, CCE, CD(DONA), CLC
See website for various locations in NYC.
347-276-2819
email: info@mindfulbirthny.com
www.mindfulbirthny.com
Mary teaches childbirth classes with the Bradley Method in Relaxation Techniques, Mind-Focusing Practices, Massage and Labor Positions, Anatomy and Physiology of Labor, Pregnancy Nutrition, and Breastfeeding & Postpartum.

Water Labor and Water Birth

Water birth, popular in Russia since the 1960s, has attracted a small but enthusiastic number of supporters in the United States. Studies have shown that warm water can reduce the hours and stress of labor, offers support to the laboring woman, and helps relax blood flow which makes the baby's journey into the world easier.

Some women use this method's water-filled tub only as a comfort during labor. Others deliver while still in the tub, and the baby takes his first breaths while most of his body is submerged in water, a gentle and familiar medium from his time in the womb.

The Birthing Center at Roosevelt Hospital makes water labor and water birth available as an option. Our friend Judy delivered her daughter there with Judith Elaine Halek attending (see page 27) and was thrilled with her experience. Should you wish, you can rent a birthing tub and have a water birth at home with the help of a midwife.

childbirth educators, classes, and other resources

If you are having a normal pregnancy, you're happy with your OB or CNM, and you've signed up for childbirth education/Lamaze classes through your doctor's office or hospital—congratulations! You are in good shape for a successful pregnancy and delivery.

If you want to know even more about what's going on with your body and what's to come during pregnancy, labor, delivery, and after, New York has many experts who work on a one-on-one basis or in a small group.

Here is a list of resources. These private practitioners specialize in a variety of birth-related areas: Lamaze, Bradley, water birth, labor support, and childbirth education. Some practitioners offer more than one kind of service; make some phone calls, and you may find just the right match for you.

Class lengths vary, but most childbirth series cost between $200 to $400+ per couple. If you use more than one service from a practitioner, you can probably negotiate a package deal.

The following are specialists in pregnancy and childbirth education:

❊ *Ellen Chuse, C.C.E.*
718-789-1981
www.ellenchusechildbirth.com
Ellen Chuse has been working with birthing women and their families since 1984. She has served as president of the Childbirth Education Association of Metropolitan New York, and remains active on the Board of Directors. She offers group classes focused on labor, birth, breastfeeding, and newborn care; classes are held in Brooklyn and cost $375 per couple. These classes fill up quickly, so call early. Ellen also offers private classes, as well as pregnancy and birth counseling in both Brooklyn and Manhattan. Additionally, she facilitates a New Mothers' Group at RealBirth (see page 29 as well as website for locations; www.realbirth.com).

❊ *Choiceful Birth and Parenting*
Ellen Krug, MSW, LCSW, CCE
718-768-0494
www.choicefulbirth.com
A certified social worker and childbirth educator, Ellen Krug has been offering childbirth classes and counseling since 1984. Classes cover birth planning, labor support techniques, and relaxation; private classes are available. Counseling focuses on supporting pregnant women and

new moms by allowing them to openly discuss issues and concerns related to pregnancy, birth, and parenting in a safe and nurturing environment. Ellen also runs the Pregnancy Circle and New Mom/Newborn circle: support groups for moms before and after giving birth. Parenting issues, adjustment to new family roles, sleeping issues, health care, and ways to balance work and parenthood are among the topics discussed. All classes and counseling are offered at a Park Slope, Brooklyn, location.

⁂ Fern Drillings, RN, MSN, CCE

390 West End Avenue between 78th and 79th streets
201 East 80th Street between Second and Third avenues
212-744-6649
Fern is a well-known name around town. She is an excellent Lamaze/childbirth instructor and a faculty member at NYU School of Nursing. Many of our friends have used her for childbirth classes and think she is terrific. She also teaches CPR/Baby Saver classes and does lactation consulting. Fern offers both individual and group classes.

⁂ Expectant Parenting Seminars

Ronni Soled/ Pamela Weinberg
212-744-3194
Ronni Soled (founder of the original New Mothers Luncheons and parent educator) and Pamela Weinberg have created a series of unique seminars for expectant parents. Their most popular is a two-hour seminar that covers Getting Ready: What you need to buy, borrow, or don't need for your new baby and Adapting to Parenthood—the first three months. They also do a seminar called Help!: Choosing a child-care provider, doula, baby nurse, and pediatrician. Call for seminar dates and times.

⁂ Mary Lynn Fiske, CCE, AAHCC

718-855-1650
Mary Lynn Fiske has been teaching the Bradley method for over ten years. She offers an eight-class series at a few locations in Cobble Hill, Brooklyn, and also teaches privately in her own and her clients' homes. Classes focus on pain coping techniques, good birth planning, coaching tools for partners, and what to expect during labor and birth. Classes include labor rehearsals and role-play, discussion of interventions and cesarean, videos, and relaxation practice. Mary Lynn is an open and generous instructor; she makes her clients feel comfortable with the decisions they reach about their pregnancy and birth.

⁂ Judith Elaine Halek

Birth Balance
309 West 109th Street bet. Broadway and Riverside Drive
212-222-4349
email: judith@birthbalance.com
www.birthbalance.com
One of the first labor support doulas in New York City, Judith attended the city's first water birth in 1987. She writes and speaks nationally on birth issues, and is a hypnotherapist, filmmaker, and "doulatographer" (doula/photographer) as well as a specialist in pregnancy, labor, birth, and

postpartum documentation. She is also the author of the self-published book Perceptions, Connections, Reflections, which is available on her website. Judith works with clients in their home, birth center, or hospital.

The Jewish Community Center in Manhattan

334 Amsterdam Avenue at 76th Street
646-505-4444
www.jccmanhattan.org

The JCC offers a plethora of classes for expectant parents. It offers an eight-week series that includes everything from how and where to purchase your layette (sometimes taught by Pamela), to planning your baby's bris or baby naming and everything in between. It also offers pre- and postnatal swim and yoga classes. Check out the schedule online.

Fritzi Kallop, RN, BS

212-906-9255

Fritzi Kallop is a certified childbirth educator and a registered nurse with years of experience in assisting with labor and delivery. She offers private childbirth classes that cover topics such as body changes in late pregnancy, the labor and delivery process, the father's role as coach, pain relief, and Lamaze breathing techniques. Kelly took Fritzi Kallop's childbirth class and loved her and the class.

Gayatri Martin, RN

Choices for Childbirth
220 East 26th Street bet. Second and Third avenues

212-725-1078
email: info@choicesforchildbirth.com
www.choicesforchildbirth.com

Gayatri has been teaching childbirth preparation classes since 1990. Her classes encourage expectant mothers to be central to the experience of planning and preparing for birth. They offer practical support strategies for partners and breathing and relaxation techniques in addition to hands-on practice. Gayatri is also a certified yoga instructor, as well as certified Prenatal Holistic Counselor and uses body-centered hypnosis to help women address the emotional and psychological aspects of birth. She conducts private and group classes.

Mary Oscategui

415-937-1602
email: mary@thebabyplanner.com
www.thebabyplanner.com

The Baby Planner is a baby planning and consulting service for expecting, adopting, and new parents designed to guide, educate, and support you throughout your pregnancy and beyond. They specialize in health, fitness, nutrition, going green, and safety.

Mom Prep

1316 Madison Avenue at 93rd Street
212-608-2036

An offshoot of Rosie Pope Maternity, this brand new space offers a wide range of classes for expectant and new moms including CPR, prenatal yoga, and childbirth education.

Power of Birth

Tara Brooke CD (DONA), PCD (DONA)

212-226-2656

email: info@powerofbirth.com

www.powerofbirth.com

Tara Brooke is a DONA-trained doula who lives in Manhattan. She has been working with pregnant women since 2000, and is the director of the Power of Birth. Her background enables her to empower and support women, both during and after the birth of a child. She offers private childbirth education in your home, which covers labor, birth, breastfeeding, and newborn care. Tara also offers one-on-one consultations during the last weeks of pregnancy to help you prepare for your baby.

RealBirth

715 Ninth Ave at 49th Street

212-245-0796; 212-367-9006

email: education@realbirth.com

www.realbirth.com

Erica Lyon, an experienced childbirth educator, opened RealBirth in 2003 as a stand-alone, comprehensive center for expectant and new parents. RealBirth offers childbirth classes that explore the many labor methods and pain management options available to pregnant women. The center provides pregnancy and childbirth education, breastfeeding support, and extensive new parent education for modern women and families. It is also one of the few places in the city to run drop-in postpartum groups. Erica is the author of The Big Book of Birth, as well as co-owner of Bump-to-Baby (www.bump-to-baby.com), a store dedicated to helping parents

find greener products for their babies.

Diana Simkin

917-602-6456

A certified personal trainer, Diana has been offering one-to-one fitness for pre- and post-natal women for over twenty years. She has a master's degree in dance education from NYU and is the author of The Complete Pregnancy Exercise Program and coauthor of Preparation for Birth: The Complete Guide to the Lamaze Method. Diana offers in-home personal training, as well as group and private Lamaze instruction. Diana teaches at various Upper East Side and Upper West Side fitness locations, but is happy to travel within Manhattan to provide private training.

Dr. Sidney Wu

New Mommy Knitting Circle at String Yarns

130 East 82nd Street at Lexington Avenue

917-902-4075

www.stringyarns.com

Dr. Wu is a wonderful (and much in-demand) obstetrician in private practice in NYC (affiliated with New York Presbyterian). She's also a compulsive knitter! Soon-to-be moms can learn to knit a baby item (the staff at String gets you started), meet other moms, and chat with Dr. Wu in a relaxed, friendly setting. It meets at her favorite knitting store on the Upper East Side.

If you are looking for more information on nontraditional childbirth educators/labor support practitioners, here are three organizations that can help:

Association of Labor Assistants and Childbirth Educators (ALACE)

P. O. Box 382724

Cambridge, MA 02238

888-22ALACE

www.alace.org

This is a nonprofit educational organization that offers parents and professionals referrals for both childbirth preparation classes and professional labor support. It also provides information on pregnancy, childbirth, and breastfeeding.

Doulas of North America

www.dona.org

Doulas of North America is an international association of doulas who are trained to provide quality labor support to birthing women and their families. The website provides general information on the role of the doula, and information on locating a labor support doula or postpartum doula in your area.

Childbirth Education Association of Metropolitan New York

www.ceamny.org

CEA/MNY is a nonprofit organization of childbirth professionals and consumer advocates that are committed to family-centered maternity care. While they support each woman's right to choose her preferred birthing method, they strongly enforce viewing pregnancy as a natural physiological process. CEA/MNY

teaches and encourages Cooperative Childbirth Education (CCE), a birthing method originally developed entirely by women who experienced pregnancy, childbirth, and breastfeeding for themselves.

It has come to our attention that there is another new choice that expectant parents are faced with: whether or not to store the baby's umbilical cord blood. Umbilical cord blood has been used with much success to treat over forty diseases (blood and marrow diseases, such as leukemia) and is expected to be even more effective in the future. There are a few different resources for private blood banking. The cost is approximately $2,070 plus a fee of $125 per year to store the blood. Your OB/GYN will most likely discuss this option with you. If you want to research it for yourself, Viacord has a comprehensive website that explains the options (www.viacord.com).

taking care
of yourself

Once you have assembled your support team, from Lamaze instructor to lactation consultant, checked out the hospital room or birthing center in which your baby will first set eyes upon the world, it's time to be good to yourself. Since we published the first edition of *City Baby New York*, being pregnant has become truly chic. Like so many supermodels and Hollywood actresses, many New York women have discovered the benefits, physical and emotional, of staying fit during the whole nine months.

Pamela's friend Debby didn't even appear pregnant until her seventh month. She had perfect skin and hair that got thicker and shinier. She looked and acted as if she felt like a million bucks. She may be the luckiest woman we know. If you are like the rest of us, however, the weight gain, the bulging belly, and the exhaustion might make you feel unattractive on occasion. Now is the time to pamper and indulge yourself. Take advantage of some of the terrific body-strengthening and spirit-lifting services New York has to offer. Treat yourself to a manicure when you're in your ninth month and feel as though you can't stand to be pregnant for one more day.

Most importantly, get involved with a physical fitness program early on. It will help you feel your best throughout your pregnancy and prepare you for labor. Our friend Matty worked until ten days before her delivery, taking the subway from her Upper West Side apartment to her downtown East Side office and back again every day. She said climbing up and down all those stairs, carrying what turned out to be her ten-and-a-half pound son, gave her legs of steel. This is good. Strong leg muscles are useful for getting you through the last months of pregnancy, as well as labor and birth.

You can do even more for yourself by checking out one or another of the facilities described in this chapter. You'll find information about health clubs, exercise studios, and private practitioners that offer pre- and postnatal exercise classes, fitness training, yoga, and massage, all fine-tuned and appropriate for pregnant women.

Kelly swears by the Medical Massage Group (see p. 44); the massages she had there relaxed her and the foot reflexology helped her morning sickness. The second time around Kelly tried massage more frequently, worked out regularly, and had a much easier pregnancy.

exercise

Most experts agree that exercising throughout your pregnancy is safe, healthy, and beneficial to your overall well-being. If your pregnancy is low risk and normal, you can participate in a moderate exercise program throughout your nine months. If you're a long-time jock or have exercised regularly prior to pregnancy (at least three times per week), you should be able to safely maintain that level of activity, with some modifications, throughout pregnancy and postpartum. Of course, check with your obstetrician or midwife before starting or continuing any exercise regimen, whether you are low- or high-risk. Also, be aware of the following recommendations adapted from guidelines issued by the American College of Obstetricians and Gynecologists (ACOG):

❊ Regular exercise (at least three times per week) is preferable to intermittent activity.

❊ Avoid exercise that involves lying flat on your back after the fourth month. Lying on your back is associated with decreased cardiac output in pregnancy. Also avoid prolonged periods of standing.

* During pregnancy, you have less oxygen available for aerobic exercise. Modify the intensity of your exercise. Stop exercising when fatigued, and never exercise to the point of exhaustion.

* Weight-bearing exercises, such as jogging, may be continued throughout pregnancy, at lower intensities. Nonweight-bearing exercises, such as cycling and swimming, minimize risk of injury.

* During exercise, be sure that your heart rate does not exceed 140 beats per minute.

* Avoid exercise that could cause you to lose your balance, especially in the third trimester. Avoid any type of exercise with the potential for even mild abdominal trauma.

* Be sure to eat enough prior to your workout. Pregnancy requires an additional 300 calories a day just to maintain your weight.

* Drink water and wear comfortable clothing to augment heat dissipation during exercise.

Many of the body changes of pregnancy persist four to six weeks postpartum. After your baby is born, resume your pre-pregnancy routines gradually, according to how you feel.

Fitness/Health Clubs

If you don't already have an exercise routine and want to get started, walking is a safe way to stay in shape. For those who desire a more structured workout environment, the following health clubs offer special classes and/or training for pregnant women. Many personal trainers in these health clubs are cer-

Top Ten Tips for Prenatal Exercising

1. Do it!
2. Try as many classes as necessary until you find one you like.
3. Remember to do your Kegels.
4. Don't lie on your back after the fourth month.
5. Drink plenty of water.
6. Don't exercise on an empty stomach; make sure to have a snack first.
7. Exercise with other pregnant women; you won't feel as big.
8. Try yoga for excellent stretching and relaxation.
9. Don't let your heart rate exceed 140 beats per minute.
10. Consult your obstetrician before starting any kind of new exercise.

tified to work with pre- and postnatal women; just inquire. (In many clubs, pregnant women work out right next to their non-pregnant counterparts.)

Membership fees in most full-service health clubs (Equinox, New York Sports Club, New York Health & Racquet Club, Reebok Sports Club, and David Barton) range from $900 to $2,000 per year, with a one-time initiation fee between $200 and $500. These fees are often negotiable and may be discounted if you join with a friend or spouse, or pay the entire amount upon joining, or work for an affiliated company. The fee for a personal trainer varies from club to club but is normally $55 to $100 per hour. With some club memberships, you can use all locations in the chain; others limit workout locations.

Private clubs offer pleasant accoutrements: roomy changing areas, lots of towels, and nice snack bars. Check your local Y classes as well. They are the most economical and offer a wide range of classes and equipment.

❈ Bally Total Fitness

Check website for locations throughout NYC.
www.ballyfitness.com
While Bally only has child-care facilities at their 106th Street location, it does offer personal trainers with experience in pregnancy exercise and postnatal workouts. As we feel location, i.e. proximity to home, is the key to many successful workout regimens, we have listed Bally's website in the hopes that one of these may be on your doorstep. Please visit the club nearest you for more information.

❈ David Barton

30 East 85th Street bet. Madison
and Fifth avenues
212-517-7577
215 West 23rd Street bet. Seventh
and Eighth avenues
212-414-2022
8 Astor Place between Broadway and
Lafayette Street
212-505-6800
www.davidbartongym.com
David Barton offers personal trainers who are specialists in working with pre- and postnatal women and will design a regimen that is right for your level of fitness. Barton is small and

tightly packed with equipment so it is difficult to move around. The design and low lighting give it a nightclub feel. There is no baby-sitting available.

❈ Equinox

Check website for locations throughout NYC.
www.equinoxfitness.com
The Equinox clubs offer a few pre- and postnatal exercise classes but recommend using a personal trainer certified in pre- and postnatal fitness to work with you. There are many trainers available, but you must be a member of the club to hire one, and the cost is not included in the membership fee. Equinox is known for its outstanding instructors and offers a wide range of exercise classes, including spinning. Their locker rooms are immaculate. The Tribeca, Columbus Circle, and Broadway at 92nd Street Equinox locations have child-care facilities for an additional fee. Kelly exercised at the East 85th Street location before and after both her pregnancies and lost 25 pounds with Equinox after each birth. (She had gained 50 to 55 pounds with each baby.)

❈ 14th Street Y

344 East 14th Street between First and
Second avenues
212-780-0800
www.14streety.org
The 14th Street Y offers tons of classes for expectant parents, new moms, and young families. Be sure to check out Wow Mommy: Work Out with Mommy, as well as New Moms Stroll-In and Mommy and Me classes with social

worker / parenting expert Kiki Schaffer. Membership plans are among the most affordable in the city, and offer fitness classes, gym time, pool access, and more (family memberships include nannies). Baby-sitting is offered for children from six months to six years old, and a ten-session pass only costs $40.

✢ Homebodies

1841 Broadway at 60th Street, Suite 905
212-586-7160
www.homebodies.com
Getting to the gym is often the biggest challenge for new moms and Homebodies has the answer. After an initial assessment, a personal trainer will come to your home with a customized workout plan that includes yoga, weight training, and Pilates. Initial assessments are $150, and one-hour workout sessions are $110.

✢ JCC of Manhattan

The Jewish Community Center in Manhattan
334 Amsterdam Avenue at 76th Street
646-505-4444
www.jccmanhattan.org
The JCC offers lots of classes: it's like a modern-day Y. There are exercise programs for infants, kids, and everyone in the whole family, with a complete gym, a pool, and changing facilities. The JCC has exercise classes, too. Membership fees vary and you can buy ten- and twenty-week passes based on the different classes. There's swimming, basketball leagues for boys and girls, and all the same activities you find at a local YMCA. Baby-sitting is offered ($10 per hour for members; $12 per hour for nonmem-

bers) for a maximum of two hours at a time. Reservations are recommended; 646-505-4467.

✢ New York Health & Racquet Club

See website for multiple locations throughout NYC.
800-HRC-BEST
www.nyhrc.com
New York Health & Racquet Club offers prenatal lectures and exercise classes through the Maternal Fitness program. Call Maryanne Donner (212-220-0774) to find out when and where classes are available. Lectures are free to members, and the six-week workshop is about $350 for members, $375 for nonmembers. Lecture topics include safe exercise during pregnancy, aerobic dos and don'ts, muscle strengthening, and flexibility. NYHRC offers baby-sitting at the York Avenue location only.

Prenatal certified personal trainers

✢ 92nd Street Y

1395 Lexington Avenue at 92nd Street
212-415-5729; 212-415-5722 (Exercise class listings)
92YTribeca
200 Hudson Street at Canal Street
212-601-1000
www.92y.org
These are two of the most complete Y's in the city with everything imaginable! The Pregnancy Exercise class (currently offered at the 92nd Street location only) is fifty-five minutes, helping expectant moms ease the discomfort of

pregnancy, develop body awareness, and maintain fitness through yoga and dance exercises. A four-session class is $92 for nonmembers and $76 for members, and a six-session class is $150 for nonmembers and $120 for members. Pick up a catalog; you will definitely want to sign up for a Mommy and Me class here as well. Its baby-sitting fees are nominal.

Peggy Levine

2726 Broadway bet. 104th and 105th streets, 3rd Floor
212-222-3637
www.peggylevinefitness.com
Peggy teaches prenatal and postnatal fitness classes at Bridge for Dance Studio on Broadway between 104th and 105th streets. You can also contact Peggy for private training lessons.

New York Sports Clubs

See website for multiple locations throughout NYC.
800-796-NYSC
www.nysc.com
The New York Sports Club offers an eight-week prenatal yoga program suitable for all stages of pregnancy (physician's release form is required) that is focused on helping women adapt to their changing bodies during pregnancy. We like New York Sports Club because it provides more value than some of the more chic athletic clubs. Baby-sitting services are offered for children ages three months to ten years, for both members and nonmembers (reservations are recommended or required, depending on the club).

Reebok Sports Club NY/Sports Club LA

160 Columbus Avenue at 67th Street
212-362-6800
330 East 61st Street bet. First and
Second avenues
212-355-5100
45 Rockefeller Plaza bet. 50th and 51st streets, and Fifth and Sixth avenues
212-218-8600
www.thesportsclubla.com
Reebok offers low-impact water aerobic classes and personal trainers who specialize in working with women during and after their pregnancies. All sorts of yoga—prenatal, postnatal, etc.— classes are offered. Prenatal exercise classes focus on the key physical toning, stretching, and breathing that pregnant women need to do; this class covers Kegels, stretching, and, of course, moderate resistance training to keep pregnant women in shape. All pregnant women participating in this program wear heart-rate monitors. Be sure to check out Family Day Yoga, Buddha Mama, and Baby Weights (for an extra charge) classes!

Once your baby is six months old, you can leave him in the state-of-the-art Kids Club while you exercise. This is probably the largest and most expensive health club in the city; a yearly membership costs over $2,000. Pamela, an exercise guru, has worked out and tried everything Reebok has to offer. And if her figure has anything to do with Reebok, they're doing something right!

Diana Simkin

212-348-0208

For ten years, Diana was the pre- and postnatal exercise instructor for the Marymount Manhattan Fitness Certification Program. She is the author of The Complete Pregnancy Exercise Program and co-author of Preparation for Birth: The Complete Guide to the Lamaze Method. She is a Certified Personal Trainer and Lamaze instructor with a Master's degree in dance education from NYU. She offers in-home personal training with a specialty in pre- and postnatal exercise, as well as group and private Lamaze instruction. Diane travels to Upper East Side and Upper West Side locations only.

Spabébé

917-911-9344

Spabébé was established in 2002 by Heidi Moon, a fitness and spa industry veteran of fourteen years and mother of two. Formerly partnered with Maternal Fitness until 2006, Spabébé continues to independently offer fitness programs and seminars at host locations all over Manhattan. Classes include Prenatal Fitness Fusion, Functional Fitness Fusion, Functional Fitness For Moms (bring your baby!), Prenatal Fitness Workshop, and AbRehab. Prices are around $26 for a single session and $85 for the four-week series.

Strollercize, Inc.

800-Y-STROLL

www.strollercize.com

Created by Lizzy Trindade, Strollercize is a terrific way to meet other new moms, spend time with your baby, and have a great [...] once. This is a fun, interactive fit[...] incorporating strollers and babies [...] mother's workout. Pre- and post[...] are held in various parks and gyms throughout the city, and personal training programs are also offered. Workouts are safe, tough, and effective, and create a great atmosphere for both baby and mom. Strollercize offers 150 classes per month, year-round, throughout Manhattan (and now Naples, Florida, and Seattle, Washington, too). Discounted memberships are available. Call for locations and times; and check out workshops as well as Lizzie's new class, Mommy Bootie Camp.

In addition to Strollercize, there are two other stroller exercise classes that have recently debuted in the New York area:

Mommy Moves

732-539-7711

www.mommy-moves.com

Mommy Moves offers stroller fitness classes, small group training, private training, nutritional consulting, kids' fitness classes, running programs, health and wellness lectures, and so much more!

Stroller Strides

866-FIT-4MOM

email: info@strollerstrides.com

www.strollerstrides.com

Stroller Strides is a total fitness program that new moms can do with their babies. It includes power walking and intervals of body toning using exercise tubing and the stroller. Taught by specially trained instructors, it's a great workout for any level of exerciser.

❖ *Vanderbilt YMCA*

224 East 47th Street bet. Second and
Third avenues
212-912-2500
www.ymcanyc.org

The YMCA's Vanderbilt location has an hour-long prenatal yoga class, which includes a combination of aerobics and stretching and toning exercises. Classes are held twice a week; an eight-week series is free for members and $135 for nonmembers. A physician's approval is required. They also offer early childhood development and pre-nursery programs, as well as child and parent classes. Individual membership to the Y is $1,080 per year (which can be paid in monthly installments) with a one-time initiation fee of $125. Family memberships are also available.

❖ *YWCA*

500 West 56th Street at Tenth Avenue
212-937-8700
www.ywcanyc.org

The YWCA offers a forty-minute Water Exercise for Pregnancy and Postpartum class twice a week, from 11:40 a.m. to 12:20 p.m. Mondays and Thursdays. The class is a combination of water aerobics and stretching. The price is $90 for an eight-class card, plus $60 for the annual YWCA membership. Individual classes are $10 for members, $15 for nonmembers. A doctor's note may be required.

Private Trainers

Here are some personal trainers who offer pre- and postnatal private training at your home, gym, or office: Ana Lerner, 212-355-3109; Debby Peress, 212-249-3972; and Diana Simkin, 212-348-0208; Janet Cook, 347-306-8864; and Adam Todd Rifkin, 917-312-2000 or foundationsfitnessnyc@gmail.com. Pamela has been working with Adam and has gotten excellent results with his patented "attack mode" fitness methods for getting your body into shape. Their fees range from $100 to $200 per hour.

yoga

There has been a huge yoga explosion since our first book. (Madonna's yoga practice throughout her pregnancies surely didn't hurt any.) But yoga is great exercise for pregnant women—aiding relaxation, maintaining flexibility, and providing an excellent way to work out without risking injury.

Many health clubs have yoga classes. If you have taken yoga before your pre-pregnant days and want to continue, do so. Make sure you tell your instructor you are expecting, however, and ask for alternatives that will be safer and more comfortable.

Yoga instructor Gayatri Martin tells us that prenatal yoga emphasizes the strengthening of pelvic floor muscles to get women ready for pregnancy and birth. Prenatal classes usually allow more time than traditional yoga for resting and relaxation. You'll learn breathing and postures that are helpful for birth and labor.

The following yoga instructors or studios specialize in pre- and postnatal yoga classes:

Aquamom

Check website for locations throughout Manhattan.

212-744-6622

www.aquamom.com

Aquamom offers an eight-week water workout that's made up of a mix of dance, aerobics, yoga, and Pilates. Since the entire class is held in the pool (don't worry, it's a stable 84 degrees and completely private), you feel weightless while you exercise, which takes pressure off of the back, sciatic nerve, and pelvic area. The cardio program increases energy, endurance, and strength, while relieving sciatica and controlling weight gain. Classes are limited to ten people and fill up quickly. Midday, evening, and late evening sessions are offered.

Baby Om

Check website for multiple locations throughout NYC.

Karma Yoga

37 West 65th Street, 4th Floor

bet. Broadway and Central Park West

212-615-6935

www.babyom.com

A unique yoga experience for moms and their babies, parents bring baby and participate in a yoga class run by Sarah Perron or Laura Staton, the founders of Baby Om, or one of six other extremely qualified instructors. Baby Om is a challenging yoga class designed to stretch and tone the postpartum mom, while providing a playful and stimulating atmosphere for baby. Baby Om also offers Mommy Om, a yoga class designed to strengthen alignment that can be weakened by pregnancy, and help the new mother connect to a vital and reawakened sense of her own body.

Mary Ryan Barnes

Yoga for Two

Check website for yoga studios that host classes.

212-360-1888

www.yogafortwo.com

Mary Barnes has created her own style of teaching called The Barnes Method, which combines anusara yoga, breath work, alignment, sound vibration, strength training, and therapeutics. Her prenatal yoga method also aids in the birthing process, helping women feel centered and strong during labor and delivery. Postpartum women can enjoy Mommy & Baby Yoga for Two™ classes, New Mom & Baby Yoga Sanctuary with mothering expert guests, and yoga with baby-sitting. (Pamela has been a student of Mary's and believes she is truly terrific!)

Charlotte Blake

Pre and postnatal Pilates

email: charblake@gmail.com

www.findyourbalance.wordpress.com

Charlotte Blake is a personal trainer, dancer, and instructor of cardio-sculpt, cycling, and Pilates, with her Pilates certification from the Kane School of Core Integration. Charlotte teaches a series of Pilates classes called Mama Moves and has a focus on working with pregnant and postnatal women. Charlotte works with people of all ages to better their strength, confidence, well-being, and body awareness.

Her classes and sessions are holistically based and focus on working correctly and efficiently.

Beth Donnelly Caban

718-753-6164

www.essentialyogabrooklyn.com

An integral yoga instructor and co-author of New York's 50 Best Places to Keep Your Spirit Alive, Beth Donnelly Caban specializes in prenatal yoga, yoga for labor and delivery, childbirth preparation, and yoga for new moms and babies. She is also a certified midwife assistant through Ina May Gaskin and The Farm Midwives, as well as a labor support doula. Beth teaches mostly in Brooklyn but will do private instruction. Call for more information.

Rebecca Gardiner

Pain Relief Specialist and Guild Certified Practitioner: Feldenkrais & The Anat Baniel Methods

35 Park Avenue at 35th Street

212-736-3331; 646-732-3026

email: rebecca@learningfrommovement.com

www.learningfrommovement.com

Rebecca offers a service that is invaluable to new moms looking to get in shape and restore their self image, relieve the stress and strain of parenthood, or both.

Integral Yoga Institute

227 West 13th Street bet. Seventh and Eighth avenues

212-929-0586

www.iyiny.org

The Integral Yoga Institute offers a multitude of classes for all levels, including prenatal and postpartum yoga, at various times throughout the week. The prenatal classes are for women who have entered their second trimester of pregnancy. The classes focus on movements, postures, and practices especially beneficial to pregnant women. Soothing and relaxation practices are emphasized. Postpartum classes are for moms and newborns ages one month to eighteen months, and include one hour of gentle stretching, chanting, and breathing and a half hour of sharing and discussion. A single class is $17; ten classes are $150; and twenty classes are $260. Unlimited class cards are also available.

Iyengar Yoga Institute of New York

150 West 22nd Street, 11th Floor

bet. Sixth and Seventh avenues

212-691-9642

www.iyengarnyc.org

Iyengar Yoga Institute offers prenatal, gentle, and restorative classes that focus on postures for the physical and psychological aspects of women's health. Prices per class range from $18 to $25. Seasonal memberships as well as three- and five-class cards can be purchased.

Jivamukti Yoga Center

841 Broadway, 2nd Floor

bet. 14th and 15th streets

212-353-0214

853 Lexington Avenue, 2nd Floor,

bet. 64th and 65th streets

646-290-8106

www.jivamuktiyoga.com

The Jivamukti Yoga Center offers two classes for soon-to-be and new moms. Prenatal Yoga meets on several weekday mornings. Jivamukti focuses on breathing, stretching, and strengthening, as well as adapting yoga postures to the needs of the changing pregnant body. The classes are structured to be a "community" that connects pregnant women with one another. Baby and Me, a postpartum class for moms and dads with babies six weeks to twelve months, emphasizes postures, and is designed to realign the inner body and tone the abdominal muscles. Special postures are taught for infants, and the class addresses postpartum issues. Family Yoga classes bring together adults with their young children (ages two through four) through activities including asana practice, imaginative games, and action and movement. Each class costs $20 and is available as a series.

Gayatri Martin, RN

Choices for Childbirth
220 East 26th Street
bet. Second and Third avenues
212-725-1078
Gayatri, a registered nurse, has been a certified childbirth educator and yoga teacher since 1988. Her private classes emphasize "discovering your strengths, feeling your flexibility, and experiencing breath as the bridge between body, mind, baby, and heart." Gayatri is available for in-home instruction for a cost of $90 per hour.

NYC Pilates

Randi Stone
Check website for multiple locations throughout NYC.
917-951-5004

email: info@nyc-pilates.com
www.nyc-pilates.com
Pilates, MELT, Tupler, and more. Randi is an Upper West Side mom and Pilates trainer to the stars who offers classes of varying levels as well as mommy and baby Pilates. Check out the new website for upcoming classes, events, and programs. Private, semi-private, and small group in-home sessions are also available upon request.

New York Yoga

212-717-9642
1629 York Ave at 86th Street
www.newyorkyoga.com
NYY has great yoga classes for all ages including prenatal yoga, mommy and baby, parent and child, and more!

Prenatal Yoga Center

251 West 72nd Street, Suite 2F
bet. Broadway and West End Avenue
212-362-2985
www.prenatalyogacenter.com
The Prenatal Yoga Center specializes in pre- and postnatal. Run by the dynamic Debra Flashenberg, this studio offers fabulous classes for pregnant/postnatal women, plus seminars and workshops on a variety of pregnancy/baby-related topics. The prenatal yoga classes help to strengthen your body and works toward alleviating many of the discomforts of pregnancy. The postnatal class helps women regain strength and energy while providing a great opportunity to meet other new moms. Classes are purchased in eight-week sessions, and are also now held at many loca-

tions throughout NYC. (Pamela's friend Abby swears by the Pilates class here, too!)

✢ Rhythm for Life

917-907-2025

www.maternaldance.com

Suzanne Caesar's Prenatal Belly Dance Workout is a contemporary and fresh prenatal workout that is a fun, safe, and effective way to stay fit during pregnancy.

✢ Mikelle Terson

37 West 76th Street

bet. Central Park West and Columbus Avenue

212-787-1116

www.yogablossom.com

Mikelle is available for private yoga instruction at your home for $175 per seventy-five-minute session.

✢ Elana Weiss

917-882-1643

212-452-2922

email: freetobeyoga@yahoo.com

www.freetobeyoga.com

Elana Weiss is a private yoga instructor and special education teacher who has been teaching children and adults Hatha yoga for nearly ten years. She can come to your apartment and work with you, your baby, or you and your baby together!

✢ Wellpath

1100 Madison Avenue at 83rd Street

212-737-9604

www.thewellpath.com

Wellpath approaches women's medical health with holistic and Western techniques in order to treat women, especially pregnant women, for various health issues. Wellpath offers photo rejuvenation, laser hair removal, Epicurean facials, and endermologie, the process that reduces cellulite and increases blood circulation. Wellpath has a private Pilates studio on-site and also offers medical consultations with Dr. Jamé Heskett upon request.

✢ WellRoundedNYC

Stephanie Clarke, MS, RD, CDN

212-752-6770

515 Madison Avenue at 53rd Street, Suite 1906

email: staff@wellroundednyc.com

www.wellroundednyc.com

WellRounded NYC classes are comprehensive two-hour courses offered twice per month (one prenatal, one postnatal) that combine nutrition education with physical therapy techniques in a fun, interactive, and intimate setting. A program founded by a team of registered dietitians and physical therapists, WellRoundedNYC classes are uniquely designed to supplement a woman's other healthcare and exercise programs, giving the mom-to-be practical knowledge that enables her to have the safest, healthiest, and most positive pregnancy experiences.

✢ Yoga Works/Be Yoga

See website for locations throughout Manhattan.

www.beyoga.com

Be Yoga evolved from Alan Finger's Yoga Zone studios in 2001, with co-owners Beverley Murphy and Bob Murphy. Alan Finger has been at the forefront of expanding yoga in the West and is considered one of the leading yogis. Alan founded Yoga Zone in 1990. Under the Yoga Zone™ name, Mr. Finger opened five studios, and created over fifty videos and a national TV show. He has been practicing and teaching for over forty years. All the teachers at Be Yoga have been trained to work with pregnant women. Senior instructors prepare women for the deep internal work of pregnancy and postpartum life, concentrating on breath and unique physical characteristics. Be Yoga offers prenatal yoga classes at most locations as well as age-appropriate yoga programs for babies five months to crawlers and kids ages three to teens. Log onto the Be Yoga website to get schedule information on the studio nearest your home or office.

massage

Many pregnant women suffer from back pain and strain, especially during the later months. Why not get a massage?

A massage therapist should be licensed by New York State, certified in prenatal massage, or have experience working with pregnant women.

Communication with your therapist is critical. If you feel lightheaded, short of breath, or uncomfortable, let the practitioner know. Many women feel uncomfortable lying on their backs after the fourth month (remember, ACOG recommends that you do not lie on your back after this time), so prenatal massages are often given to a woman as she lies on her side with pillows between her legs. The Medical

Massage Group has a special table with a cut-out middle so that you can lie on your stomach when you might be uncomfortable on your side.

Every massage therapist listed is licensed by the state of New York. Some specialize in prenatal massage, and many will come to your home for an additional fee. All work is by appointment only, so call ahead.

✳ *Laura Favin, LMT, LCSW*

220 West 71st Street, Suite 2A
bet. Broadway and West End Avenue
917-209-6534
Laura has been a licensed massage therapist, specializing in massage for pregnant women and new moms, for over twenty-two years. She is certified in prenatal and postpartum massage, trigger point therapy, deep tissue, and craniosacral therapy. She charges $95 for a one-hour massage, $140 if she travels to your home or office. She also teaches infant massage—a lovely way to bond with your new child.

✳ *Mama Spa*

212-591-1630
www.mamaspa.com
Mama Spa is a mobile prenatal massage spa that delivers VIP prenatal pampering in the comfort of your own home. Founded by Marie Scalogna-Watkinson, who has over eighteen years of prenatal massage/spa experience, Mama Spa is fully focused on mothers' safety and education. Masseuses educate each client and give women clear reasons for what is done (or not done) during the treatment. They do not use pregnancy massage tables—all treatments are performed

with women either in a side-lying or semi-reclining position on a special incline pillow. Prices start at around $200 per treatment. Mama Spa also offers the Daddy-O massage, a one hour Swedish/deep tissue combo for the mom-to-be's partner, as well as spa-themed baby showers through sister company Spa Chicks On-the-Go (www.spachicksonthego.com).

❋ Maternal Massage and More

Janet Markovits
73 Spring Street, Suite 201
bet. Lafayette and Crosby
212-533-3188
www.maternalmassageandmore.com
Maternal Massage and More offers prenatal massage, labor support, postpartum massage, and baby massage with Janet Markovits, a licensed massage therapist with over twelve years of experience. Each treatment, around $125, is catered to your specific stage of pregnancy with the use of bodyCushion™ support system. Janet also offers Pregnant New Yorker events, alternative health events teaching the pregnant community how to have an easy and healthy pregnancy (www.thepregnantnewyorker.com).

❋ The Medical Massage Group*

328 East 75th Street, Suite 3
bet. First and Second avenues
212-472-4772
www.medicalmassagegroup.com
The Medical Massage Group is run by Donna and Harvey Manger-Weil. The practice is mostly pre- and postpartum medical massage and

staffed with massage therapists. It has specially designed massage tables for pregnant women: tables that have a hole in the center so pregnant women can lie down comfortably and their stomachs are supported by adjustable slings. We highly recommend this group of licensed physical therapists. Kelly has had massages with both Donna and Harvey and they are superb!

❋ Prenatal Massage Center

123 West 79th Street, Suite LL2
bet. Amsterdam and Columbus avenues
212-330-6846
www.prenatalmassagecenter.com
The Prenatal Massage Center is run by Anne Heckheimer, a New York–licensed massage therapist, who has specialized in prenatal and postpartum massage for over five years. After receiving her massage license, Anne became additionally certified as a prenatal and labor massage therapist through the Mother Massage® method of prenatal and postpartum massage therapy.

❋ The Quiet Touch

317 West 35th Street
bet. Eighth and Ninth avenues
212-246-0008
800-946-2772
www.massageinc.com
The Quiet Touch is a national service that provides a licensed, insured, and fully equipped massage therapist at your door within a few hours. It has specialists in all types of massage, including prenatal. Massages are $125 per hour; membership packages are available for a

discounted rate, and there is a 10 percent discount for first-time clients.

nutrition

You know that good nutrition is a critical part of producing a healthy baby, and there are many books available addressing this subject. Two of the best are: *What to Expect When You're Expecting*, the pregnant woman's bible, which has an excellent section called the "Best Odds Diet," with guidelines on how to eat every day; and *What to Eat When You're Expecting*. Your OB or CNM should talk to you about nutrition, but if he or she doesn't, bring it up yourself.

If you are underweight, overweight, diabetic, or need extra help managing your diet, you can consult a nutritionist to set up a diet that meets your needs. Weight Watchers also offers a healthy plan for overweight pregnant women. You might want to keep them in mind for after the pregnancy, too. . . . We sure did.

Eating Right While You're Pregnant

What you should know about nutrition during your pregnancy:

* *Eat regularly and well.* This is no time to diet. You will gain weight, and most obstetricians today say a gain of 25 to 35 pounds or more is normal. Increase your calorie intake by about 300 calories a day during the last two trimesters, as you will need more energy during this time.

* *Eat healthy foods.* That means ample daily servings of grains (cereal, whole-grain bread, crackers), fruits, vegetables (steamed are best), protein (eggs, meat, fish, peanut butter), and calcium (milk, cheese, yogurt, tofu).

* *Avoid junk food.* When you want sugar, reach for fresh fruit, which will also help you avoid the ubiquitous affliction of pregnancy: constipation.

* *Drink water.* Your core body temperature is higher than normal when you are pregnant, and you need to take in at least two quarts of liquid a day, especially before, during, and after exercise.

* *Do not drink alcohol.*

* *Don't drink caffeinated beverages* (coffee, tea, colas) during your first trimester, and restrict intake to one cup a day after that. Caffeine reaches the baby through the placenta.

* *Listen to your body.* Those infamous cravings for pickles and peanut butter may have a basis in physiology. Your body may need a little extra salt.

The following nutritionists have worked with pregnant women. Initial consultations cost around $125, with follow-up visits ranging from $50 to $85. You can also call the New York State Dietetic Association for certified dietitian nutritionists (CDNs) in your area at 212-691-7906, or look for them on the web at www.eatrightny.org.

Nutritionists

Joy Bauer Nutrition

116 East 63rd Street
bet. Park and Lexington avenues
212-759-6999
www.joybauernutrition.com
Joy Bauer has built one of the largest nutrition centers in the country. With two locations, in Manhattan and Westchester, Joy Bauer Nutrition provides counseling to both adults and children dealing with a variety of nutritional concerns.

Janet Cook, CHHC, CPT

347-306-8864
www.janetcookhealthcounseling.com
Certified health counselor and personal trainer Janet Cook can show you how to enjoy a healthy pregnancy and postpartum experience—with a personal-training and nutrition program designed to nourish you and your growing family.

Allyson Mechaber

718-797-0310
201-615-6143
email: AMechaber@nyc.rr.com
Allyson specializes in pre- and postnatal nutrition as well as nutrition for children. Allyson comes to your home and works with you one-on-one. She will look through your pantry and offer healthy suggestions (she will even take you food shopping). She will also advise you on a vitamin program.

MMMunch

917-771-6114 (Amy)
917-699-5509 (Jackie)
email: amy@mmmunch.com
email: Jackie@mmmunch.com
www.mmmunch.com
MMMunch offers classes on self and family wellness providing easy, nutritious recipes that are well-balanced and kid approved. Their motto is "You wouldn't give your kids hormone-laden, genetically modified, over-processed hugs. So why would you do it with dinner?"

Simply Beautiful Mom

917-439-8328
email: Hillary@simplybeautifulmom.com
www.simplybeautifulmom.com
Registered dietician Hillary Irwin will help you customize a nutrition program that's right for you and your family. Hillary was the nutritionist at Exhale Spa (www.exhalespa.com).

Lauren Slayton

Food Trainers
212-769-4300
www.foodtrainers.net
A mom herself, Lauren knows the issues facing pre- and postnatal women, and her practice has many of them. For her prenatal clients, she does a consultation in the third trimester going over all the things to keep in the house and stock when the new baby arrives. She of course sees many postnatal women who want to get

back to their pre-pregnancy weight, too. Her practice has recently started Family Foodtraining where they see Mom or Dad and discuss a family meal plan complete with recipes/items for each family member. Lauren will also send weekly care packages of "afternoon ammunition" to your home or office complete with healthy low carb/high-fiber snacks. Pamela speaks from experience in saying that Lauren is a terrific nutritionist who truly gets results! Lauren now offers Market Foodtraining programs, which are supermarket tours geared towards weight loss and healthy family eating, as well as refrigerator makeovers.

❈ Bonnie Taub-Dix, MA, RD, CDN
212-737-8536; 516-295-0377
Bonnie is the spokesperson for the American Dietetic Association, the organization that helps people to eat in a healthy and realistic way. She practices in both New York City and parts of Long Island.

Food Delivery
If you are too tired to cook and prepare your own food (and your baby's food when the time comes) there are solutions besides that take-out Chinese menu by the phone. For (an often high) price the following outfits will cook and deliver your food to your door fresh and healthy.

❈ Baby Time Chef
212-592-3077
www.babytimechefs.com
Baby Time Chef's personal chef service offers healthy, home-cooked meals to enjoy at your leisure. A week or more of meals from this professional service is a popular shower or baby gift for new parents. New parents also can treat themselves to these great meals by the week or month. Baby Time Chefs will do the shopping, cooking, and clean up in your home ,too.

❈ Evie's Organic Edibles
212-544-2122
email: info@eviesorganicedibles.com
www.eviesorganicedibles.com
Evie provides homemade food for children six months to eight years old. As a new mother Evie had a hard time finding healthy food for her colicky child, and began a business by cooking food for her own child out of her kitchen. She shops and cooks for her clients in their home and will also deliver her healthy food to moms all over New York City. Evie offers new menu selections each week, which are available to order online every Thursday for the following week. Be sure to order early because quantities are limited!

❈ Happy Baby
25 Washington Street, Suite 601, Brooklyn
718-852-7606
email: helen@happybabyfood.com
www.happybabyfood.com
Happy Baby is the leading premium brand of baby and toddler meals in the U.S.—sold in over 5,000 stores with five different lines of optimally delicious organic foods for your growing family.

Mothers & Menus

646-522-9591

www.mothersandmenus.com

Mothers & Menus is a food delivery service that customizes organic, gourmet meals around your nutritional needs and food cravings. The goal is to provide increased energy and optimum nutrition for your postnatal needs. One new mom that we know found out that her baby was allergic to wheat and dairy, and Mothers & Menus was able to prepare her great food to eat that wouldn't upset that baby's allergies. Within the past few years the company has focused on media and communication, and now offers daily podcasts as well as coaching for expectant moms and parents with children ages newborn to three.

home organizers

You may be feeling overwhelmed at this point with all of the "stuff" you are getting for your new baby. With a typical city apartment, it is often difficult to find room to store all of your gear and still have the baby's room be tidy and organized. A home organization specialist may be the answer. We think highly of Sonya Weisshappel, who is a new mom herself and well-suited to the challenges of new parents.

Sonya Weisshappel

Seriatim, Inc.

115 Central Park West, Suite 2G

212-877-3267

www.seriatim.net

email: info@seriatim.net

The owner of Seriatim (a professional organiza-tion firm), Sonya Weisshappel is a mother herself. She has specific services that are particularly beneficial for new moms everywhere. Seriatim can prepare a room for the new baby, sort out gifts from the baby shower, and organize toys and clothes. Another terrific service is photo album organization and upkeep.

A Moving Experience

917-270-9006

www.outoftheboxorganizing.com

A Moving Experience helps people prepare for and get organized after residential moves. They will do everything including sort, de-clutter, fine-tune, and pack/unpack for those who are moving, trying to sell their home, or just needing some organizational help. Complimentary consultations are offered as well.

Gifted at Birth

212-785-0285

www.giftedatbirth.com

Confused about what newborn care products you'll need? Gifted at Birth delivers weekly packages of diapers, wipes, receiving blankets, and more for twelve weeks, right to your door. Choose from eight different configurations, or have them customized to your specifications. Postpartum doula support is included, guiding parents on the use of the products. Owners Tara Brooke and Ari Nave will make sure you have exactly what you need so you can focus on caring for your baby.

The Joyful Organizer, LLC

Bonnie Joy Dewkett
203-731-4651
email: bonnie@thejoyfulorganizer.com
www.thejoyfulorganizer.com
Professional organization services to fit your various needs.

Sacred Currents

Feng Shui Advisory
Integrative Design and Color Consultation
Judith Wendell
212-410-1832
917-903-9390
email: judith@sacredcurrents.com
www.sacredcurrents.com
Judith is a feng shui consultant who works primarily with expecting moms to set up the nursery and ready the whole house for the baby. She has recently been on the PBS special "Real Savvy Moms" talking about feng shui and the nursery and has been published in *Baby Talk* magazine.

Simply Staci LLC

212-714-8005
email: staci@simplystaci.com
Staci's mantra is "Organize your life simply," and she works with new moms and families to just that.

spas for baby and you

In Manhattan, there are spas everywhere, but now there are two that we can recommend taking your baby to and that were created specifically with baby and mommy in mind.

DevaSpa

425 Broome Street at Crosby Street
212-274-8686
www.devachansalon.com
DevaSpa is a gorgeous and Zen-like spa in Soho. They offer prenatal massages that are truly wonderful as well as manicures, pedicures, and facials in a relaxing atmosphere.

The Gravity Fitness & Spa

at the Le Parker Meridien Hotel
119 West 56th Street
bet. Sixth and Seventh avenues
212-708-7340
This spa supplies their younger guests with special diapers for the pools and cribs. The postnatal massage is $110 and is great to help restore energy to sleep-deprived moms. It's one of the few New York City spas that allow you to bring your infant in and take a day of relaxation. For those who want a quick way to relax, the Water Babies 101 tutorial for kids and parents in the indoor pool is great and it's only $75.

from healthcare
to day care

Sometime toward the end of your pregnancy, you should begin searching for the people who will help care for your little one. This is a toughie. The very idea of entrusting your baby to another person can be terrifying. You'll feel more comfortable with the idea if you take the time to do the necessary research—scout around, ask questions, make phone calls, pay visits.

First, you will need to find a pediatrician. Your goal is to find one you and your husband or partner connect with and who can provide your baby with the best available medical care. But, that is just the beginning. You may wish to hire a baby nurse or doula (see page 54) to help out in your home the first few days or weeks after your baby is born. After that, your child-care needs depend on what else is going on in your life. If you are returning to a job after a maternity leave, you will probably require full-time help, either in your home or elsewhere. If you work at home or are involved in activities that will take you away from your child a period of time each day or week, you will need child care part-time. Also, if you simply want to get out of the house now and then, sans baby, you should have one or two reliable baby-sitters to call upon. If you have family nearby, you may be lucky enough to have occasional free baby-sitting come your way.

We have each changed nannies several times since the first edition was published in 1997. The transitions were difficult both for our kids and ourselves, but we learned a valuable lesson: the most important person in your child's life is you, the parent. Kids eventually adjust to a new nanny or caregiver. That said, get the best nanny you can find, and keep looking until you find that person.

In this chapter, we'll show you how to find reliable child care. To help get the ball rolling, we'll give you names and numbers and our impressions.

pediatricians

You should begin looking for a pediatrician during the last few months of your pregnancy. Your baby's doctor will be noted on the record form that your obstetrician will send to the hospital about a month prior to your due date, and the pediatrician will then come by the hospital to examine your baby before the two of you are released.

Here's how to find a pediatrician, and what you should look for:

- Ask your obstetrician for a recommendation. If your doctor lives in the city, whom does she use for her own children? This is how Pamela found her pediatrician.
- Ask relatives, neighbors, and friends about pediatricians they use.
- Call any of the hospitals in the city, and ask for a referral from the pediatric department.
- Go to the New York Public Library and look up listings in the American Academy of Pediatrics directory. New York magazine's yearly edition of "The Best Doctors in New York" is a great resource as well.
- Consider location. Your newborn will be going to the doctor often, and having a pediatrician with an office near your home is practical, especially during an emergency or nasty weather.
- Consider whether you place importance on the doctor's age, type of practice (group, partner-

ship, or solo practitioner), or gender (some parents prefer to have a pediatrician the same sex as their baby).

Once you have the names of two or three pediatricians who sound promising, set up a consultation. Most will agree to make appointments in the early evening after regular office hours. Good doctors should be willing to take the time to meet with you and your husband or partner. Kelly requested consultations with five pediatricians. One did not conduct prenatal interviews; the other four were happy to meet with her and her husband to answer their questions and give them a brief office tour. It was time-consuming, but Kelly has been very happy with her pediatrician, and has never had to change. (If your prospective pediatrician is part of a group practice, it's a good idea to meet with most of the doctors; chances are each one will be treating your child at one time or another.)

Prepare a list of questions in advance and write down the doctors' answers. That way, you can compare pediatricians and discuss everything with your husband/partner, who may not be with you at each consultation. And, while you are waiting, take a look around the waiting room.

* Is it child friendly, with enough toys, pictures, and books to keep a baby or toddler busy during the wait to see the doctor?
* Is the receptionist friendly, or does she seem curt and harried?
* If you're visiting during office hours, ask parents in the waiting room about their experiences with the doctor; have they been positive?
* Find out how long they typically wait to see the

Top Ten Things to Look For in a Caregiver

1. Track record and references (strong ones!). How long does she stay in a job?
2. The ability to speak and read English or your native language.
3. Personality—it's hard to be around someone who never smiles.
4. Experience—especially with children the same age as your own (newborn experience is a must!)
5. Honesty—this is fundamental to any relationship between employer and employee, and particularly in regard to someone hired to watch your children.
6. Patience.
7. Positive attitude.
8. Nice appearance.
9. Reliability and responsibility.
10. Instinct—trust your gut.

doctor. A forty-five minute wait with a sick toddler is no fun.
* Do sick and healthy children wait in the same waiting room? Kelly's pediatrician has eight examination rooms, and babies under one year old automatically go into one of these. The office tries to keep only healthy children in the waiting area.
* Is there an on-site lab for quick blood tests, strep tests, etc.?

When you sit down with the doctor, be sure to ask the following questions:

* How does the doctor answer parents' non-emergency calls throughout the day? Is there a call-in hour or does the doctor take calls all day and return them intermittently between patients? Is there a nurse or physician's assistant who can answer questions?
* How are emergencies handled? Is the doctor affiliated with a nearby hospital? Is the practice affiliated with more than one hospital? (A good pediatrician will meet you at the hospital or have a specialist meet you there in case of an emergency.)
* How does the pediatrician feel about breastfeeding? (Whether or not you choose to breastfeed, you will want a pediatrician who is supportive and encouraging of your decision.)
* What are the pediatrician's views on circumcision, nutrition, immunizations, and preventive medicine? (It is important that you and your doctor are in sync on most of these issues.)
* If the pediatrician is a solo practitioner, who handles phone calls when she is on vacation?

If you don't feel rushed during the consultation, and the pediatrician is patient with you, these are good indicators of how the doctor will be with your baby. Again, don't be afraid to ask any questions. Even after you select a pediatrician, don't be afraid to change. We've had many friends do just that, and it is worth it! There are hundreds of pediatricians in New York, so just persevere. Like all aspects of childcare, the right one for you is out there.

baby nurses/doulas

Immediately after the birth of your baby, you may wish to have a baby nurse or doula.

Baby nurses usually come the day you bring the baby home and live with you in your apartment for a week or two or longer. An in-home nurse works twenty-four hours a day, seven days a week. She cares for the baby, gets up in the middle of the night to change and feed him or bring him to you for breastfeeding, and generally allows you to sleep later and rest up. Baby nurses are expensive, costing from $18 to $25 per hour. Some live-out and work for shorter periods (not a full day).

A doula comes to your home for a few hours each day and almost always lives out. She helps and pampers you: she does the grocery shopping, laundry, and fixes meals, so you have more time with your baby. She may also assist you in taking care of your baby by bathing or changing him, and she should be able to answer questions regarding breastfeeding.

When you hire a doula, typically you buy a set block of visits or hours with a fifteen-hour minimum. Each visit is at least three hours, and costs approximately $25 to $50 per hour.

The best way to find a baby nurse or doula is through a trusted friend who has used one herself. Or call one of the many agencies that have baby nurse divisions. Kelly hired her nurse, Olga, through an agency and was extremely pleased. Olga had been taking care of babies for more than twenty years, and her references were impeccable. So good, in fact, that one family kept her for five years! Pamela hired a baby nurse that she found through a friend, and she is so great, she continues to work for the family one day a week.

An agency will send three or four candidates for you to interview while you are pregnant. You may then reserve the baby nurse or doula of your choice, and the agency will try not to place her for two weeks around your due date. If you are late or early, the nurse you've requested may be on another job, but this rarely happens. Agencies are very good at monitoring their baby nurses' schedules.

Baby nurses get booked way in advance, so plan early. Kelly started asking friends for recommendations when she was five months pregnant, and three of the names she received were already booked.

Of course, your mother or mother-in-law may offer to stay with you. If you feel comfortable with a family member living in and helping out, great. However, we've found that many new parents prefer to hire short-term professional help, which allows them to get the rest they need without having to impose on—or be nice to—a relative.

The following is a list of baby nurse and doula agencies in the New York area. Also see www.4nanny.com/agency_directory/new_york.htm for a complete directory of various nanny agencies.

❊ Absolute Best Care
274 Madison Ave, Suite 503 at 40th Street
212-481-5705
email: dkozinn@absolutebestcare.com
www.absolutebestcare.com

❊ All Metro Health Care
50 Broadway, Lynbrook, New York
516-887-1200
80 Broad Street at South William Street
212-876-6530
www.all-metro.com

❊ Baby Nurses and Doulas
646-645-6922; 877-506-2585
email: info@babynursesanddoulas.com
www.babynursesanddoulas.com

❊ Baby Nurses and More/ Gentle Hands
See website for locations throughout NYC.
212-767-9173
email: gentlehands@gentlehandschildcare.com
www.babynursesandmore.com
www.gentlehandschildcare.com

❊ Bohne's Baby Nursing
16 East 79th Street at Madison Avenue, Suite G4
212-879-7920

❊ Doula Care
Ruth Callahan
70 West 93rd Street at Columbus Avenue
212-749-6613
www.doulacare.com
e-mail: ruth@doulacare.com

❊ Fox Agency
30 East 60th Street, Suite 904
bet. Park and Madison avenues
212-753-2686
www.classicbabynurse.com

❊ Frances Stewart Agency, Inc.
1220 Lexington Avenue, Suite 2B at Lexington Avenue
212-439-9222
www.francesstewartagency.com

In a Family Way

124 West 79th Street, Suite 9B
bet. Amsterdam and Columbus avenues
212-877-8112
email: inafamilyway@kealy.com
www.inafamilyway.com

Lullaby Staffing Services

914-816-3085
www.newyorkbabynurse.com

Mother Nurture

Doula Service
Glen Oaks, New York
718-631-BABY (718-631-2229)
email: doulacomp@aol.com
www.mothernurture.com

Penelope's People

226 East 54th Street, Suite 306
bet. Second and Third avenues
212-444-1313
email: info@penelopespeople.com
www.penelopespeople.com
Penelope's People offers the placement of nannies, baby-sitters, baby nurses, and companions for seniors for permanent, temporary, live-in, live-out, full-time, part-time, on-call, and emergency care. They follow a strict seven-step process in order to properly match clients.

nannies

Hiring someone to look after your child while you're at work or away is stressful and nerve-racking. You want someone who is good, kind, smart, honest, sober, reliable, loves kids, knows infant CPR, bakes cookies, and is going to think your baby is the most adorable child she's ever seen. You want another you.

Of course, you won't find another you, but if you're determined and keep your ears open, you will locate someone who will be an affectionate, caring, responsible child-care provider for your youngster.

You may want a nanny who lives with you or one who comes to your home each morning and leaves each evening. You may need this person's help on a part-time or full-time basis. There are several ways to go about finding her. As is true for so many services, word of mouth is the best place to start. Ask friends who have child care whether their nannies have friends looking for work. When we were in search of help, we stopped nannies in the park, talked to mothers and nannies at the classes we took with our children, and looked at bulletin board notices in child- and religious-oriented institutions and at our pediatricians' offices. Many schools as well as the Parent's League also post nanny information on their bulletin boards.

Craigslist.com has tons of ads placed by employers looking for a nanny and nannies looking for work. Use Craigslist.com at your own risk, and be sure to screen candidates carefully over the phone, and never meet with anyone alone at your home for the first time. Pamela successfully hired her last nanny through Craigslist.com by responding to an ad. Another great new resource is the nanny board on www.babybites.net. All of the listings on the nanny board have references that have been checked by babybites.

If you get nowhere by word of mouth, try the newspapers. Many parents have successfully found child care by advertising in newspapers or by answering an ad. We'll show you how to do that shortly. Finally, a number of agencies specialize in nanny placement. We list those agencies as well.

We cannot sufficiently stress the importance of checking references and thoroughly questioning candidates. On more than one occasion, we have heard stories of falsified references in which nannies listed friends or relatives instead of former employers. Toward the end of this section, we'll give you a list of some of the most important questions to ask your future nanny. You may also want to read *How to Hire a Nanny* by Elaine S. Pelletier. This step-by-step guide helps you through the nanny search. Another excellent resource, written by two experienced British moms, is *The Good Nanny Guide* by Charlotte Breese and Hilaire Gomer. Although geared to the English nanny system, it is full of practical advice and guidelines.

Prices for nannies vary according to experience, education, checkable references, and legal status, but start at around $600 a week. For an experienced, educated caregiver, you can expect to pay as much as $700 to over $1,000 per week.

Newspaper Advertisements

Placing a classified ad can be an excellent way to find a nanny. *The Irish Echo*, the *Irish Voice*, and *The New York Times* are popular nanny-finding papers (all of these papers are online, so you can scan every day). A number of newspapers are published for various nationalities and many nannies look in them for jobs. Explore them if you would prefer a nanny from a specific country, would like

your child to learn a foreign language, or if your spouse is from another country.

When you place an ad, be as specific as possible. If you must have a nonsmoker, live-in help, or someone with a driver's license, say so. If you need someone to work on Saturdays or stay late in the evening, state it. Check the classified sections to see examples of help-wanted ads, or follow the sample we've provided here:

Upper East Side Nanny Needed.

Live-in nanny needed for a two-year-old boy. Light housekeeping, shopping, and errands. Must have two years experience with toddlers and excellent checkable New York references. Nonsmoker. Must swim, drive, and cook. Must have legal working papers. Willing to travel with family. M-F, weekends off. Own room, TV-DVD, A/C. Call 555-5555.

When Kelly ran an ad similar to this one in two newspapers three weeks before Christmas, her phone began ringing at 6 a.m. the Wednesday morning the *Irish Echo* came out and she had received sixty calls by 11 a.m.

Interview candidates on the phone before you bring them to your home. Tell them about the job, find out what they are looking for, and ask about their past work experience. Screen them carefully; it will save you time later. Kelly needed a caregiver who could work on Saturdays and travel with the family, and she was able to eliminate a number of candidates who could not fill those requirements over the phone.

We recommend making a list of the three most appealing and the three least appealing aspects of your job. Discuss them with the applicant over the phone. Start with the three worst aspects: she must arrive at 7:30 every morning, she must baby-sit three nights a week, and she will be expected to work on Saturdays. If the applicant is still interested and if you are pleased with her responses to your key questions, proceed from there with an interview in your home or office.

The following four newspapers are reliable and frequently used. When you call, check their deadlines. Ads can be phoned, faxed or emailed, and can be paid for with a credit card.

❖ Irish Echo
11 Hanover Square
New York, NY 10005
212-482-4818; 212-482-6569 (fax); 212-482-7394 (fax 2)
www.irishecho.com
Call for exact submission details and deadlines. Three lines cost $35 and each additional line is $10. Lines consist of 30 characters, including spaces.

❖ Irish Voice
875 Avenue of the Americas, Suite 2100
New York, NY 10001
212-684-3366, ext. 22; 212-244-3344 (fax)
e-mail: classifieds@irishvoice.com
www.irishvoice.com
Prices are reasonable, but vary. Please call or email Robert Hogan for current info.

❖ The New York Times
620 Eighth Avenue
New York, NY 10018
212-556-1234
www.nytimes.com
Ad rates vary per day. Call for details regarding deadlines and submission details.

❖ The Polish Daily News
333 West 38th Street
New York, NY 10018
212-594-2266, ext. 31; 212-594-2374 (fax)
email: listy@dziennik.com
www.dziennik.com
This daily paper (except Sundays) is written in Polish, but many of the classifieds are in English. Ads must be submitted by noon to run in the next day's paper. Call or email for specific pricing and submission deadline details.

Agencies

On one hand, good word of mouth and a sterling reputation keeps a service business alive. On the other hand, the more people they place, the more money agencies make; high turnover is oddly beneficial to their business. This is contrary to what you are looking for—someone who will stay with you a long time. So, a few words of caution when using an agency: although agencies claim they check references, many have been known to send a candidate on an interview with skimpy or weak references. Some have never even met the candidate face to face. Be on guard if, for example, a nanny's previous employer has moved and now has an unlisted phone number somewhere in Florida, or if the applicant hands you a hand-written letter of reference with grammatically incorrect sentences and misspelled words.

❉ A Choice Nanny

850 Seventh Avenue, Suite 706
212-246-KIDS
email: nyc@achoicenanny.com
www.achoicenanny.com

❉ Absolute Best Care

274 Madison Ave, Suite 503
212-481-5706
email: dkozinn@absolutebestcare.com
www.absolutebestcare.com
This is a well-run agency that specializes in placing families with highly qualified nannies in New York, New Jersey, and Connecticut. Absolute Best Care's goal is to match families with caregivers who are highly qualified, capable and sensitive to the needs of children. It also offers nanny training classes and workshops.

❉ Absolute Best Care Nanny Learning Center

274 Madison Avenue at East 40th Street, 5th floor
212-481-5705
www.abcnlc.com
info@absolutebestcare.com
Absolute Best Care Nanny Learning Center is an offshoot of the Absolute Best Care nanny agency (see above). It is a licensed nanny training school dedicated to offering nannies and caregivers the highest level of education through a forty-hour curriculum that teaches nannies childcare standards such as milestones, organization, discipline, security and safety, education, entertainment, and much more, as well providing them with a full first-aid and CPR certification. They will also be trained in administration, maintenance, household communication, which are key ingredients to a successful nanny career. This is the only nanny training school that is licensed by the New York State Education Department and is designed to offer nannies a true career option in this field.

❉ Child Care, Inc.

322 Eighth Ave, 4th Floor
212-929-7604 (General); 212-929-4999 (Child Care Referrals)
email: info@childcareinc.org
www.childcareinc.org
Child Care, Inc., is a child-care resource and referral service that provides a consultation service to parents to help educate and choose the most efficient class for their child's needs.

❉ College Nannies & Tutors

College Nannies & Tutors NYC Metro
Julia Bardach, Placement Coordinator / Marketing Associate
860-302-8420; 203-504-7916 (fax)
email: jbardach@collegenannies.com
www.collegenannies.com
www.collegetutors.com
All nannies are college educated and available for workdays anywhere from one afternoon to fifty hours per week. All special needs

and requests are customized to meet each family's needs.

Domestic Job Picks

535 Fifth Avenue, Suite 1201
212-687-7876 (fax)
email: elizabeth@domesticjobpicks.com
www.domesticjobpicks.com

Fox Agency

516-984-3356
email: info@classicbabynurse.com
www.classicbabynurse.com

Frances Stewart Agency, Inc.

1220 Lexington Avenue, Suite 2B
212-439-9222
www.francesstewartagency.com

Greenhouse Agency, Ltd.

55 West 39th Street, Suite 700
bet. Fifth and Sixth avenues
212-889-7705; 212-889-3673 (fax)
email: reception@greenhousestaffing.com
www.greenhousestaffing.com

Mommy Mixer

email: info@mommymixer.com
www.mommymixer.com
MommyMixer connects busy moms with part-time sitters through face-to-face events, akin to speed dating. Mixers are held at hot spots throughout the city where parents can person-ally meet and interview a number of locally recruited candidates. At the end of the night, parents leave with the golden resource, the

Babysitting Book, featuring an A+ list of sitters including their contact information, availability, skills, and more. And mixers are fun, too! Events generally feature swag bags, shopping dis-counts at the venue, and giveaways (like a Mutsy stroller and a $200 Sephora gift bag).

The New York Nanny Center, Inc

250 West 57th Street
212-265-3354
email: info@nynanny.com
www.nynanny.com

Not Just Babysitters

917-523-0065
www.notjustbabysitters.com
Fully screened, top-notch, experienced, col-lege-educated sitters for short-term, long-term, or last-minute bookings.

NYC Nanny Finder

20 West 20th Street, 2nd Floor
646-660-2401
email: info@nycnannyfinder.com
www.nycnannyfinder.com

Pavillion Agency

15 East 40th, Suite 400
212-889-6609
www.pavillionagency.com

Professional Nannies Institute

501 Fifth Avenue, Suite 908
212-692-9510
email: pni@msn.com
www.profnannies.com

Robin Kellner Agency

2 West 45th Street, Suite 1503

212-997-4151

email: robin@robinkellner.com

www.robinkellner.com

Sitter City

888-SIT-CITY

email: support@sittercity.com

www.sittercity.com

Sittercity.com is America's largest database for baby-sitters and nannies. It has over 50,000 caregivers in fifteen major markets (including New York, of course), and provides an alternative to agencies or message boards as a way for parents and caregivers to contact each other and set up child-care jobs. All of its sitters are over the age of seventeen, and are skilled in areas like pre-med, early childhood education, CPR, first aid, disability, and more. Most sitters are college students, but there are also nannies and other child-care providers posted. Membership costs $39.99 for the first month, $9.99 each month after that, or $119.88 ($9.99 per month) for the entire year. Parents pay the sitters themselves on an hourly basis. Sittercity.com does not screen its applicants, so you must check references carefully.

Town and Country Companion and Nursing Agency, Inc.

286 Madison Avenue, Suite 905

212-921-5588

email: info@towncountryagency.com

www.towncountryagency.com

Urban Nurture

Sally Wilkinson, Founder

212-925-1400; 212-925-1414 (fax)

email: sally@urbannurture.com

www.urbannurture.com

Urban Nurture is a child-care consultancy based in Tribeca that opened for business in November 2006. Their philosophy is deeply routed in the British tradition of professional nanny care. Nannies in the U.K. are professionally trained, well respected, and highly paid, and Urban Nurture is seeking to offer New Yorkers the world-class nanny services they have long deserved.

The Interview

Nothing is as important as the interview to determine whether a candidate is the right person to take care of your little one. Be conscious of the atmosphere you create. Are you interviewing potential nannies at your office, in your formal living room, in the playroom, family room, or at the kitchen table? Are you looking for someone to join the family, or will this person be more of an employee with a formal working arrangement?

Pamela always likes to interview nannies with her husband present. It's useful to get a second opinion, and to have another person asking questions you might forget to ask. It's also good to have your child nearby so you can see how the potential candidate interacts with him.

Here's our suggested list of interview questions:

* Tell me about yourself. Where are you from? Where did you grow up? How many brothers and sisters do you have? Did your mom and dad work?

* Why do you want to be a nanny? What is it you like about being a nanny?

* What previous child-care experiences do you have? Tell me about those jobs.

* What was a typical day like? What did your duties/responsibilities include? (Look for someone who has held a child-care position similar to the one you are offering. If she cooked and cleaned on the last job and you are looking for light cooking and cleaning, she probably won't be upset if you ask her to grill a chicken breast or wipe off the kitchen counter.)

* How many children did you take care of in your previous positions? How old were they?

* Do you have children of your own?

* What did you like best about your previous jobs? What did you like least?

* Why did you leave your last job(s)?

* Did Mrs. X work? How did you two interact on a daily basis?

* Do you smoke?

* Do you have CPR or first-aid training?

* Can you stay late during the week or work on weekends if necessary?

* Describe an emergency or stressful situation in your past job? How did you handle it?

* What are your child-rearing philosophies or views on discipline? Do you believe in spanking and time-outs?

* What are your interests? What do you like to do when you're not working?

* Do you have any health restrictions or dietary preferences I should know about?

* What are you looking for in a family?

* Would you travel with the family if needed?

* Do you know your way around the city?

* Do you drive, swim, bicycle (or whatever else is important to you)?

* Do you like to read? What is your favorite children's book?

* When could you start? What are your salary requirements?

Checking References

Checking references with previous employers can be one of the most challenging parts of finding child care. Who are you calling? How can you be sure the name you have been given is not a candidate's friend or relative? And then, some people just aren't very talkative on the telephone. They reveal very little that can help you reach a decision.

Use your common sense and intuition; be open and friendly; and identify yourself in detail. For example: "Hello Mrs. X, this is Mrs. Y, and I am calling to check a reference on Susan Jones, who told me she worked for you. My husband and I live in New York City on East 53rd Street and we have a three-year-old daughter." Tell her a little about your family. This will help break the ice and allow you to ask about her family and work situations. It's important to know the kind of household in which your potential nanny has worked, because it may be very different from your own. If Mrs. X had a staff of three, and Susan had no household duties, she may not be happy in your home if you ask her to cook, clean, and do the laundry. Be realistic.

Here are some questions you may want to ask:

- How did you meet Susan? (agency, friend, ad?)
- How long was Susan with you?
- Why did she leave?
- How many children do you have? How old are they?
- Do you work? What do you do? Were either you or your husband home during the day or was Susan pretty much on her own?
- What were Susan's responsibilities?
- What were her hours?
- Was there ever an emergency or difficult situation that Susan had to handle on her own?
- How would you describe her overall personality and attitude?
- Was it easy to communicate with her? Did she give you daily feedback on your children? Did she take direction/instruction well?
- Did she cook, clean, drive, run errands, swim, iron (or whatever you need most)?
- Did you trust her? Did you find her reliable and honest?
- How did your children like her? Did you like her?
- Would you hire her again?

Several agencies verify references on nannies. Documented Reference Check (800-742-3316 or 909-629-0317; www.badreferences.com; email: customerservice@badreferences.com) investigates employment references and sends a report to you for $87.95. American International Security in Virginia (276-346-3400, www.aisc-online.com) charges $95 (+$50 in NY), for which you obtain a motor vehicle record, a New York City criminal convictions record, and a social security number track report, and a DMV check. A credit check is an additional $35, and other services are available, including

National Criminal Check Only, $150; National Criminal Check with DMV and SSN, $195; and Criminal Check in a Foreign Country, $95.

When the Nanny Starts

After you have found the right person, it is important to watch how she and your baby and/or children interact in order to make sure they are comfortable with each other. It's a good idea to have prepared a list of duties as well as what is expected of the nanny on a daily basis aside from child care, such as cooking, cleaning, laundry, and grocery shopping. Be specific. Sit down and go over everything again within the first few days to make sure she understands and accepts the responsibilities of the job. Set a date for a follow-up meeting in two weeks to discuss how things are going, what's working well, and what is not.

We are big on giving the nanny a "trial" period. We try her out for a week or so and see if it's a match hiring her full time. If you are going back to work, it is a good idea to have your new nanny begin at least two weeks before you start. This will give you an opportunity to observe her with your baby and to show her around your neighborhood. Take her to your supermarket, dry cleaner (or to whatever other places she may need to visit while working for your family), as well as to the pediatrician's office so that she can feel comfortable going there without you, if necessary.

You may also want your nanny to have a physical examination. Certainly, inquire about her health and vaccinations. Depending on where your nanny is from and how long she has been in this country, she may not be vaccinated against measles, mumps and rubella, or chicken pox. If she's not, arrange with your doctor for her to get these shots, as well as a flu shot and an H1N1 vaccination if your family members have decided to get theirs.

Once a nanny is on the job, you may want to monitor her activities in your absence. Parents who have had to hire a caregiver very quickly and have little time to train and supervise may find that having in-home video surveillance, or a "nanny cam" provides peace of mind.

The following is a list of additional companies that provide video surveillance and other nanny-related services. Some companies now have remote monitoring packages that allow parents to view their children via the Internet. Many people are divided over whether or not to utilize video surveillance (or nanny cams). It is an ethical decision that only you can make. You may want to tell your nanny that you have a camera so that she is always on her best behavior; other parents just let the camera run without informing the nanny. Best practice is that if you suspect that there may be a problem (your baby seems fussier, unhappy, or unwilling to go to the nanny), then talk to her first. If you are unsure, best to let her go and find someone else.

❋ *Best Nanny Cam*
www.bestnannycam.com

❋ *Homestep*
212-760-5959; 516-375-8492
email: homestepsafety@yahoo.com
www.homestepsafety.com

❋ *Know Your Nanny*
866-364-0967
www.knowyournanny.com

❋ *Mind Your Business*
888-758-3776; 732-302-9104 (fax)
email: jyarbrough@mybinc.com
www.mybinc.com

❋ *Video Surveillance.com*
877-478-1911
email: info@videosurveillance.com
www.videosurveillance.com

Taxes and Insurance

Remember that once you hire a nanny, you have become an employer. Check out "Nanny Taxes for Dummies" for an easy way to calculate which taxes you need to pay and how to set yourself up as an employer. (www.dummies.com/how-to/content/considering-nanny-taxes-when-choosing-childcare.htm.)

The Basics are:

1. Apply for an employer identification number with the IRS using form SS-4 (www.irs.gov).
2. File Schedule 1040H (a tax form that replaced Form 942). Employers should report wages paid to household workers or nannies on their income tax returns. Schedule H, which is filed with your 1040, simplifies the work of calculating social security, Medicare, and federal income taxes.
3. Give your nanny a W-2 form, listing total wages and taxes paid, by January 31.

4. File a W-3, a summary of all your W-2s, by February 28. File quarterly and annual state reports.

Other forms to fill out include federal unemployment and state unemployment tax forms. These cover anyone who earns more than $100 a quarter. The federal unemployment tax form 940 can be obtained from the IRS; the New York State Labor Department supplies state unemployment forms.

Other areas of concern are compensation and disability policies. If you employ a child-care provider for more than forty hours a week, you should buy a workers' compensation and disability policy. These start at around $300. Call the New York State Insurance Fund for more information (212-312-9000). The IRS publishes two booklets to help employers through this maze: "Employment Taxes for Household Employers" (Book 926) and "What You Need to Know If You Hire Domestic Help" (Book 27). To receive these booklets, call the N.Y.S. Department of Taxation and Finance at (800) 462-8100. Call the New York State Department of Labor, 518-457-9000; 888-4-NYSDOL to request the "Employer's Guide to Unemployment Insurance." For even more information about taxes, contact the IRS at 800-829-1040.

au pairs

Hiring an au pair is a child-care option many parents find practical and economical.

Au pairs come to the United States from various countries, but they are usually European. They can remain in this country legally for one year and work a forty-five-hour week. Generally, an au pair has a week-long orientation just after she arrives in this country, and she takes one academic course during her stay. In addition, she is provided with support counselors and a health plan by her umbrella organization.

Au pairs are not permitted to care for babies younger than three months, and must have two hundred hours of child-care experience to care for children younger than age 2. Current wages for an au pair are $195.75 per week plus room and board. Families also pay $500+ toward academic coursework for the au pair. Au pairs can work forty-five hours per week, no more than ten hours per day. Always interview a prospective au pair over the phone or in person if possible. Most agencies provide background information on several candidates.

Au pairs tend to be inexperienced child-care providers. They most often work in homes with stay-at-home mothers. They are not allowed to remain alone with children overnight, so an au pair is not a good option for parents who travel. Pamela's friend Margot has employed close to half a dozen au pairs in seven years. She was extremely satisfied with one out of six; the rest were mediocre to decent, but none fabulous. One drawback with au pairs is that they are young, and many of them want an active social life. In New York, that is not always compatible with child care.

If you are interested in hiring an au pair, contact the following agencies:

❖ *Agent Au Pair*
Stacey Frank, Director
1450 Sutter Street, #526
San Francisco, CA 94109
415-376-0202
email: info@agentaupair.com
www.agentaupair.co/uk

Au Pair in America

River Plaza
9 West Broad Street
Stamford, CT 06902
800-9AU-PAIR (800-928-7247)
email: aupair.info@aifs.com
www.aupairinamerica.com

Au Pair Care

600 California Street, 10th Floor
San Francisco, CA 94108
800-428-7247
email: customercare@aupaircare.com
www.aupaircare.com

Au Pair Foundation

866-428-7211; 631-651-2871
Gail Scamoni, NY Director
email: gail@aupairfoundation.org
www.aupairfoundation.org

Au Pair International

888-649-2876
email: hostfamily@aupairint.com
www.aupairint.com

Au Pair USA/Interexchange

161 Sixth Avenue, 10th Floor at Spring Street
New York, NY 10013
800-AU-PAIRS (800-287-2477); 212-924-0446
email: aupair@interexchange.org
www.aupairusa.org
www.interexchange.org

Cultural Homestay International

800-432-4643
www.chiaupairusa.org

EurAupair

250 North Coast Highway
Laguna Beach, CA 92651
800-713-2002
Tiare Toulon, Eastern Regional Director
email: east@euraupair.com
www.euraupair.com

Go AUPAIR

151 East 6100 South, Suite 200
Murray, UT 84107
888-AUPAIR-1 (888-287-2471)
email: inforequest@goaupair.com
www.goaupair.com

Great Au Pair

775-215-5770
email: support@greataupair.com
www.greataupair.com

day-care centers

New York City has more than twenty-five hundred day-care centers where you can bring your child early each morning and pick him or her up by 6 p.m. Centers must meet rigid requirements in order to be licensed by the State of New York.

One of the best professionally run day-care centers we know is the Bright Horizons Center at 435 East 70th Street (212-746-6543). This nationwide chain has an excellent reputation as a leader in upholding stringent day-care standards, with over fifteen locations in NYC alone. In addition, there are approximately 5,300 in-home care centers or family day-care providers in the city. In family day care, an individual takes care of a few children (by law, no more than twelve) in her home. The provider must be licensed by New York State and must register with the Department of Health. Even so, be cautious. Pay a personal visit to the center, speak with other parents, and trust your instincts.

Investigate options offered by your employer. More and more companies are offering on-site day care, or are willing to contribute to day-care costs.

House of Little People

122 East 91st Street, # 1
bet. Lexington and Park avenues
212-369-2740
www.houseoflittlepeople.org
This daycare center is in Pamela's neighborhood and she knows many parents who have happily used their services for their own babies and children. It is a lovely facility and a sought after daycare center in an area where there aren't many.

Love A Lot Preschool

99 Suffolk Street
bet. Delancey and Rivington streets
21 Clinton Street at Stanton Street
212-529-2650
email: info@lovealotpreschool.com
www.lovealotpreschool.com
Ages: 2 months to 5 years old
Love A Lot preschool is a combination preschool/day-care center and it provides all-day care, following a preschool curriculum. Love A Lot takes children as young as two months old. It offers full, partial, half, or extended-day options, two to five days a week. Love A Lot is licensed by the NYC Department of Health and is a great new day-care option for downtown families.

For more information contact:

Child Care Inc.

322 Eighth Avenue at West 26th Street, 4th Floor
212-929-7604 (general); 212-929-4999 (child care referrals)
This nonprofit organization serves as an information and referral resource for New York parents. Its excellent guides include "Choosing Child Care for Your Infant or Toddler," "Choosing an Early Childhood Program," and "In-Home Care." Other handouts cover finding and working with in-home care or nanny agencies, and it has samples of contracts for household employment. Child Care will also prepare lists of day-care centers and in-home care providers by zip code.

❋ The Department of Health:

This city agency regulates day-care centers and will tell you whether a specific center is licensed. Call 212-676-2444 and ask for the child-care bureau.

❋ The Daycare Council of New York

12 West 21st Street at Fifth Avenue, 3rd Floor
212-206-7818
email: info@dccnyinc.org
www.dccnyinc.org
The Council will refer you to twenty-five centers free of charge. Centers are listed by zip code, and you can request referrals in three zip codes. You will probably want to look at centers that are in your home and office zip codes to compare and contrast.

baby-sitting

You may be a stay-at-home parent who requires only a little child care on a Saturday night or a few afternoons a week. The solution here is a baby-sitter. Ask your doorman, superintendent, or neighbor whether there are teenagers in the building available for baby-sitting, or check out colleges that have baby-sitting services or a baby-sitting agency. Each service works differently; often there is an initial registration fee between $25 and $50. Many require a two-hour minimum and have varying rates, starting at $12 an hour. Look for a sitter who has experience with children the same age as your child, and check references. Don't assume that just because someone is enrolled in a local college she is trustworthy.

Finally, tell everyone you know that you're looking for a sitter. Ask other baby-sitters or nannies for recommendations. Oftentimes an experienced nanny is looking to make some extra money and will be happy to watch your child on a Saturday night; check bulletin boards at your pediatrician's office and play spaces. Pamela has used Barnard Baby-Sitting Service and always finds the students reliable and competent.

You may want to consider having a sitter come for an afternoon when you are at home to watch how she interacts and plays with your child. It is better for your child to have regular sitters whom she knows and you trust.

Baby-sitting services include:

❋ Absolute Best Care

274 Madison Avenue at East 40th Street, Suite 503
212-481-5705; 732-972-4090 (NJ office)
email: dkozinn@absolutebestcare.com
www.absolutebestcare.com

❋ Baby Sitters Guild

60 East 42nd Street at Park Avenue, Suite 912
212-682-0227
email: babysittersguild@cs.com
www.babysittersguild.com
It has been in business for over fifty years and can send you a sitter who is bilingual. The company has sitters who speak over sixteen different languages. Rates start at $20 an hour.

❋ Bank Street College

610 West 112th Street
bet. Broadway and West End Avenue
212-875-4400; 212-875-4404; 212-875-4678 (fax)

Bank Street College will post baby-sitting employment positions for graduate students for free. It is open Monday through Friday from 9 a.m. to 5 p.m.

❈ Barnard Baby-Sitting Service at Barnard College

49 Claremont Avenue at 119th Street,
2nd Floor of Elliot Hall
212-854-2035
email: bbsitter@barnard.edu
www.eclipse.barnard.columbia.edu/~bbsitter/index.html

❈ Metropolitan Sitters LLC

Brooke Woodard, Founder
917-575-7370
email: info@metropolitansitters.com
www.metropolitansitters.com
Metropolitan Sitters offers on-call baby-sitting, part-time nannying, full-time nannying, traveling sitters for family vacations, overnight sitters, and event sitters at a monthly membership fee of $25. Hourly rates vary, starting at $16 per hour.

❈ NYC Artist Babysitting

328 West 83rd Street at Riverside Drive,
Suite 3E
646-707-3281
Shannon Darin, Owner and President
email: Shannon@artistbabysitting.com
www.artistbabysitting.com
NYC Artist Babysitting Agency is a unique baby-sitting agency that inspires creative artistic exploration for kids of all ages by employing professional, established artists to engage in creative child care.

❈ NYC Nanny Finder

20 West 20th Street at Fifth Avenue, 2nd Floor
646-660-2401
email: info@nycnannyfinder.com
www.nycnannyfinder.com
NYC Nanny Finder believes in a fair and reasonable pricing structure. There is no sign-up fee to become a member. At the time a family decides to hire a candidate for a nanny, baby-sitter, or temporary help position, a placement fee is paid.

❈ Pinch Sitters

275 Madison Avenue at East 40th Street,
14th Floor
212-260-6005
email: pinchsitters@yahoo.com
www.nypinchsitters.com
All sitters have at least three years experience and two recent references, a background and reference check, plus personal interviews are conducted with each sitter. Sitters are college graduates, American citizens, and English-speaking women between the ages of twenty-two and fifty. Bookings are designed for last-minute needs and can be made with as little as two hours notice, however there is a $35 cancellation fee for bookings cancelled with less than twenty-four hours notice. Most sitters are fun college grads who are pursuing careers in the arts. Baby-sitters charge $20 per hour with a four-hour minimum and cab fare ($10 max) after 9 p.m.

❋ Sensible Sitters

175 East 96th Street at Third Avenue, #27M

646-485-5121

email: vanessa@sensiblesitters.com

www.sensiblesitters.com

❋ Sitter City

222 Merchandise Mart Plaza, 22nd Floor

Chicago, IL 60654

888-SIT-CITY

email: support@sittercity.com

www.sittercity.com

Sittercity.com is America's first website for parents and college baby-sitters. Now over eight years old, Sittercity.com has aided more than 50,000 sitters in fifteen major markets to find local jobs in their area. Parents joining Sittercity.com get access to local sitters for a subscription fee of $39.99 for the first month, $9.99 each month after that, or $119.88 ($9.99 per month) for the entire year. Parents pay the sitters themselves on an hourly basis. Sittercity.com does not screen its applicants, so you must check references carefully. Baby-sitting rates vary by location.

adjusting to
new motherhood

After you bring your newborn home, your bulging belly won't be the only thing missing—all semblance of control over your life will have vanished too . . . but that's okay.

The first few weeks at home are going to be turbulent. Many new mothers feel a bit blue or depressed. Having a baby is an emotionally draining experience, and to complicate things, those hormones really kick in after the birth. You may feel tired all day. Life will seem to be reduced to baby feedings, diaper changing, and laundry, laundry, laundry. The state of your apartment will deteriorate right before your very eyes.

Our advice? Let the place get messy. Use the time between feedings, changes, and naps to take care of yourself, rest, and think about what an adorable child you have. Allow willing friends and grandparents to throw in a load of laundry for you or pick up your dry cleaning.

If you actually cook, forget about it now. Order in. (Try www.menupages.com or www.delivery.com or www.seamlessweb.com for delivery ease!) New York is take-out heaven, and there is wonderful prepared food all around you. Come to think of it, order all your necessities! Most pharmacies will take phone orders and deliver. The big drugstore chains, such as Duane Reade and Rite Aid, all deliver formula by the case, disposable diapers, and baby wipes by the package. Or get online and order formula and diapers from www.diapers.com. Have your food and supplies delivered from your local supermarket or www.freshdirect.com. Make it easy on yourself.

This book suggests dozens of places to meet new mothers and learn from the experts. We can't say enough about forming or joining a playgroup, or a group of moms with babies who are the same age as your own. Playgroups usually meet once a week in rotating homes. If you don't have friends with babies your age, don't worry, you'll meet some.

Take a Strollercize class, attend a Babybites Luncheon, sign up for a hospital class—before you know it, you will have friends all over town.

Forming a playgroup was a lifesaver for Pamela, whose children were both born in the winter. The women she met in Rebecca's group sixteen years ago are some of her best friends to this day. A playgroup should have four to six moms and babies and meet at a specific time each week. You can serve lunch, or just cold drinks, and let the babies do their thing while the moms discuss everything from breastfeeding to sleep deprivation and more. These get-togethers become vital to a new mother's sanity, and definitely will become one of the highlights of your week.

new mother classes

Once your baby is a few weeks old and you have settled into something of a routine, you'll enjoy swapping baby stories with other mothers and sharing advice on caring for your infant.

A number of hospitals offer classes you can attend with your baby. They provide an opportunity to hear from pediatricians, child psychologists, child-safety experts, and other skilled professionals. Plus, you'll be able to ask questions and meet other new parents.

When Alexander was six weeks old, Kelly attended the five-week New Mother Discussion Group at New York Hospital. This class, led by Jean Schoppel, RN, and Ronni Soled, became the highlight of her week. Pamela took the New Mother/New Baby class, for mothers with children newborn to twelve months, offered by the 92nd Street Y, and loved it.

Hospital Classes

The hospitals listed below offer new mother classes. Fees vary from hospital to hospital and change frequently; most range from $40 to over $100+ for one-time classes or workshops, and from $300 to $400+ per couple for a series of classes or new mother support group meetings. Most hospital classes and support groups are open to all women, not just those who delivered at that hospital. So, if you want to take a class at New York Hospital but deliver at Beth Israel, just call New York Hospital to sign up. New moms are encouraged to bring their babies to all classes.

❉ *Beth Israel Hospital*
16th Street at First Avenue
212-420-2000 (General); 212-420-2999 (Classes)
email: biparented@aol.com
www.wehealny.org/familyed
Beth Israel offers a variety of classes and intensive workshops for the new mother, including a childbirth preparation series, a baby care and parenting class, a CPR course, a class in child safety, a breastfeeding class, a sibling preparation course, a new mothers' support group, and more.

❉ *Lenox Hill Hospital*
100 East 77th Street
bet. Lexington and Park avenues
212-434-2000 (General); 212-434-2273 (Parents Education)
www.lenoxhillhospital.org

Parent education classes for childbirth preparation, infant care, CPR, and physical fitness are offered in cooperation with the 92nd Street Y.

❉ *The Mount Sinai Hospital of Mount Sinai NYU Health*
The Jo Carole and Ronald S. Lauder Center for Maternity Care
One Gustave L. Levy Place
Klingenstein Pavilion
The Kravis Children's Hospital
1176 Fifth Avenue at 98th Street (enter at Madison and 100th Street)
212-241-6500 (General); 212-241-7491 (Women & Children's Office); 212-241-6578 (Breastfeeding Warm Line)
www.mountsinai.org
Mount Sinai offers classes in caring for newborns, CPR, breastfeeding, cesarean birth, siblings, and Lamaze. Its new mothers' support group meets once a week.

❉ *New York-Presbyterian Hospital / Columbia University Medical Center*
420 East 76th Street at First and York avenues, Suite 131
212-305-2500 (General); 212-305-2040 (Lactation Consultants); 212-746-3215 (Preparation for Parenthood Program)
www.columbiaobgyn.org/obstetrics/ob_classes.html
Columbia Presbyterian offers a three-week or a five-week Lamaze curriculum, a breastfeeding workshop, and classes in baby care and parenting.

Top Ten Things to Keep You Sane with a Newborn

1. Stock the freezer before the baby is born—lasagna, soup, etc.
2. Get help—a friend, mother, sister, or baby-sitter, if possible. Remember: any relief is better than no relief at all.
3. Sleep when the baby sleeps.
4. Order take-out food the first few weeks; it's too tiring to cook.
5. Buy in bulk and have it delivered—a case of formula, a box of diapers, and several packages of baby wipes will make life much easier.
6. Open up charge accounts at stores in the neighborhood that will deliver.
7. Let the house get messy.
8. Make friends with other new moms, and call them.
9. Try to go outside every day.
10. Attend a new moms' event or class.

❖ New York-Presbyterian Hospital/ Weill Cornell Medical Center

525 East 68th Street at York Avenue
212-746-5454 (General); 212-746-3215 (Preparation for Parenthood Office)
www.cornellpediatrics.org
New York Hospital offers a multiples class, for women delivering twins or multiple babies; a baby care class; and a new mothers' discussion group that meets once a week. The Preparation for Parenthood staff maintains a telephone information line for new mothers.

❖ New York University Medical Center

660 First Avenue, Room 470
bet. 37th and 38th streets
212-263-7300 (General); 212-263-7201 (Classes)
www.nyubaby.org
New York University Medical Center offers very extensive classes in childbirth preparation, infant, child and adult CPR, first aid, and a sibling class. Additionally, they offer a breastfeeding support group for new mothers that meets once a week.

❖ St. Luke's Roosevelt Hospital Center

1000 Tenth Avenue at 58th Street
212-523-4000 (General); 212-523-6222 (Parent/ Family Education); 212-523-BABY (Appointments)
www.nywomenshealth.com
St. Luke's Roosevelt Hospital offers classes in family education, baby care, infant CPR, child CPR, and breastfeeding, and has a new mothers' support group. They also cater to those having twins or more with a multiples Lamaze or breastfeeding for multiples class, as well as an older sibling prep class for ages three to six and seven to twelve. St. Luke's holds workshops for fathers, second-time mothers, and even pet owners. Not enough variety? Try their prenatal yoga class for a calming time-out.

CPR Classes

Baby Be Safe

See website for locations throughout NYC.
888-SAFE-557
email: natania@babybesafe.com
www.babybesafe.com
Baby Be Safe teaches infant and child CPR and first aid classes that include preventative segments on childproofing, emergency prevention, and safety tips for individuals, groups, and organizations. You can also get a group of friends together and arrange your own CPR/first aid class at your home or office.

Downtown Babies

See website for locations throughout Manhattan and New Jersey.
212-502-7996
email: info@downtownbabies.com
www.downtownbabies.com
Downtown Babies is a parent education resource and social club for parents, caregivers, and children (birth to five years). Downtown Babies also offers creative play packages for infants, toddlers, and preschoolers that focus on a variety of areas important to a child's physical growth and development (feelings, sharing, caring, pretend play, music, creative movement, and so on).

Enjoy CPR

273 Bowery Street at East Houston
718-233-2599; 800-939-0236
general email: info@enjoycpr.com
class information email: classes@enjoycpr.com
www.enjoycpr.com
Enjoy CPR offers infant, child, and adult CPR classes at your home or a local facility during mornings, evenings, and weekends. Their classes are conducted in an enjoyable, effective, and efficient way, allowing for same-day certification. The price of class includes a textbook and DVD.

Fern Drillings, RN, MSN, CCES

Call for locations throughout Manhattan.
212-744-6649
Besides being a childbirth educator, Fern also gives infant CPR and baby safety classes. She is also a nurse on staff at NYU Hospital. Contact her to get the schedule for the East and West Side locations, or put together your own group and inquire about personalized private sessions.

Little Hearts CPR

688 Sixth Avenue at 22nd Street, Suite 202
212-691-5989
email: info@littleheartscpr.com
www.littleheartscpr.com
CPR/baby safety classes from GotCPR at Little Hearts are held on the Upper East Side, Upper West Side, Downtown, and Brooklyn. They offer comprehensive training in a fun and enjoyable atmosphere in group settings, and private sessions as well. Classes are available daytime, evenings, and weekends, too, so there is no excuse not to take a class! If getting a baby-sitter is not possible, young babies are also welcome.

Northeast CPR

606 Columbus Avenue
bet. 89th and 90th streets

857-991-6509

email: contact@northeastcpr.com

www.northeastcpr.com

Classes held every Sunday at 6 p.m. at Super Soccer Stars. This straightforward class taught by licensed paramedics and firefighters provides personalized training and group sessions at affordable rates.

❉ *Save-A-Tot*

317 East 34th Street at Second Avenue

212-725-7477

email: info@saveatotcpr.com

www.saveatotcpr.com

Save-A-Tot offers private or group infant/child CPR at your home or in midtown Manhattan for parents, expecting parents, grandparents, and caregivers. Private childbirth education classes and safety and baby-proofing classes are also available.

Other Classes, Groups, and Seminars

There are excellent non-hospital-based support and discussion groups throughout the city. Many of them, like the hospital classes, teach infant CPR, which every new parent should learn. Some of the classes listed are fun to take with your child.

Schedules and fees are always subject to change. Call for the most up-to-date information.

❉ *92nd Street Y "New Parent Get-Togethers"**

92nd Street YM-YWHA

1395 Lexington Avenue

bet. East 91st and 92nd streets

212-415-5611 (Parenting Center);

212-415-5500 (General)

www.92y.org

New parent get-togethers (birth to twelve months) features speakers who discuss topics including working and parenting, child care, sleep, babies, and your marriage ($5 for members of the Y's Parenting Center, $10 for nonmembers; $175 for annual membership). See website for a detailed schedule. Other classes for new moms include postpartum exercise, caring for a newborn, and a breastfeeding workshop. The Y also offers a New Mother/New Baby class that tackles different topics each week. The Y offers baby-sitting for children four months to four years; $12 per hour for nonmembers and $11 per hour for members. For more information on baby-sitting, please call 212-415-5617; this is a separate phone line just for baby-sitting rates.

❉ *Apple Seeds*

10 West 25th Street

bet. Broadway and Sixth Avenue

212-792-7590

email: hello@appleseedsnyc.com

www.appleseedsnyc.com

Appleseeds is a 15,000-square-foot play space with a playground, various classes, camp, birthday parties, special events, a boutique, children's salon, and cafe for all of your parenting needs. Classes for newborns include Baby Fingers, an American Sign Language class; Music Together, a music class; Chat & Snack, a parent's group class; Prenatal Yoga; and Developmental Movement, a sports and movement class that aids in the crawling-to-walking process. All prices vary; see website for further information.

✳ Babybites

See website for locations throughout NYC, as well as in New Jersey and Westchester.
email: manhattan@babybites.net
www.babybites.net
Babybites, run by Laura Deutsch, a mother of two, is a fast-growing social and educational community for moms and moms-to-be. At various locations throughout Manhattan, they host numerous events like new mom luncheons, sample classes, seminars, new mom support groups, and special events (like Infant Massage and Mommy Happy Hour!) Pamela is a frequent speaker at these luncheons and events. Truly a gem in the world of moms!

✳ Birth Day Presence

Terry Richmond, Jada Shapiro, and Anna Merrill
291 8th Street
bet. Fifth and Sixth avenues
917-751-6579
email: doulas@birthdaypresence.net
www.birthdaypresence.net
Birth Day Presence provides birth and postpartum doula support, childbirth education classes, seminars, chiropractic care, and pregnancy, birth, and child photography.

✳ CitiBabes

52 Mercer Street, 3rd Floor
800-697-0107

email: info@citibabes.com
www.citibabes.com
Citibabes is the only family membership club that has offerings for both children and adults. A Citibabes annual membership costs around $2,100 for an all-access pass that includes access to an indoor play space, cafe, adult gym, yoga and fitness classes, adult lounge, e-learning centers, travel concierge, retail boutique, family events, and parenting seminars. Membership also includes a package of prenatal products and services including a Preparing for Parenthood workshop.

✳ The Early Childhood Development Center

Becky Thomas, ECDC Director
163 East 97th Street at Third Avenue
212-360-7803
ww.cchphealthcare.org
The center conducts one-hour weekly meetings to discuss sleeping, feeding, crying, and other early child-raising issues. Call for up–to-date information on schedules and pricing.

✳ Educational Alliance Parenting and Family Center at the Sol Goldman YM-YWHA*

344 East 14th Street
bet. First and Second avenues
212-780-0800, ext. 236
email: info@14streety.org
www.14streety.org
The Educational Alliance, a nonprofit organization, is a great city resource with a variety of wonderful workshops for parents and classes

for children of all ages. For new moms, the Alliance offers New Moms Stroll-In, an open discussion led by the director of the Parenting and Family Center, Kiki Schaffer. The groups are ongoing. It's five sessions and it costs $50 for members, $65 for nonmembers. A trial class costs $15. (Ms. Schaffer, a CSW, is available for private counseling sessions as well. She can be reached at 212-780-0800, ext 4335.) The Alliance also offers a workshop entitled Preparing Your Marriage for Parenthood, counseling groups for mothers suffering from postpartum depression and mothers returning to work, co-parenting classes for the divorced/separated, nanny partnering classes, parenting classes for special-needs children, classes in infant massage, and prental, postnatal, and mommy/baby yoga. Kiki Schaffer is a consummate professional, and we only wish we lived closer to the Sol Goldman Y.

Sandra Jamrog, CCE, AAHCC, LMT

600 West 111th Street at Broadway, #3B
212-866-8527
email: sandy@sandrajamrog.com
A mother of four, Sandra Jamrog has been a childbirth educator for over thirty years. She teaches pre- and postnatal classes as well as childbirth education and is also a New York State–licensed massage therapist. In addition, Sandy teaches infant movement sessions, which stimulate appropriate infant development, with the caretakers' cooperation. This helps parents to better understand their infant's development.

Jewish Community Center on the Upper West Side

334 Amsterdam Avenue at 76th Street
646-505-4444; 646-505-5700 (Membership)
email: info@jccmanhattan.org
www.jccmanhattan.org
The 120,000-square-foot JCC offers a wide range of activities for new parents, including new parents' luncheons, childbirth education, infant/child first aid/CPR classes, and classes like New Moms, New Babies, Baby Teeth Basics, Postpartum Depression, and Massage for Babies: Connecting to Your Child. The JCC is a valuable local resource for parents.

Karma Kids Yoga

104 West 14th Street bet. Sixth and
Seventh avenues
646-638-1444
email: downdog@karmakidsyoga.com
www.karmakidsyoga.com
For new moms, Karma Kids Yoga offers many classes like a prenatal yoga class, Mom & Baby Yoga and Dad & Baby Yoga (both for ages six weeks to walkers), Parent & Child Yoga (walkers to three years), Story Time Yoga (infants to five years), and private yoga instruction. They also have classes for children in their teens. See their website for info on special free trials.

Phyllis LaBella, LCSW, BCD

Adoption Specialist, Domestic and
International
212-987-0077
Phyllis treats an entire range of emotional problems and issues affecting adopted children, adoptive couples, and birth moms.

Mindful Parenting:

750 Park Avenue at East 72nd Street
212-327-3624
email: jsherwitz@verizon.net
www.rie.org

Johanna Herwitz, PhD, leads this parent and baby playgroup and encourages moms to trust their instincts, do less, and observe their child more. The RIE method (popular in L.A. and meaning "Resources for Infant Educators") teaches parents how to recognize the unique needs of their baby and how to have realistic expectations for themselves and their child in fulfilling those needs. Johanna also sees moms and dads through her private practice.

The Parent Child Center

Alice Rosenman, MS, CSW, Program Coordinator
247 East 82nd Street
bet. Second and Third avenues
212-879-6900
email: alice@theparentchildcenter.org
www.theparentchildcenter.org

The Parent Child Center, affiliated with the New York Psychoanalytical Society, offers weekly learning-while-playing groups to parents and children (from birth to three years). These groups are limited to seven or eight families in order to provide an intimate and cohesive environment. Call for up-to-date information on class offerings and costs.

The Parents League of New York*

115 East 82nd Street
bet. Park and Lexington avenues
212-737-7385
email: info@parentsleague.org
www.parentsleague.org

The Parent's League, a nonprofit organization founded thirty years ago, is a vital resource for New York parents. For a $125 annual fee, you'll have access to lectures, literature, and counseling services, plus a calendar and guide to citywide events and programs for children, a birthday party reference guide, a list of emergency telephone numbers, a newsletter, and information on schools and after-school activities. The league maintains an advisory service for schools and camps, as well as a listing of nannies, mother's helpers, and baby-sitters. You'll also receive the Parent's League Toddler Book, which contains information on classes you can take with a toddler. The Parent's League sells a guidebook to private schools that describes all of the Independent Schools Admissions Association of Greater New York (ISAAGNY) member schools. It's $24 by mail.

Parenting Horizons*

Julie Ross/Carolyn Meyer
212-765-2377
405 West 57th Street, #1F
bet. Ninth and Tenth avenues
email: info@parentinghorizons.com
www.parentinghorizons.com

Julie Ross teaches Practical Parenting, which covers how to handle tantrums, and how to help children sleep at night, learn to brush their teeth, get dressed for school, and perform other daily tasks. Julie works to build parental confidence and gives practical examples of what to do when a particular situation arises. Kelly and Pamela have both had wonderful experiences with Julie and Carolyn. Classes meet weekly for eight weeks, three semesters per year. Fees are $600 per person and $1,100 per couple. This is an excellent class for parents of toddlers. Private instruction is also available.

❈ The Parenting Program

Temple Shaaray Tefila
250 East 79th Street at Second Avenue
212-535-8008, ext. 248
email: parentingprogram@tstnyc.org
www.shaaraytefilanyc.org

The Parenting Program provides social interaction for you and your toddler (dads and grandparents, too). There are daytime classes for parents and toddlers, evening classes for toddlers and employed mothers, and evening playtimes for dads and toddlers. Classes offer children between ages twelve and thirty months (classes are divided by age) developmentally appropriate challenges that foster self-confidence and curiosity in the world around them. This unique program incorporates Sabbath celebrations, Hebrew songs, and holiday rituals. See website for cost and session information.

❈ Prenatal Yoga Center

See website for locations throughout NYC.
212-362-2986
email: info@prenatalyogacenter.com
www.prenatalyogacenter.com

An excellent source for all types of yoga, the PYC holds classes in prenatal yoga, postnatal yoga, mommy and me yoga, music for babies, infant massage, and Baby Fingers.

❈ Real Birth

715 9th Avenue at 49th Street
212-245-0796; 212-367-9006
email: education@realbirth.com
www.realbirth.com

Real Birth offers various classes in the city including a new parents' class, a dads' workshop, a 9-to-5 workshop, a CPR and safety class, baby sign language, infant massage, sibling workshops, Baby & Me Yoga, and many others. Most classes are structured in a casual, drop-in format that require only class cards instead of membership fees.

❈ Rhinelander Children's Center/ The Children's Aid Society

350 East 88th Street
bet. First and Second avenues
212-876-0500
www.childrensaidsociety.org/rhinelander

The Rhinelander Center is part of the Children's Aid Society. For expectant or new moms, classes include Enhanced Lamaze, Lamaze Refresher, and Infant Massage. Rhinelander is also an early childhood center and offers a full nursery school. For parents of older children, there are daytime and evening discussion groups, with topics that include gaining cooperation, calming temper tantrums, learning to share, and reducing sibling squabbles. Kelly has had positive experiences over the years at Rhinelander.

Nancy Samalin, MS

212-787-8883

www.samalin.com

Nancy has worked with parents, educators, and health-care professionals since 1976, teaching positive discipline and improved communication skills for toddlers through teens. She is also a prolific author of parenting books such as Loving Your Child Is Not Enough: Positive Discipline that Works. She is a former contributing editor to *Parents* magazine, and her newest book is Loving Without Spoiling.

Lisa Schuman, LCSW, CASAC

590 West End Avenue at West 89th Street, Suite 1A

212-874-1318

www.drcopperman.com/lisa-schuman-lcsw.aspx

Lisa Schuman is a psychotherapist who specializes in family issues. She works with couples, individuals, and groups on child-rearing issues, relationship difficulties, and a wide range of parenting questions. She also works with parents in the area of infertility, adoption, and specializes in reproductive medicine. She is currently on the Reproductive Medicine Associates of New York's (RMA of NY) team at Mount Sinai.

Elizabeth Silk, MSW, CSW, BCD

172 West 79th Street, Suite 18A

bet. Amsterdam and Columbus avenues

212-873-6435

www.therapists.psychologytoday.com

Elizabeth Silk, a psychotherapist with over thirty years expertise in women's reproductive issues, postpartum depression, and mothering, holds weekly groups for new mothers. The women focus on adding new dimensions of motherhood to their identity. Individual and couples sessions are also available.

The SoHo Parenting Center

568 Broadway at Prince Street, Suite 402

212-334-3744

email: info@sohoparenting.com

www.sohoparenting.com

The Parenting Center, a respected downtown resource for new moms, organizes various mother/infant support groups during the day and in the evenings. The center offers a second-time mother's group and both private and group parent counseling sessions. It also offers mother/toddler programs, sleep counseling, and pre- and postnatal yoga. The directors of the center—Jean Kunhardt and Lisa Spiegel—along with Sandra K. Basile, wrote *The Mother's Circle*, which is about the first year of motherhood.

Spabébé

Various partner locations in New York City

email: info@spa-bebe.com; registration@spa-bebe.com

www.spa-bebe.com

Started by Heidi Moon in 2006, Spabébé is a rare facilitator of maternal fitness with classes such as Prenatal Fitness, Pregnancy Prep, Prenatal Pilates, Mom & Baby Pilates, Ab Rehab, and many more. Spabébé has locations all around the country, so email them for your specific class information. See also page 37.

Swellbeing

212-924-1913

email: info@swellbeing.com

www.swellbeing.com

Swellbeing is a parenting resource that offers consultations, discussion groups, and workshops aimed at solving parenting problems like breastfeeding, baby blues, sleep issues, infant prep for moms-to-be, and more. Classes and workshops are intended for parents of children pre-delivery to four years old.

Tot-Saver

10 East 101st Street at Mt Sinai Hospital Basic Science Building

212-241-6222 (Class Info); 212-241-7491 (Class Registration)

www.mountsinai.org

Conducted at Mount Sinai Hospital, these classes teach CPR techniques for infants and children as well as safety and injury prevention. The fee is $75 per person or $135 per couple per two-session course. Class is limited to six participants. Call for further information and registration.

Uptown Mommies

Sarah Klagsbrun, MD

200 East 94th Street at Third Avenue, Suite 2411

212-996-4300

email: drk@uptownmommies.com

www.uptownmommies.com

Sarah Klagsbrun, a child, adolescent, and adult psychiatrist and mother of three, runs new parent discussion groups on the Upper East Side.

The groups help new moms learn about their child's social, emotional, cognitive, and language development so they can parent with confidence. Topics include establishing sleeping and eating patterns; temper tantrums; limit-setting; self-esteem; toilet training; sibling relationships and more. Email Dr. Klagsbrun for pricing info.

entertainment for new moms

Big City Moms

917-488-8542

email: info@bigcitymoms.com

www.bigcitymoms.com

Big City Moms was started almost six years ago by Risa and Leslie, two sisters who believe that new moms need a night away from their babies to socialize with each other and just have fun. They offer exciting events for moms each week such as luncheons, classes, workshops, seminars, and outings. Past events have been with Child magazine, Vicky Iovine, FAO Schwarz, Dr. Harvey Karp, Kidville NY, Little Maestros, and more. See website for pricing and membership information.

Divalysscious Moms

Lyss Stern, Founder

917-601-0068

email: lyss@divamoms.com

www.divalysscfousmoms.com

Divalysscious was started by Lyss Stern, a dynamic new mom who wanted to enjoy all of the exciting things that NYC had to offer—but found that most movie premieres, day spas, and cooking schools weren't baby friendly at all. Divalysscious Moms offers all sorts of lifestyle events throughout the city for moms, babies, and grandmas, too. Recent events have included parties at Dylan's Candy Bar, a shopping outing at Barney's, and moms-night-out at a trendy hotel. Lyss's events are fun for moms and babies alike. She brings an elegance and panache to every event she does and makes all the moms feel at home. Prices vary by event.

❖ Mamapalooza

207-504-3001

email: joy@mamapalooza.com

www.mamapalooza.com

Mamapalooza brings together musicians, artists, dancers, filmmakers, writers, business owners, educators, and moms of all kinds to celebrate motherhood and to highlight the challenges caregivers face in an ever-evolving personal, social, cultural, sexual, and political landscape.

❖ Metropolitan Moms

212-206-7272

email: info@metropolitanmoms.com

www.metropolitanmoms.com

Molly has created Metropolitan Moms, "the cultural oasis for city dwellers of all ages." MMs offers a series of once-a-week classes for new moms, to be taken with or without your baby. Each class in the series takes place at a different museum, gallery, or neighborhood. Recent classes have included a walking and architectural tour of Greenwich Village, a gallery tour of Chelsea, culinary adventures, auction house previews, and artists' studio visits. Classes are led by experts, and mom-and-baby classes include baby-sitters. Prices vary greatly as some classes meet once while others meet once weekly for a month.

❖ Rattle & Reel

Sunshine Cinema

143 East Houston Street

bet. First and Second avenues

212-330-8182

www.landmarktheatres.com

The Sunshine Cinema welcomes caregivers and their babies Wednesdays at 11 a.m. Adults pay normal admission and babies are free—and free to scream with joy!

hotlines, warmlines, and other special help

There may be times during your baby's first few weeks or months when you need more specialized help or support than your pediatrician, mother, or friend can provide.

During these weeks it is a good idea to keep handy the telephone number of the nursery of the hospital in which you delivered. Often, the nurses can easily answer your questions and help you through a minor crisis. Some hospitals also have special telephone numbers set up to assist new moms. Inquire about your hospital's policy for new mother call-ins. Following are a variety of additional support groups and referral programs, as well as some important numbers to have in case of an emergency.

Adoption

ABSW Child Adoption, Counseling, and Referral Service
1969 Madison Avenue
212-831-5181

Adoptive Parents Support Group
212-475-0222

Adoptive Parents Committee
212-304-8479
An adoptive parents' support group with chapters in New York, Westchester, and on Long Island.

Advocates for Adoption, Inc.
362 West 46th Street
212-957-3938

Association to Benefit Children
419 East 86th Street
212-831-1322

Children's Aid Society
Adoption and Foster Home Division
150 East 45th Street
212-949-4961

Children's Village
2090 Adam Clayton Powell Boulevard,
9th Floor
212-932-9009

Jewish Board of Family and Children's Services, Inc.
120 West 57th Street
212-582-9100

Jewish Child Care Association
Ametz Adoption Program
120 Wall Street, 12th Floor
212-558-9949

New Alternatives for Children
37 West 26th Street
212-696-1550

New York Council on Adoptable Children
589 Eighth Avenue, 15th Floor
212-475-0222

New York Foundling Hospital
590 Avenue of the Americas
212-727-6828

Adopting.com
www.adopting.com
Adopting.com is a wonderful resource with tons of helpful information for the adopting parent including website suggestions, hotlines across the country, and tips to aid you in your process.

Breastfeeding

❀ Beth Israel Medical Center

Board-Certified Lactation Consultants Warm-line Program

212-420-2939

www.wehealny.org

A warmline to answer breastfeeding questions and provide support for nursing mothers.

❀ La Leche League International

212-569-6036 (Hotline)

www.llli.org

A worldwide volunteer organization founded by a group of mothers to support other moms who choose to breastfeed their babies.

La Leche's services are free, nonsectarian, and supported by membership fees ($40 per year). La Leche has group leaders in various parts of New York who run monthly meetings to discuss breastfeeding. It also provides a valuable telephone help service. When you call, a recording gives you the name and number of a woman who can be reached that day. A new mother who couldn't figure out how to work her electric breast pump called La Leche, and a volunteer spent twenty minutes on the phone explaining it to her.

❀ Màire Clements, RN, IBCLC

The Breastfeeding Salon

212-595-4797

www.thebreastfeedingsalon.com

Màire Clements (pronounced "Moira"), RN, is a breastfeeding expert and lactation consultant who teaches women how to breastfeed correctly. She gives breastfeeding classes at St.

Luke's-Roosevelt Hospital and other locations. She also sponsors luncheons where she speaks, offering mothers additional support and guidance about breastfeeding and other issues concerning new mothers. Màire offers a working mother's group and a breastfeeding Toddler Teas group, all of which she personally caters at mothers' homes (locations rotate).

❀ The National Association of Mothers Centers

Jericho, NY

877-939-MOMS

email: info@motherscenter.org

www.motherscenter.org

A support group and referral service for mothers' groups in your area.

Special Parenting Help

❀ Big Brothers Big Sisters

223 East 30th Street

bet. Second and Third avenues

212-686-2042

www.bbs.org

Offers mentoring and social relationship opportunities for children growing up with one parent.

Hotline Help

❀ Child Abuse and Maltreatment Reporting Center

800-342-3720

www.ocfs.state.ny.us

A hotline to report cases of suspected child abuse.

❊ Emergency Children's Service

ACS (Administration for Children's Services)

212-341-0900 (general); 212-966-8000 (nights, weekends, holidays)

Emergency assistance for abused, assaulted, mistreated, or neglected children.

❊ LIFE NET

800-LIFENET

Operates 24 hours a day, 7 days a week. Assists people who are experiencing a crisis and provides a prompt, professional response to callers in urgent need of psychiatric assistance.

❊ National AIDS Hotline

800-342-AIDS

email: hivnet@ashastd.org

www.cdc.gov

Trained specialists answer questions about HIV infections and AIDS.

❊ National Center for Missing and Exploited Children

800-843-5678

❊ National Sexual Assault Hotline

800-656-4673

❊ National Youth Crisis Helpline

800-999-9999

Operates 24 hours a day, 7 days a week. Offers crisis intervention and referrals for youth and families nationwide. Affiliated with Covenant House for runaway youth.

❊ New York Foundling Hospital Crisis / The Crisis Nursery

212-472-8555

An emergency placement for a child up to the age of ten whose parent is under stress. This free service provides some cooling-off time for parents, for a period of one day up to three weeks.

❊ Poison Hotline

800-222-1222

A service that offers immediate advice and direction in cases of poison ingestion.

❊ Prevention Information and Parent Helpline

800-342-7472

Operates 24 hours a day, 7 days a week. Provides help for parents who need guidance and support by giving information and referrals.

❊ United States Missing Children Hotline

800-235-3535

❊ Youth Hotline (NYC)

800-246-4646

Operates 24 hours a day, 7 days a week. Provides information about youth programs, as well as crisis intervention and other services.

Premature Infants

The best place to get advice and counseling or to find out about support groups for parents of premature babies is through your hospital's Intensive Care Nursery. Many ICNs automatically provide such sup port. If yours does not, ask the staff to direct you to a group in your area.

* ❈ *First Candle/National SIDS Resource Center*
800-221-SIDS; 800-221-7437; 410-653-8226
www.firstcandle.org
This center provides Sudden Infant Death Syndrome (SIDS) information to parents.

Single Parents

* ❈ *The Single Fathers' Lighthouse*
www.lighthousedad.com
Provides resources from one single father to another.

* ❈ *Single Mom*
www.singlemom.com
An all-in-one online resource for single mothers.

* ❈ *Parents Without Partners*
800-637-7974
www.parentswithoutpartners.org
A self-help group providing support and information about single parenting issues.

* ❈ *Single Mothers by Choice*
212-988-0993
www.singlemothersbychoice.com
A support group for women who have had a baby on their own.

* ❈ *Single Parents Support Group*
212-780-0800, ext. 239
This group meets at the Parenting Center at

the 14th Street Y. Baby-sitting is available with advance reservation.

* ❈ *Single Spouse*
www.singlespouse.com
An online community for single parents.

* ❈ *Single Women's Alliance Network (SWAN)*
205 West 13th Street at Seventh Avenue
212-414-0529
SWAN provides support for single mothers and single mothers by choice.

Twins or More

* ❈ *Manhattan Twins Club*
212-774-7488
email: manhattantwinsclub@hotmail.com
www.manhattantwinsclub.org
Offers information and social networking for every possible issue facing NYC parents of twins.

* ❈ *M.O.S.T. (Mothers of Super Twins)*
248-231-4480
email: info@nomotc.org
www.mostonline.org
A support group for parents of triplets, quadruplets, or quintuplets. Also offers information and support for parents of premature babies.

* ❈ *Multiples*
www.multiples.about.com
Offers current updates about parenting multiples.

※ *National Organization of Mothers of Twins Clubs, Inc.*
877-540-2200
www.nomotc.org
This club provides information on local twin, triplet, and quadruplet (or more) support groups.

LGBT Parents

※ *Gay Parent Magazine*
718-380-1780
email: gayparentmag@gmail.com
www.gayparentmag.com
Offers specialized publication for information on gay parenting.

※ *Lesbian, Gay, Bisexual, Transgender Center: Centerkids*
208 West 13th Street at Seventh Avenue
212-620-7310
email: terryboggis@gaycenter.org
Offers support, guidance, and groups for individuals and couples considering and preparing for parenthood. Also offers monthly social networking events, age-appropriate "family playdays," playgroups, and networking opportunities.

Older Parenting

※ *Mothers Over 40*
www.mothersover40.com
Provides a source for information and support for older parents.

※ *"Plum Magazine"*
www.plummagazine.com
An informative magazine for older parents.

Special Needs Groups

※ *Center for Hearing and Communication*
50 Broadway, 6th Floor
bet. Morris and Wall streets
917-305-7700
www.lhh.org
Provides information on speech and hearing programs and clinics.

※ *Cerebral Palsy*
United Cerebral Palsy of New York City
877-UCP-CONNECT
www.ucpnyc.org
This organization offers comprehensive services for children and their families, beginning at infancy.

※ *Cystic Fibrosis Foundation*
212-986-8783
www.cff.org
A foundation providing advice, counseling, and hospital referrals for families of children with Cystic Fibrosis.

※ *Educational Alliance*
197 East Broadway at Jefferson Street
212-780-2300
email: info@edalliance.org
www.edalliance.org
Educational Alliance runs workshops to help parents through pregnancy loss.

The Lighthouse/New York Association for the Blind

212-821-9200

email: info@lighthouse.org

www.lighthouse.org

The Lighthouse works with blind children throughout the city and provides comprehensive services and resources for them and their families.

National Down's Syndrome Society

666 Broadway at Bond Street, 8th Floor

212-460-9330; 800-221-4602

email: info@ndss.org

www.ndss.org

This society offers general information, parent support, and assistance with identifying programs at local hospitals for Down's Syndrome babies and children.

Pregnancy and Infant Loss Center (Bereavement Group)

612-473-9372

email: donnarail@aol.com

This center provides information on local support groups for women or couples recovering from a miscarriage or the loss of an infant.

Resources for Children with Special Needs

212-677-4650

116 East 16th Street at Irving Place, 5th Floor

email: info@resourcesnyc.org

www.resourcesnyc.org

An information, referral, advocacy, and support center for parents of children with special needs.

Spina Bifida Information and Referral

800-621-3141

email: sbaa@sbaa.org

www.spinabifidaassociation.org

Williams Syndrome Hotline

570 Kirts Boulevard, Suite 223

Troy, MI 48084-4156

800-806-1871; 248-244-2229

email: info@williams-syndrome.org

www.williams-syndrome.org

The Williams Syndrome Association was formed in 1982 by, and for, families of individuals with Williams syndrome. The WSA is the only group in the U.S. devoted exclusively to improving the lives of individuals with Williams syndrome. The WSA supports research into all facets of the syndrome, and the development of the most up-to-date educational materials.

YAI / National Institute for People with Disabilities Network

212-418-0323

email: hchusid@yai.org

www.yai.org

Called Life Start, YAI / NYL Early Intervention Program is a federally funded agency that has an agreement with New York City to run Life Start for children under the age of three who have mental, physical, emotional, social, or cognitive development difficulties. All sorts of physical, speech, and occupational therapies are available free of charge to children in New York State.

Autism

❊ *New York Center for Autism*

477 Madison Avenue at East 51st Street,
Suite 420
212-759-3775
email: info@newyorkcenterforautism.com
www.newyorkcenterforautism.com

❊ *New York Families for Autism*

718-641-3441
www.nyfac.org

important supplies

❊ *Kids RX*

523 Hudson Street
bet. West 10th and Charles streets
212-741-7111; 212-741-7110 (Fax)
email: info@kidsrx.com
www.kidsrx.com
Kids RX, voted Best Pharmacy in New York
magazine in 2007, customizes prescriptions to
suit your child's needs in a fun, welcoming
atmosphere for you and your child. All insurance plans accepted (grown-ups, too!), free
delivery, and they ship.

Diaper Services

In our environmentally conscious age, some people
may want to use cloth diapers to help the earth.
Since our last edition, many diaper services have
closed down or consolidated. There is only one diaper service in the tristate area that still provides cloth

diapers. We have also included the Walgreens website for easy online ordering of disposable diapers;
see below.

❊ *www.walgreens.com*

❊ *Cloth Diaper.com*

877-215-9004
email: customerservice@clothdiaper.com
www.clothdiaper.com
ClothDiaper.com is a web-based retail infant
cloth-diapering products store, owned and
operated by a family-owned business called All
Together Diaper Enterprises.

❊ *Diapers.com*

800-DIAPERS
email: CustomerCare@diapers.com
www.diapers.com
Founded in Montclair, New Jersey, by Marc
Lore and Vinit Bharara, Diapers.com is the
largest online specialist offering baby-care
necessities in the United States. They buy in
bulk, so prices are highly competitive. They
offer fast delivery and comprehensive options
for all your baby's needs.

❊ *Seventh Generation*

800-456-1177
10 Farrell Street
South Burlington, VT
www.seventhgeneration.com
This catalog company in Vermont offers
biodegradable diapers in three sizes, as well as
cloth diapers. Costs vary depending on your
order and you can even set up a monthly deliv-

ery order. See their website for a complete service listing in your area.

⁂ *Tidy Diapers*
50 Commerce Street
Norwalk, CT 06850
203-866-2568; 800-732-2443
email: tidydiapers@aol.com
$16.95 per week
Tidy Diapers will deliver cloth diapers to your door every week in Brooklyn, Queens, Manhattan, Westchester, and some counties in Connecticut.

⁂ *Walmart*
www.walmart.com
Walmart sells cloth diapers and reusable diapers as well as thousands of items for all of your complete shopping needs and a delivery option.

Breast Pumps

For breastfeeding working moms or other women who would like their husbands or caregivers to feed baby an occasional bottle of breast milk, an electric breast pump is a wonderful convenience. Electric pumps are faster and easier to use than manual or battery-operated pumps. If you plan to breastfeed for three months or less, we recommend renting an electric, hospital-grade pump. Pumps can be rented by the day, week, or month. They can also be purchased through The Right Start catalog. Buying is a good idea if you plan to breastfeed for an extended time or if you are planning to have more children. The Medela Lactina is a good one to rent or purchase. For the nearest outlet, call Medela at: 800-TELL-YOU. The La Leche League (212-569-

6036; www.llli.org) can also tell you where to rent a breast pump.

Prices for pump rental vary depending on the type of pump and your desired rental period. The single pump allows you to pump milk from one breast, and the double from both breasts at the same time.

Breast pumps can be rented at the following locations in Manhattan:

upper east side

⁂ *Beth Israel Medical Center*
305 First Avenue, #7
bet. East 17th and 18th streets
212-420-2377

⁂ *Caligor Pharmacy*
1226 Lexington Avenue at 83rd Street
www.caligorrx.com
212-369-6000

⁂ *Cherry's Pharmacy*
207 East 66th Street
bet. Second and Third avenues
212-717-7797
email: cherryspharmacy@rcn.com
www.cherryspharmacy.com
Cherry's Pharmacy is unique, as it is one of the only pharmacy in the city that caters directly to kids and families. Cherry's pharmacists prepare children's medication with flavors that actually taste good, and good tasting medicine is easier to administer. You will find all children's medication and products here, even some toys and gifts. Delivery is free.

❋ *Falk Drug*
259 East 72nd Street at Second Avenue
212-744-8080

❋ *Goldberger's Pharmacy*
1200 First Avenue at 65th Street
212-734-6998; 800-288-5382
www.goldbergpharmacy.com

❋ *Health Care Pharmacy*
53 East 122nd Street at Madison Avenue
212-369-5555
www.healthcarerxny.com

❋ *Planet Kids*
247 East 86th Street
bet. Second and Third avenues
212-864-8705
email: contact@planetkidsny.com
www.planetkidsny.com

❋ *Timmerman Pharmacy**
799 Lexington Avenue
bet. 61st and 62nd streets
212-838-6450
email: sales@newtimrx.com
www.newtimrx.com

❋ *Yummy Mummy*
1201 Lexington Avenue
bet. 81st and 82nd streets
212-87-YUMMY
www.yummymummystore.com

upper west side

❋ *Apthorp Pharmacy**
2201 Broadway
bet. 78th and 79th streets
212-877-3480
email: staff@apthorprx.com
www.apthorprx.com

❋ *Chateau Drug*
181 Amsterdam Avenue
bet. 68th and 69th streets
212-877-6390
email: info@chateaudrugandhomecare.com
www.chateaudrugandhomecare.com

❋ *Joseph Pharmacy*
216 West 72nd Street at West End Avenue
212-875-1718
www.josephspharmacy.com

❋ *Planet Kids of Amsterdam Avenue*
191-193 Amsterdam Avenue
bet. 68th and 69th streets
212-362-3931
email: contact@planetkidsny.com
www.planetkidsny.com

❋ *Suba Pharmacy*
2721 Broadway at 104th Street
212-866-6700

❋ *The Upper Breast Side*
135 West 70th Street, Suite 1L
212-873-2653 (Store);
917-513-3129 (Emergency)
www.breastvillage.com;

www.upperbreastside.com
Messenger service available in Manhattan.

midtown

⁂ *Chelsea Mobility & Medical Equipment*

327 Eighth Avenue at 26th Street
800-249-1188; 212-255-5522
www.chelseamme.com

⁂ *NYU Medical Center*

560 First Avenue at 32nd Street
212-263-BABY
www.nyubaby.org

⁂ *St. Luke's-Roosevelt Hospital Center*

1000 Tenth Avenue at 58th Street
212-523-4000
www.wehealny.com

downtown

⁂ *Barren Hospital Medical Center*

49 Delancey Street
bet. Eldridge and Forsyth streets
212-226-6164
email: baronmed@verizon.com
www.baronmedical.com

⁂ *C.O. Bigelow Apothecaries*

414 Sixth Avenue
bet. 8th and 9th streets
212-533-2700; 800-793-5433
www.bigelowchemists.com

⁂ *Elm Drugs*

298 First Avenue bet. 17th and 18th streets
212-777-0740

⁂ *Kings Pharmacy*

5 Hudson Street at Reade Street
212-791-3100
241 Bedford Avenue, Brooklyn
718-782-1000
email: kingspharmacy@gmail.com;
kingspharmacy11211@gmail.com (Brooklyn location)
www.kingspharmacy.org

⁂ *Little Folks*

123 East 23rd Street
bet. Park and Lexington avenues
212-982-9669

⁂ *BabyBucks Card*

Susan Barr
646-284-2333
www.babybucksnyc.com
The clever "BabyBucks" card (created by mom Susan Barr) is a must-have for anyone who wants to save money and the cost of raising children in the city. When you purchase a Baby-Bucks card ($30 per year) and show it at participating merchants, you are entitled to a 10- to 20-percent discount on items like birth announcements, children's furniture, clothes, toys, birthday parties, and more. There are over sixty ways to save and new places are added every couple of months. The list of participants includes popular merchants like One Step Ahead (www.onestepahead.com), Little Eric

Shoes (see page 183), Bookberries (see page 262), and The Art Farm in the City (www.theart farms.org).

* A final note: The BabyBucks card is a great way to save money on classes, products, and more. A smart purchase while you have a new-born, because you can begin saving right away!

entertainment for
kids and moms

You've survived the first couple of months; you have packing the diaper bag down to a science, you're getting a handle on this motherhood business—it is time to venture out with your little one and have some fun!

You and your baby can roll around on a mat together at the 92nd Street Y, get some culture at the Temple of Dendur at the Met, relax at an outdoor cafe, or stroll to a neighborhood playground and meet other moms and their babies.

In this chapter, we'll give you a rundown of the Mommy and Me classes and activities available in the city. (Unless otherwise indicated, caregivers, dads, or grandmas are also welcome to take their young charges to these classes.) Then we'll turn to New York's playgrounds and parks, museums, and other special spaces where you and your baby can have a good time.

Given our considerable experience with all of these classes and activities, we have a few thoughts on monitoring your child's schedule. With our first kids, we both overdid it with classes. Beginning at three months old, Rebecca and Alexander "learned" music, art, gym, French, ballet, tumbling, soccer, swimming—you name it. You get the idea; we overbooked them. The second time around, we were smarter and realized that playgroups and time with mom in the park are just as valuable as Gymboree.

Once Benjamin was a year old, he and Pamela began a gym and music class. It paid to wait because he enjoyed it much more at one year than Rebecca had at six months. Angela took her first music class with Kelly at age one and she is more advanced and talkative now at age two than her brother was at that age, although he had been introduced to everything under the sun by the time he was two years old.

mommy and me classes and programs

As your child grows, she is going to learn to run, jump, tumble, sing songs, and scribble pictures all on her own. But classes can help her develop social skills, learn how to function in groups, be disciplined, and acquire a host of other skills. Above all, children enjoy themselves in these programs, and it's nice to have some places to go during New York winters.

All these places and programs offer classes for children age three and under. Some take babies as young as three months. However, you and your child will find an organized class much more enjoyable if she is able to sit up on her own, so it's a good idea to wait until your baby is at least six to nine months old before signing up.

Here are some guidelines to follow as you check out these programs:

❋ Take a trial class or attend an open house before you sign up. You may have to pay for it, but you'll have a better sense of what you are getting into.

❋ Look for classes with children the same age as your own.

❋ Look for big, open, clean rooms with plenty of space and light, accessible by elevator or ramp. You should not have to walk up five flights of stairs carrying your baby, diaper bag, and stroller.

❋ Equipment should be scaled down to small-child size, and any gymnastic-type facilities should include lots of mats and other safety features.

* Small- to medium-size classes are best. Do not be too concerned if a class is very big on the first day, because everyone is not there every week. Illnesses, naps, and vacations normally account for a quarter of a class being absent in any given week.

* The teacher makes all the difference; some are better than others. The other children and their mothers and nannies also can affect the atmosphere of a class. If you are the only mom in attendance, for example, you may feel awkward spending time with ten nannies every Thursday afternoon at two o'clock. (You can always ask to switch to a class with more moms.)

* Location is important. Enroll in a class near your home. If you can push your baby in a stroller less than ten blocks, you will be more likely to attend and to make it there on time.

Prices and schedules change almost every semester, so call ahead for the latest information. Classes often run in sessions of seventeen to nineteen weeks; prices range from $300 to $475. During the summer, many places—Jodi's Gym and the 92nd Street Y, for example—offer four- , six- , and nine-week sessions that cost from $95 to $200.

❋ The Art Farm in the City

419 East 91st Street
bet. York and First avenues
212-410-3117
email: info@theartfarms.org
www.theartfarms.org
Ages: 8 months to 7 years
In each week's forty-five-minute class, the children are visited by a live animal such as a

Top Ten Things to Do with Your Family on the Weekend

1. Visit Chelsea Piers (skating, gymnastics, bowling, etc.).
2. Go to Central Park to see the Alice in Wonderland sculptures and feed the ducks (mid-park at 72nd Street).
3. Go to dinner at the restaurant at the 79th Street boat basin (79th Street and the Hudson River). Eat good food in a kid-friendly environment and watch the boats.
4. Go down to Battery Park City. Stroll by the water, eat ice cream cones, and people-watch.
5. Visit the Brooklyn Botanic Garden. It has a great kiddie area with all types of hands-on activities.
6. Invite a few other families to a potluck picnic in Central Park. Bring bubbles, balls, and blankets.
7. Take a drive out into the country for fall apple-picking/pumpkin-picking.
8. Visit the penguins in the Central Park Zoo (infants love to look at black and white).
9. Form a "daddy" playgroup—dads get to bond with other dads and babies, and you get some time off.
10. Go to a playground in a neighborhood other than your own.

rabbit, frog, or pig, and learn about the animal's habitat, eating habits, etc. Classes alternate each week between music and art (music only for six- to fourteen-month-olds). At the end of class, the children have fifteen minutes to visit all of the animals in the 1,000-square-foot indoor "farm." Kids three to seven years old can take animal care classes. Call or see website for all class schedules and pricing.

Asphalt Green Inc.

The A.G.U.A. Center
1750 York Avenue at 91st Street
212-369-8890
www.asphaltgreen.org
Age: 4 months and up
Asphalt Green, a huge fitness and sports complex, offers classes in swim, gymnastics, sports, high performance, camps, and parties. Swimming classes for young children are held in the warm water teaching/exercise pool (not the Olympic-size pool) under excellent supervision. Water Babies is for four- to eighteen-month-olds. It accustoms them to being in the water through soothing games and songs. Water Tots, for children eighteen to thirty-six months, teaches kicking, arm movements, prone floating, and safety jumps. The curriculum incorporates the teaching methods of both the American Red Cross and the American Swim Coaches Association. Adults must go in the water with children under three. Asphalt Green also hosts parties and offers delightful puppet shows for children eleven months and older, as well as various art and fitness classes such as Toddlercise, Tumble Tots, and Kinder-

musik. This is one of the best places for swimming lessons in the city, and parents travel from across town to downtown so their kids can swim here. Book your classes early! Prices vary between classes.

Baby Fingers

See website for locations throughout NYC.
212-874-5978
email: info@mybabyfingers.com
www.mybabyfingers.com
Age: newborn to 6 years
A unique program for children ages one month to six years old offering American sign language (ASL) instruction through the arts. Classes involve music, signing, and singing. Founder Lora Heller is certified in early childhood education, special education, and speech therapy. She is also a musician with a magical voice. Some class examples include baby and toddler ASL, Creative Play & Sign, music for babies, Baby Fingers Sign & Stretch, adult ASL, and kid ASL. They also offer parties, musical therapy, guitar lessons, family and school workshops, as well as webinars.

Bloomingdale School of Music

323 West 108th Street
bet. Broadway and Riverside Drive
212-663-6021
email: info@bsmny.org
www.bsmny.org
Age: newborn and up
Bloomingdale's preschool programs are an ideal way to introduce children to the world of music. Baby's First Music Class offers a wealth

of fun activities like singing, dancing, rocking, and exploring instruments, and shows adults how to help their children develop musically. While Music and Movement encourages children age eighteen months to three years to improvise and stretch their imaginations through music. It also offers classes—Musical Adventures and More Musical Adventures—for three- and four-year-olds, respectively. A number of private and group classes are offered for older kids, too, without parents or caregivers, including Musical Adventures, Dalcroze Eurythmics, Guitar, Keyboard, Violin, and more.

❖ Broadway Babies

St. Jean's Community Center
184 East 76th Street at Lexington Avenue
212-717-0703
Applause Westchester
114 West Boston Post Road
Mamaroneck, New York
914-835-2200
www.broadwaybabies.com
www.applauseny.com
Age: 4 months to 12th grade
Each week, a different Broadway musical sets the stage for this energetic, interactive, and educational Mommy and Me class. Four professional teacher/performers along with a live pianist sing out the show tunes in harmony while everyone performs and plays along with different props, toys, and musical instruments. Guided by highly accredited teachers and pediatricians, owner Audrey Kaplan's curriculum weaves educational activities such as pre-K development of motor skills, color and letter recognition, counting, and socialization through the stories and songs of each musical. While Broadway Babies is their original and best-known class, they now offer very successful classes in various performing arts categories. Prices and schedules vary per class.

❖ C.A.T.S. (Children's Athletic Training School)*

235 East 49th Street
bet. Second and Third Avenues
212-832-1833
Long Island C.A.T.S.
188 Maple Avenue
Rockville Centre, NY
email: catsturtlebay@gmail.com
www.catsny.com
Ages: 1 year and up
CATS is the only comprehensive children's sports training program for one- to twelve-year-olds in the United States. Baby CATS and Kiddie CATS meet once a week for forty-five minutes in a large auditorium-like space; children under two years play on gym equipment such as slides and tunnels. Classes are large, with eighteen toddlers and moms or caregivers, plus three coaches for each session. Many children stay with the program for years, going on to take lessons in tennis, soccer, golf, hockey, basketball, dance, and martial arts. Alexander loved CATS and even participated in CATS summer programs for two years.

Chelsea Piers

Pier 62, 23rd Street at Twelfth Avenue
212-336-6500, ext. 0
email: info@chelseapiers.com
www.chelseapiers.com
Age: 6 months and up

In addition to its extensive adult offerings, Chelsea Piers, the largest sports complex in New York, offers various programs and facilities for very young children, such as basketball, baseball, dance, gymnastics, rock climbing, soccer, ice-skating, golf, and a highly acclaimed summer camp. Tiny Tots, for ages twelve months to twenty-four months accompanied by caregivers, uses directed play such as games, art, and drama to encourage children to share and ask questions. For physical activity, enroll your child in the pre-school gymnastics program (seventeen months to five years), or take her to the toddler gym, where she can crawl, roll, and jump on mats and equipment designed to help develop basic skills. Chelsea Piers also offers an excellent introduction to soccer for three- to five- year-olds. Benjamin played there, and learned all the soccer moves and about teamwork. One session at the toddler gym is $11; call for other prices.

The Children's Garden Studio

240 West 98th Street at Broadway
212-678-2997
email: cgkiamesha@aol.com
www.childrensgardenstudio.com
Age: infant to 5 years

The Children's Garden Studio uses music, art, and sensory development to help children grow toward their natural potential while providing a warm and rich learning environment that meets their developmental needs. Music classes are teacher-led, group experiences. The Art Studio and Montessori Garden are independent learning programs for parents or caregivers to use with the guidance of resource teachers.

Child's Play

See website for locations throughout Manhattan.
212-879-2019
email: childsplaynyny@aol.com
www.childsplaynyc.com
Age: 4 months to 4 years

Child's Play is a playgroup program for parents only and their children that uses circle time, music, movement, art, free play, story time, and parachute activities to engage the children. Playgroups are one and a half hours long and include parent discussion and workshops.

Children's Tumbling

9 Murray Street
bet. Broadway and Church Street (East Entrance at City Hall)
212-233-3418
www.childrentumbling.com
Age: 16 months to preteen

Downtown moms think highly of this tumbling and gymnastic program for children over eighteen months. Classes are a special combination of dance, gymnastics, and theater. Toddlers climb large mats, swing on trapeze and rings, jump on the trampoline, and play with equipment that encourages their gross motor skills. The culmination of each semester is a show, with dramatic lighting, music, and stilt walking, in which the children showcase what they've learned. Classes for toddlers are kept small (six or seven children), last an hour, and meet once a week.

Church Street School for Music and Art

74 Warren Street at West Broadway
212-571-7290
email: info@churchstreetschool.org
www.churchstreetschool.org
Age: 16 months and up
This well-regarded program teaches music, movement, art, and instruments. Church Street School features the Dalcroze method of music instruction, which combines music awareness and movement.

Columbus Preschool and Gym*

606 Columbus Avenue
bet. 89th and 90th streets
212-721-0090
email: columbuspreschool@yahoo.com
www.columbuspreschoolandgym.com
Age: 6 months and up
The facilities at Columbus Gym are some of the nicest and cleanest in the city; there are tunnels, trampolines, balance beams, and hills to climb over and through. Gymnastic classes for toddlers twelve to eighteen months are with mom or caregiver. For older toddlers, there's P.E.P. (Preschool Enrichment Program), a ninety-minute mini preschool class including gym, arts and crafts, painting, music, and story time. Pamela and Rebecca (and Pamela and Ben) took the P.E.P. class for a year and enjoyed it tremendously.

Diller-Quaile School of Music

26 East 95th Street
bet. Madison and Fifth avenues
212-369-1484
email: info@diller-quaile.org
www.diller-quaile.org
Age: 4 months and up
Diller-Quaile is a New York institution that offers music classes for toddlers and moms, as well as private instruction on different instruments. Classes begin in September and run until June. Music Infants, for those ages four to eight months, incorporates singing, chanting, rhythmic taps and claps, tickles and wiggles, and bouncing and rocking, with small percussion instruments and other engaging props to help heighten the child's sense of music. Each class also has a pianist who improvises various musical styles. Music Babies, for those ages twelve to fifteen months, teaches lullabies, finger plays, nursery chants, and a variety of playful rhythmic activities. Music for Nearly Twos uses movement activities, games, and percussion instruments to guide classroom play. There are ten to twelve children in a class, with three instructors for children under eighteen months. Note: The application process begins one year in advance of classes. Call for more information and current pricing.

Discovery Programs

251 West 100th Street at West End Avenue
212-749-8717
www.discoveryprograms.com
email: info@discoveryprograms.com
Age: newborn to 14 years

Discovery Programs is a popular uptown option for families. It has recently added a Parent Education Center to its mix, which hosts professionally led discussion groups for parents. Mommy and Me classes include Baby Massage and Music, Mommy Friends and Baby Friends, and My Grandparent and Me. These classes complement the already packed class offerings of dance, music, gymnastics, and art classes. A new On My Own program for two-year-olds has also been added, which features a gradual separation process based on each child's needs.

Dribbl

212-717-7651
email: info@dribbl.com
www.dribbl.com
Dribbl has been around for a long time for "big kids" but has a brand-new program for three and four years olds that focuses on teamwork and sportsmanship while engaging kids in sports like basketball and soccer. Dribbl classes take place at Kidville locations throughout the city as well as other locations.

The Early Ear

48 West 68th Street
bet. Central Park West and Columbus Avenue
353 East 78th Street
bet. First and Second avenues
110 West 96th Street
bet. Amsterdam and Columbus avenues
212-877-7125 (for all locations)
www.theearlyear.com
Age: 4 months to 5 years
The Early Ear is a highly regarded introduction

to music for babies as young as four months. Each class has ten children, with two teachers, one to accompany and another to demonstrate. Classes are forty minutes and incorporate sing-a-longs, games, play activities and mini musical instruments. The cost of each fifteen-week session varies between locations but all have a registration fee of $35. From Pamela's own experience with Benjamin, it's best to start when the child is a year old.

Educational Alliance Parenting and Family Center at The Sol Goldman YMHA*

344 East 14th Street
bet. First and Second avenues
212-780-0800, ext. 239
email: info@14streety.org
www.14streety.org
Age: newborn to teens
The Educational Alliance Parenting Center offers Mommy and Me Two x Two play classes that concentrate on play, music, and art, and Tykercise, a sensory-movement course for children three to eighteen months. There is also a variety of multicultural classes, such as Chinese for Children (ages three to four) for adopted children, French lessons, Judaica programs, and even a Japanese parenting center. Classes last from forty-five minutes to two hours and are limited to twelve children and adults. It also has a monthly Daddy and Me group (birth to one year), a three-session workshop for new parents called From Pair to Parent, evening groups for working and single parents, and other parenting classes, as well as newborn classes. You can

join the 14th Street Y for a yearly fee, which entitles you to program discounts, special events, priority registration, and pool and gym facilities. Classes have member and nonmember fees. Kiki Schaffer, the director, creates a special sense of community and is an encyclopedic resource for the downtown parent.

Elliots Classes

See website for multiple locations throughout NYC.

917-517-8721

www.elliotsclasses.com

Ages: 6 months to preteen

Elliot Cortez has been "famous" amongst Upper West Side parents for as many as sixteen years—probably more. Before there was a dog whisperer, there was Elliot, whose ability to interact with babies is legendary. He does an amazing baby balancing trick that is truly remarkable. Elliott has taught at and owned many gymnastics studios over the years, and now seems settled into these three Upper West Side studios where gymnastics classes are offered for babies six months and up, and sports and gymnastics classes are offered for older kids. He is a skilled teacher and makes the classes a lot of fun for all.

Funworks for Kids

201 East 83rd Street at Third Avenue

917-432-1820

Age: 9 months to 3 years

Funworks has existed for over seventeen years and offers sixty- or ninety-minute classes—a preschool-type program—of combined music,

art, and movement. Classes feature free play that includes a ball pool and air mattresses, and circle time with singing, dancing, and the use of many props such as puppets, parachutes, and balls. Plus there's an art project and story time. This program has a loyal following and moms praise the extended program, especially the one for toddlers. Funworks also hosts birthday parties and playtime hours.

Free to Be Under Three

All Souls Church

1157 Lexington Avenue at 80th Street

212-988-1708

www.freetobeunderthree.com

Age: 6 months to 32 months

This very popular class was started a few years ago by Joe Robertson. It incorporates music, story time, and free play hour in a preschool-like environment. There are at least two teachers—with high energy and an understanding of early development issues—in each class. Register at birth, as the wait list is long and it can take a year or more to get a spot.

Gymboree

See website for multiple locations throughout Manhattan.

877-4-GYMWEB

www.gymboreeclasses.com

Gymboree hosts various classes for newborns to five-year-olds as well as Family Fun classes. Their Play & Learn class for newborns to infants of six months explores the senses through physical activity, light exploration, and music. This class also offers parent discussion time to help parents understand their child's development.

Gymtime Rhythm & Glues

1520 York Avenue at 80th Street

212-861-7732

email: info@gymtime.net

www.gymtime.net

Age: 6 months to 12 years

Gymtime offers organized play classes that feature songs, games, and circle time for mother and child in clean, bright rooms with gymnastic-style equipment. You'll also find a variety of classes, including cooking, sports, tae kwon do, and art for toddlers. There can be up to ten children in a class with two instructors; classes meet once a week for forty-five minutes to one hour. Gymtime will prorate its prices for latecomers.

Hands On! A Musical Experience, Inc.

See website for locations throughout Manhattan.

212-628-1945

www.handson4music.com

Age: 4 months to 5 years

Samari Weinberg (no relation to Pamela), a seasoned early-childhood music teacher, uses a specially formatted program, Hands On!, to present musical activities that also enhance other types of learning such as the acquisition of language, listening skills, auditory discrimination, social understanding, and personal discovery. Young students learn to listen and sing everything from popular American folk songs to Broadway tunes. Classical themes are introduced as well. Classes are approximately $600 for a fifteen-week session, plus a $35 yearly fee.

Samari is a former Early Ear instructor, and is wonderful with children.

Imagine Swimming

41 Union Square West at East 17th Street, Suite 1528

212-253-9650

email: info@imagineswimming.com

www.imagineswimming.com

Age: 15 months and up

Classes by Imagine Swimming are $40 per 40-minute class and have a very small (one to four) teacher/student ratio. Locations around the city include Hunter College, Chelsea, Financial District, Midtown East, 25th Street at First Avenue, North Moore Street in Tribeca, Lower East Side, River Club, and Brooklyn Heights. Call for schedules or check it out online.

The Jewish Community Center on the Upper West Side

334 Amsterdam Avenue at 76th Street

646-505-4444

email: info@jccmanhattan.org

www.jccmanhattan.org

Age: newborn and up

What doesn't the JCC have for kids? With arguably the best swimming pool in Manhattan (with a hydraulic floor!), new facilities, and top-notch instructors, the West Side truly got lucky when the JCC opened a few years back. Now in full swing, classes include gym, swim, art, music dance, science, cooking, Jewish culture, and more. Grab a catalog or get your name on the mailing list so you and your baby can sign up. They also have brilliant classes for new moms (see page 78).

Jodi's Gym*

244 East 84th Street
bet. Second and Third avenues
212-772-7633
www.jodisgym.com
Age: 6 months to 12 years

Classes in this brightly colored, well-padded facility feature free playtime, singing, stretching, and an obstacle course. Jodi personally trains all her instructors, who are certified by the USA Gymnastic Federation. Jodi's Gym holds Mommy & Me Gym and Music classes (for ages nine months to three years), preschool gymnastics (for ages three to five years), school-aged gymnastics (kindergarten to sixth grade), Jodi's GymFit, camps, open playtime, playgroups, and birthday parties. Classes for children under three feature slides, ladders, tunnels, balls, and parachutes that are just right for tiny hands and feet. Classes are forty minutes, and there is a maximum of sixteen children to a class with two instructors.

Kids at Work

See website for locations throughout Manhattan.
347-933-8293
email: info@kidsatworknyc.com
www.kidsatworknyc.com

Kids at Work is a wonderfully affordable music program that offers MusicPlay, Jam Sessions, Piano Games, and age-appropriate music and piano lessons for young children. Their Jam Sessions classes are for newborns to age four and features music that will appeal to parents and kids alike to foster parental involvement.

Kidville

See website for locations throughout NYC, Long Island, New Jersey, and abroad.
212-772-8435
email: mayor@kidville.com
www.kidville.com
Age: newborn to 5 years

Kidville has been the talk of the town since it opened in January 2005. It is a four-story entertainment complex with over one hundred classes for kids and grown-ups, plus a cafe, toy and clothing boutique, kid's hair salon, and movie theater. Enrollment in a class gives you automatic Silver membership, which provides discounts at the cafe and boutique and other perks. You can upgrade your membership to Gold or Platinum for an additional cost, which entitles you to additional discounts and a list of other goodies. Kidville offers classes in music (Little Maestros), dance, gym activities, art, cooking, parenting, preschool alternatives, and a summer camp program. Classes are typically sixteen weeks long and cost around $695 per semester. They also offer complete party packages on site that are proving to be quite popular.

Kids Co-Motion

Rebecca Kelly Dance Studio
579 Broadway, 5B
bet. Prince and Houston streets
212-431-8489
email: rkballet@ix.netcom.com
www.kidsco-motion.com;
www.rebeccakellyballet.com
Age: 12 months to 8+ years

Choreographer Rebecca Kelly and her husband, dancer Craig Brashear, founded this popular, unique, and creative program in 1991. It provides a joyous atmosphere with motion, tumbling, song, and music for young children with their caregivers. Kids Co-Motion emphasizes a productive, positive learning experience. Classes run in twelve-week sessions, in fall, winter, spring, and in an extended summer program. Class prices vary with the length of the session. There is a one-time registration fee of $30 per family.

❈ Kindermusik

The Greenwich Village Center
(a.k.a. The Children's Aid Society)
177 Sullivan Street at West 3rd Street
212-254-3074
email: info@kindermusik.com
www.kindermusik.com
Age: newborn to 7 years
Kindermusik is an international music program with more than twenty-one hundred teachers. This introductory music class gets toddlers singing, chanting, dancing, and playing simple instruments like rhythm sticks, bells, and drums. The sessions are forty-five minutes to an hour long, and children can participate with either a parent or caregiver. Kindermusik also holds classes in New Jersey, Long Island, Westchester, and other New York City boroughs.

❈ The Language Workshop for Children

888 Lexington Avenue at 66th Street
The Lucy Moses School, 129 West 67th Street
at Broadway

52 Mercer Street at Broome Street, 3rd Floor
800-731-0830 (for all locations)
www.thibauttechnique.com
Age: 6 months to 5 years
François Thibaut created the Language Workshops for small children in 1973, and today they are more popular than ever. In the Just for Tots program you'll find a variety of age-appropriate forty-five-minute classes for toddlers, including arts and crafts, music and movement, and gymnastics, in addition to the French and Spanish language workshops.

❈ Life Sport Gymnastics

West Park Presbyterian Church
165 West 86th Street at Amsterdam Avenue
212-769-3131
Age: 12 months to adult
Rudy Van Daele has been teaching gymnastics for over twenty years. Classes here are small, with seven to eight students, and include activities on mats, trampolines, beams, and horses. Children are encouraged to try whatever interests them, from cartwheels to flips and more. Yoga classes are also offered.

❈ The Little Gym

2121 Broadway
bet. 74th and 75th streets
*Tribeca location coming soon!
212-799-1225
email: info@thelittlegym.com;
tlgupperwestsideny@thelittlegym.com
www.thelittlegym.com;
www.tlgupperwestsideny.com
With over three hundred locations in twenty-

one countries, The Little Gym is well versed in the developing needs of your growing child. They offer gym, sports, music, karate, cheer-leading, and dance classes for ages four months to twelve years. Their youngest parent/child class, From Somersaults to Self-Esteem, infuses music and gymnastics to help advance basic motor skills, balance, body awareness, and coordination.

❊ Little Maestros*

344 East 69th Street
bet. First and Second avenues
See website for locations throughout NYC, Long Island, Westchester, and New Jersey.
212-772-8435
email: info@littlemaestros.com
www.littlemaestros.com; www.kidville.com
Age: 3 months to 5 years

Little Maestros, named the best music class in NYC by Nickelodeon's Parents' Pick Awards and by the *lilaguide*, is one of the most popular classes around right now. Each class has a full band of four teachers singing everything from "Bach to Rock" with guitar, piano, and percussion accompaniment. Every week there is musical story time, language development activities, a puppet show with an ongoing story, instruments, bubbles, and much more. Evening classes are offered and are ideal for working parents. Little Maestros is now a part of Kidville and is currently franchising across the country. Please consult their website for up-to-date pricing info.

❊ The Lucy Moses School Music and Dance

129 West 67th Street
bet. Broadway and Amsterdam Av
212-501-3360
email: lucymosesschool@kaufman-cei .c.org
www.kaufman-center.org/lucy-moses-school
Age: 8 months and up

Musical Babies is for ages eight to twelve months and encourages communication through bouncing songs, lullabies, wiggling, tickling, peekaboo, and music. They also offer advanced classes as your child gets older, such as Musical Ones, Music and Movement, Music for Toddlers, and many other classes through adulthood. Children attend with parents or caregivers.

❊ Mary Ann Hall's Music for Children*

The Church of Heavenly Rest
2 East 90th Street
bet. Madison and Fifth avenues
203-854-9797
email: mail@musicforchildren.net
www.musicforchildren.net
Age: infants, toddlers, and up

Mary Ann Hall's Music for Children is nationally acclaimed. This early childhood program nurtures young children in a musical environment, "connecting the art of the music with the heart of the child." Children discover, explore, and develop natural musical abilities. Mary Ann and Emily Hall play the piano as children walk, march, gallop, and run to the appropriate accompaniment. They lead the group in various songs and free play with a variety of musical instruments. Weekly forty-five-minute classes, not exceeding ten children, run from October to May. Kelly has used this program with both of her children.

⁂ Mommy and Me

Philip Coltoff Center at Greenwich Village
(a.k.a. The Children's Aid Society)
219 Sullivan Street at West 3rd Street
212-254-3074, ext. 19
email: rhondelld@childrensaidsociety.org
www.childrensaidsociety.org/pcc/
earlychildhood
Age: 10 months to 3 years
Children play outdoors in an enclosed playground, sing songs, listen to stories, and do art projects. Infant & Baby Classes, Sibling Time, Messy Art Time, Toddler Literacy, Speakin' Spanish, Fun in French, Baby Fingers, Baby and Toddler Yoga, Toddler Time, Toddler Gymnastics, and Kindermusik are among the featured classes. There is also a variety of classes for children up to five years old, in subjects such as woodworking, pottery, ballet, and Kung Fu. There are ten children and two teachers in every class.

⁂ Music Together*

See website for locations throughout Manhattan.
212-203-4785
email: musictogethernyc@gmail.com
www.musictogethernyc.com
Age: newborn to 4 years
Music Together is a forty-five-minute class for mommies and children (or caregivers/fathers),

where they sing, dance, chant, and play with various instruments. Classes are held in a relaxed, playful, no-pressure setting so as to encourage personal growth and comfort in playing and creating. At the beginning of the program, parents receive a compact disc and a charming illustrated songbook. They are encouraged to play the music at home and children come to know and love the songs. Music Together has ten to twelve children per class. There are classes for babies and toddlers separately and classes for infants and toddlers mixed together. Tuition is $390 for twelve weekly 45-minute classes. Pamela has taken many classes at various Music Together locations with Rebecca and Ben. Instructors do vary with each location, so we recommend a trial class before signing up.

⁂ Musical Kids International

1296 Lexington Avenue
bet. 87th and 88th streets
212-996-5898
email: info@musicalkids.net
www.musicalkids.net
Age: newborn to 7 years
Musical Kids International is the one program in New York City specializing in arts-based bilingual education. In a joyful and stimulating setting, Musical Kids International integrates the musical, kinesthetic, visual, and language arts in a second-language immersion format attuned to each child's age and stage of development. Utilizing only native-born teachers from the countries whose languages are represented, the MKI curriculum focuses on authentic songs and dances

imported from the original culture's heritage. The USA music classes have two teachers and a pianist leading children in singing, dancing, and playing musical instruments.

New York Kids Club

See website for locations throughout Manhattan.
212-721-4400
email: nykidsclub89@nykidsclub.com
www.nykidsclub.com
Age: 6 months to 12 years
New York Kid's Club is a premier facility for children's gymnastics, rock climbing, and martial arts, and also offers classes in dance, drama, music, art, and cooking. Call for schedule information on classes at all locations.

The Poppyseed Pre-Nursery

Gail Ionescu, MSW Director
424 West End Ave at 81st Street
212-877-7614
Poppyseed Pre-Nursery offers age-appropriate activities for newborns to three-year-olds that promote self-assurance, creativity, and self-expression through singing, dancing, and exploring the sensory world of art.

Rhinelander Children's Center / The Children's Aid Society

350 East 88th Street
bet. First and Second avenues
212-876-0500
www.childrensaidsociety.org/rhinelander
Age: 6 months to 4 years
Rhinelander is a very popular Upper East Side community center. Mommy and Me classes,

early childhood development programs, evening parenting seminars, as well as newborn-geared classes (see page 80) are all taught here. The Baby Fingers class teaches sign language to six- to twelve-month-olds. Children twelve to eighteen months old can enjoy Steppin' Out, an hour of free play, music, art, stories, bubbles, and snacks. Toddler Time, for eighteen- to twenty-four-month-olds and thirty- to thirty-six-month-olds, and Kiddie Crafters, an art class for toddlers age two and a half to three and a half years, are also offered. Classes usually have fifteen children with two instructors. Classes fill quickly, so apply promptly.

74th Street Magic

510 East 74th Street
bet. York Avenue and the East River
212-737-2989
email: magicinfo@74magic.com
www.74magic.com
Age: 6 months and up
74th Street Magic is held in a clean, bright, and large play space made up of two gyms. The gym for children over one year has padded tunnels, bridges, and houses, while the baby gym, for children under a year, is filled with a bubble pen and big balls. Magic holds music, art, gymnastics, cooking, science, separation, and preschool alternative classes to enrich children ages six months to teens that run from forty-five minutes to an hour. There are usually ten children per class with three instructors. Their youngest parent/child class option is for ages six to ten months, which incorporates music, bubbles, and parachute time in order to

enhance climbing, balancing, and other gross motor and social skills. They offer a drop-in option that allows you to better sample their class format.

Sokol New York Gym

420 East 71st Street
bet. First and York avenues
212-861-8206
email: office@sokolnewyork.org
www.sokolnewyork.org
Age: 10 months and up
Founded in 1867, Sokol New York offers Mommy and Me classes for infants, and a toddler gym class for one, two, and three-year-olds. Classes consist of free play, circle time, parachute play, bubbles, and more, with a different theme every few weeks. They also offer ballet, basketball, tae kwon do, and several adult-level classes. This is one of the most reasonably priced programs in New York City.

The Sports Club/L.A.

330 East 61st Street
bet. First and Second avenues
212-355-5100 ext. 4330
45 Rockefeller Plaza
212-218-8600
email: uppereastsidefko@mp-sportsclub.com
www.thesportsclubla.com
Age: 6 months to 13 years
Their For Kids Only club offers programs and camps throughout the year, music classes such as Jam with Me, and fitness-focused classes including Yogi Beans and Super Soccer Stars, or for little dancers, Tutus and Tiaras.

StoryTime By Design

1349 Lexington Avenue at 90th Street
917-543-3247; 917-533-4201
Ages: 6 months to 5 years
Storytime By Design, Inc., is a company that produces educational, musical, and interactive story hours that inspire literacy and a love for learning. Children are exposed not only to classic stories, but also to new works of fiction from exciting and upcoming authors in children's literature. Visual aides by the StoryTime By Design team include puppets, finger play, contemporary music, and simple art created during the story.

The Striking Viking Story Pirates

See website for a list of participating venues including the Jewish Community Center.
Story Pirates contact: Jamie at 310-880-4725
JCC contact: Melissa at 646-505-5729
email: afterschool@storypirates.org
www.storypirates.org
Ages: 5 and up
The Striking Viking Story Pirates (SVSP) is a not-for-profit organization founded to promote creative collaboration between adults and children by providing a wide variety of original arts and literacy programs. SVSP offers amazing writing workshops, acting classes, puppet classes, and dance programs in schools all over the tristate area. They also do private classes and parties!

Swim Jim

3 West 102nd Street (Main Office)

See website of a list of participating venues.

212-749-7335

email: info@swimjim.com

www.swimjim.com

Age: 6 months and up

Swim Jim is a proven name in swim instruction in NYC. It offers group, semi-private, and private lessons in a variety of locations or at your pool. Group classes are thirty minutes—see website for pricing info.

Take Me to the Water

See website for multiple locations in NYC, Long Island, and New Jersey

888-794-6692

www.takemetothewater.com

Age: 6 months and up

Heather Silver teaches private, semiprivate, and group swimming classes. Classes at Take Me to the Water can be as small as three babies and mothers with one instructor, and are taught at various public and private pools around the city. Classes parallel the school year; none are held in the summer.

Three Little Birds Music

266 East 78th Street at Second Avenue

212-744-0404

www.tlbmusic.com

Three Birds Music provides music education and exploration for children to enhance their development through music. This program is now equipped with a playroom on the lower level for you and your child.

True School Rocks / Bradley True and Friends

646-283-6935

email: bradley@bradleytrueandfriends.com

www.bradleytrueandfriends.com

Age: 4 months and up

Bradley has taken his skills from working for many well-respected NYC kids' music programs to developing his own, fast-growing music classes, parties, and concerts! Check out his site for all of the details.

Turtle Bay Music School

244 East 52nd Street

bet. Second and Third avenues

212-753-8811

email: info@tbms.org

www.tbms.org

Age: 18 months to adult

Turtle Bay, founded in 1925, is a full-service music school offering private music classes in all instruments. Music and movement classes start for toddlers at eighteen months, and there are programs for two- and three-year-olds as well. The Mommy and Me classes focus on movement, song, and percussion instruments. This warm and friendly school is ideal for midtown families. TBMS is involved in many community outreach programs that incorporate music, and they also offer a free two-year music program to committed school-age children and their parents.

YWHA 92nd Street*
1395 Lexington Avenue at 92nd Street
212-415-5500
www.92y.org
Age: newborn to adult
The 92nd Street Y's Parenting Center has a variety of activities and outstanding programs for parents and children, making it a nationwide model. Classes include Lamaze, Caring for a Newborn, Breastfeeding, Baby Massage, Rock 'n' Roll Baby, Little Explorers, Kids in the Kitchen, Pilates, Yoga, New Dads, Wonderplay, and Parkbench. A $190 membership in the Parenting Center allows you priority registration, special prices for every class, invitations to New Parent and Toddler-Parent Get-Togethers, members' rates for baby-sitting ($11 per hour), and special discounts at children's stores around the city.

Each of the following Y Associations offers a variety of classes for your baby, from gymnastics to music and swimming. Call your nearest Y for information, or go to www.ymcanyc.org.

YWCA of the City of New York
500 West 56th Street
212-937-8700

Vanderbilt YMCA
224 East 47th Street
bet. Second and Third avenues
212-912-2500

West Side YMCA
5 West 63rd Street
bet. Central Park West and Broadway
212-875-4101

McBurney YMCA
124 West 14th Street at Sixth Avenue
212-912-2300

Chinatown YMCA Houston Street Center
273 Bowery at East Houston
212-912-2460

Chinatown YMCA Hester Street Center
100 Hester Street at Forsyth Street
212-219-8393

Harlem YMCA
180 West 135th Street at Seventh Avenue
212-281-4100

YMCA of Greater New York Association Offices
5 West 63rd Street, Sixth Floor
212-630-9600

YWCA Polly Dodge Early Learning Center
Patricia Ferguson, Director
538 West 55th Street
bet. Tenth and Eleventh avenues
212-757-2047
Age: 2 to 6 years
Offers toddler, pre-school, and universal pre-K

mommy and me yoga classes

Since our first *City Baby* edition came out, there has been an explosion of yoga studios all over the city. There is probably one on your corner that has Mommy and Me classes but, if not, here are some good ones to check out. We have just listed them with web addresses, because many places have multiple locations and schedules change frequently.

* Baby Om
  www.babyom.com

* Be Yoga
  www.beyoga.com

* CitiBabes
  www.citibabes.com

* Educational Alliance Parenting and Family Center at the Sol Goldman YM-YWHA
  www.14streety.org

* Elana Weiss
  www.freetobeyoga.com

* Integral Yoga Institute
  www.iyiny.org

* Iyengar Yoga Institute of New York
  www.iyengarnyc.org

* The Jewish Community Center in Manhattan
  www.jccmanhattan.org

* Jivamukti Yoga Center
  www.jivamuktiyoga.com

* Karma Kids Yoga
  www.karmakidsyoga.com

* Mikelle Terson
  www.yogablossom.com

* New York Yoga
  www.newyorkyoga.com

* Philip Coltoff Center at Greenwich Village
  www.childrensaidsociety.org/pcc/earlychildhood

* Prenatal Yoga Center
  www.prenatalyogacenter.com

* Real Birth
  www.realbirth.com

* The SoHo Parenting Center
  www.sohoparenting.com

* Yoga for Two
  www.yogafortwo.com

playgrounds

New York's parks and playgrounds provide just about every activity you can think of. The park is a great place for your baby or toddler to explore, swing, slide, and climb, and for you to meet other moms with children close in age to yours. And when the weather's nice, you'll love going out, enjoying a change of scenery, and taking in some fresh air.

The Department of Parks and Recreation oversees some 1,578 parks and 862 playgrounds around the city. In the past few years, many playgrounds have been renovated and now have soft rubber mat surfaces, brightly colored metal bars for climbing, and sprinklers for cooling. One of the city's most original playgrounds is the Rustic Playground at East 67th Street, a perfect stop before or after a visit to the Central Park Zoo.

You can call the Parks Department at 311 or 212-NEW-YORK (www.nycgovparks.org) for information on events in any of the city's parks. For older children, call the department's recreation office at 24 West 61st Street, 212-408-0243, to find out about playground programs, sports, and Arts in the Park, a summer series of free activities and performances for children. Playground Partners is a wonderful organization dedicated to fund-raising to help maintain the playgrounds within Central Park. Its annual spring parties in the Park are not to be missed!

Central Park

You can easily spend a leisurely day in Central Park (www.centralpark.org). Walk around the Boat Pond (72nd Street at Fifth Avenue), or sit in an outdoor cafe and watch the miniature boat enthusiasts sail their remote-controlled beauties across the pond. Run through the Sheep Meadow (69th Street at mid-park) or Strawberry Fields (72nd Street at Central Park West); bring a ball for a game of catch and some nibbles for a picnic lunch. Or buy one from a nearby concession stand. For a complete listing of all playgrounds in Central Park, visit www.centralpark.com/pages/activities/children-s-activities/playgrounds.html.

Some of our favorite Central Park spots include:

❖ *Alice in Wonderland statue*
(74th Street at Fifth Avenue). As soon as your youngster is moving around comfortably on her own, this huge bronze statue, full of nooks and crannies to climb on, will captivate her. There are always lots of kids, with moms and caregivers sitting on the nearby benches keeping an eye on things.

❖ *James Michael Levin Playground*
(77th Street at Fifth Avenue). This renovated playground has a padded gym/slide good for eighteen-month-olds and up; space to run, play, or ride a tricycle; an enclosed swing area; a big, roomy sandbox; and a toddler-friendly water sprinkler system for those hot summer days.

❖ *Spector Playground*
(85th Street at Central Park West). A West Side favorite, this playground has an area for children under two, with a sandbox, slides, climbing equipment, and a blacktop space for tricycles and toy cars. For children over two, a

sandy section of the playground has tire and rope swings, climbing chains, and more.

Adventure Playground

(next to Tavern on the Green, West 67th Street at Central Park West). Divided into two sections, a lower play area has baby swings, a sandbox, slides, and a bridge, while the hilltop playground, for older kids, resembles an Egyptian park. Perfect for "imagination" games!

Diana Ross Playground

(81st Street at Central Park West). This is the perfect place to go with your new baby or visiting five-year-old niece; it has baby swings as well as great climbing equipment for older kids.

East 96th Street Playground

(at Fifth Avenue). This large, well-laid-out playground is the East Side stomping ground for the four-to- six-year-old set. After preschool it is the place to meet, complete with swings, sandbox, climbing gym, and fort. You'll undoubtedly find your own favorite parts of Central Park. And, of course, you'll pay many visits to these two special attractions:

The Central Park Carousel

Middle of Central Park at 64th Street
212-879-0244
The Central Park Carousel is one of this country's great antique carousels. Each ride lasts about five minutes and is accompanied by calliope music. Your baby can ride with you on a horse that moves up and down, on a stationary horse, or in one of two chariots. Each ride costs $2 per person.

Central Park Wildlife Conservation Center (Zoo)

Fifth Avenue at 64th Street
212-439-6500
Officially called the Central Park Wildlife Conservation Center, this zoo provides natural habitats for mostly small (with the exception of the polar bear) animals. Visit the rain forest, complete with monkeys; the penguin house; and, of course, the sea lions' circular pool with see-through sides. The daily sea lion feedings are sure to delight your youngster. You'll find plenty of places to sit, as well as a cafeteria.

There are scheduled tours and activities each day (story hours, arts and crafts, and animal feedings), so call ahead. Adult admission is $10, $7 for seniors, children three to twelve years pay $5, and children under three are free. These prices include admission to the newly renovated Tisch Children's Zoo's Enchanted Forest and Domestic Animal Area.

Other Parks

While Central Park is the biggest and best, New York has a variety of parks where your child can have some outdoor fun. Here are some favorites, by neighborhood:

East Side (East River)

Carl Schurz*

East End Avenue at 84th Street
This popular Upper East Side park has something for everyone: for infants, there is a play area with swings, bridges, and slides; for tod-

dlers, there is an enclosed sandbox with climbing and sliding jungle gyms; and for adults, there is a superb riverside promenade. A paved pavilion with a sprinkler fountain running in the summer is used for ball play and tricycles in the fall and spring.

❊ Ancient Playground

Enter Central Park at Fifth Avenue and 84th Street
Built in homage to the Metropolitan Museum of Art's Egyptian art collection, the newly renovated Ancient Playground has slides, chain bridges, baby and tire swings, ropes, and a sprinkler mixed in with obelisks and pyramid-like structures. Bathrooms available. Open daily, dawn to dusk.

❊ John Jay*

FDR Drive at 76th Street
This big, clean enclosed playground has slides and moving bridges, a good central sprinkler system, a sandbox with swings for all ages, and benches all around. From the Fourth of July to early September, a large swimming pool is open from 11 a.m. to 7 p.m., and there are free swimming lessons for children ages three and up. Sign up early; the playground and pool get busy and crowded in the summer months.

❊ Madison Square Park

Enter at 25th Street and Madison Avenue
www.madisonsquarepark.org
There's never a dull moment at Madison Square Park. Aside from the classic jungle gyms and slides, kids are kept busy with scheduled arts-and-crafts workshops and puppet shows. The surrounding area includes lush lawns, flowerbeds, and a restored nineteenth-century fountain. (Not to mention Shake Shack.) Culture-vulture parents will love the sculpture exhibit in the summertime. Open 6 a.m. to midnight; no bathrooms.

You might also check out these parks:

❊ Mercer Playground

Enter at Mercer Street, near Bleecker Street
212-267-9700
www.nyc.gov/parks
This half-acre park is fantastic for kids on wheels. An evenly paved space is the perfect surface for helmeted skaters, bladers, cyclers, and kids on their scooters. There's also a sprinkler and boulders to climb on. Open daily, dawn to dusk.

❊ Nelson A. Rockefeller Park

Battery Park City, enter at Chambers Street and River Terrace
www.bpcparks.org
This sprawling park has a pedal-driven carousel, a rubbery surface for chalk drawing, a sandpit, bronze animal sculptures, and a wading fountain for the tiny ones. You'll also find chess tables, slides, swings, jungle gyms, and climbing nets. River views and shady benches for mom and dad make a visit fun and relaxing for everyone. Open 6 a.m. to 10 p.m.; bathrooms available.

St. Catherine's Playground

(First Avenue at 67th Street).
Sutton Place Park
(FDR Drive at 57th Street).
MacArthur Playground
(FDR Drive at 48th Street).

West Side/Riverside Park

Hippo Park Playground at Riverside Drive and 91st Street*

This is one of our favorites, with adult and baby hippo statues ideal for climbing. It's extremely clean, and monitored by a parents' association as well as by the Parks Department. Picnic tables, benches, slides, a sandbox, seesaws, swings, and climbing equipment are shaded by fifty-year-old oak trees. This playground was specially designed for kids ages two to seven.

P.S. 87 Playground at 77th Street and Amsterdam

A few years back this playground was completely gutted and redone recently. What a clever place! Lots of interesting structures to climb on, monkey bars for kids of all sizes—even pretend kiosks for kids who want to play "store."

Riverside Drive at 76th Street*

Here you'll find nicely divided sections for infants and toddlers, plenty of climbing equipment, swings, and a gentle circular sprinkler system. There is a separate sandbox, a nice grassy area, and a basketball court for older children nearby. Bring your sunscreen; there isn't a lot of shade.

River Run Playground at 83rd Street and Riverside*

This playground is fantastic and true to its name has a "river" running through the center (with about an inch of water in it). The water is turned on in this park if the temperature reaches 75 degrees. The playground also features a sand-box with faces sculpted into the perimeter, tons of climbing equipment for all ages, a mini carousel, and swings for all sizes.

A friend of Pamela's held her daughter's third birthday party here, and the kids had a blast! You must call the Parks Department for a permit, but it's free, and there are three picnic tables there to hold your pizza and cake. And remember this is New York—you can get pizza delivered directly to the playground!

Other Riverside Park playgrounds are located at:

Riverside Drive at 97th Street

Riverside Drive at 110th Street

Riverside Drive at 123rd Street

Downtown

Hudson River Park Playground*

(Chambers at Greenwich Street). A thriving down-town favorite, this clean, enclosed playground sits across from the esplanade of the Hudson River. All the equipment is labeled by age group, and there's a separate section with tables. There are swings, a sand table, a sliding bridge, climbing structures, sprinklers, and some of the most imaginative play equipment in the city.

❋ *Battery Park* (Battery Park City).*
Located at the tip of Manhattan, this park attracts a number of tourists. While the swings and slides (across from the entrance to the Staten Island Ferry) are old and outdated, the grassy park itself has a fabulous view and is a pleasant place for picnicking.

Also for downtown parents and tots:

❋ *P.S. 40*
(Second Avenue at East 19th Street)

❋ *Union Square Park*
(Broadway at East 16th Street)

❋ *Washington Square Park*
(West Fourth and MacDougal streets)

❋ *Duane Park*
(East Stuyvesant High School)

❋ *Abingdon Square Park*
(Bleecker and Bank streets)

❋ *James J. Walker Park*
(Leroy Street and Seventh Avenue)

public libraries

Beginning at six months, children are good candidates for short library visits. Sit and relax while your toddler listens during story time, watches a short film with popular characters, or participates in an arts and crafts project.

The New York Public Library system puts out a free booklet every month listing each branch's activities for children, but proximity to your home is the key in choosing what to do. Stop in or call and see what's going on.

Library branches with children's activities are listed below, by neighborhood.

Upper East Side

❋ *96th Street*
112 East 96th Street
bet. Park and Lexington avenues
212-289-0908

❋ *67th Street*
328 East 67th Street
bet. First and Second avenues
212-734-1717

❋ *Webster*
1465 York Avenue
bet. 77th and 78th streets
212-288-5049

❋ *Yorkville*
222 East 79th Street
bet. Second and Third avenues
212-744-5824

Upper West Side

❊ *Bloomingdale*
150 West 100th Street at Amsterdam Avenue
212-222-8030

❊ *Columbus*
742 Tenth Avenue
bet. 50th and 51st streets
212-586-5098

❊ *Riverside*
127 Amsterdam Avenue at 65th Street
212-870-1810

❊ *St. Agnes*
444 Amsterdam Avenue at 81st Street
212-877-4380

Midtown

❊ *Donnell Library Center / Children's Center at 42nd Street*
Stephen A. Schwarzman Building
Fifth Avenue and 42nd Street
212-621-0208
email: childrenscenter42@nypl.org
This special branch boasts the largest collection of children's and young adult books in the city. Moreover, it houses Christopher Robin's original Winnie-the-Pooh stuffed animals (Pooh, Tigger, Eeyore, Piglet, and Kanga), who live in the second-floor children's room.

❊ *Epiphany*
228 East 23rd Street
bet. Second and Third avenues
212-679-2645

❊ *Kips Bay*
446 Third Avenue at 31st Street
212-683-2520

Downtown

❊ *Hudson Park*
66 Leroy Street at Seventh Avenue South
212-243-6876

❊ *Jefferson Market*
425 Sixth Avenue at 10th Street
212-243-4334

Lower East Side

❊ *New Amsterdam*
9 Murray Street
bet. Broadway and Church Street
212-732-8186

❊ *Tompkins Square*
331 East 10th Street
bet. Avenues A and B
212-228-4747

other activities for you and your child

Everything in this section is definitely worthy of a gold star.

❋ American Girl Place

609 Fifth Avenue at 49th Street

877-AG-PLACE

www.americangirlplace.com

Ages: 2 to teen

The American Girl Place has been a great addition to New York. It is an entire four-story emporium dedicated to American Girl dolls. Little girls can shop, see a show, get their doll's hair done, and have lunch all in one place with their American Girl doll in tow. Just be warned: this place gets really crowded. It is best to reserve in advance for lunch and a show. This is also a popular place to celebrate a little girl's birthday. When Rebecca and Pamela dined there, birthday cakes came out of the kitchen at record speed.

❋ The American Museum of Natural History

79th Street at Central Park West

212-769-5100

www.amnh.org

Even when the American Museum of Natural History fills with toddlers and their parents, it's so huge and full of hands-on exhibits and fascinating things to see that you'll hardly notice the crowd. Little children stare in wonder at the lifelike dioramas and those spectacular dinosaurs. Parents love bringing their children to the Whale's Lair, where little ones can run around on the huge floor under the giant blue whale. And for your convenience, there's a child-friendly cafeteria, located in the basement. Adult admission is $16, children are $9, and seniors and students are $12.

❋ Barnes & Noble / Barnes & Noble Junior

Check website for multiple locations throughout NYC

www.barnesandnoble.com

These are more like community centers than bookstores. Introduce your children to the kids' sections, where they can listen to you read a story or lie on the floor to look at books by themselves. In addition, the stores have special scheduled readings, Gymboree story time, and bedtime stories. Schedules change weekly, so call ahead or drop by for a listing of events. Most Barnes & Noble stores are open from 9 a.m. to 10 p.m.; all events are free. ·

❋ Brooklyn Botanic Garden

1000 Washington Avenue, near Montgomery Street

Brooklyn

718-623-7220

www.bbg.org

Brooklyn Botanic Garden is a tranquil, 52-acre urban oasis featuring more than 11,000 different kinds of plants from around the world. The BBG offers a ton of really cool and educational programs for children and their parents. Check out their website for detailed info. Adult admission is $8, seniors 65+ and students 12+ with IDs are $4, and children under 12 are free.

Brooklyn Children's Museum

145 Brooklyn Avenue at St. Mark's Avenue
Brooklyn
718-735-4400
www.brooklynkids.org

With award-winning, hands-on exhibits and innovative use of its collections, the museum engages children from preschool to high school in learning adventures. It is one of only two children's museum in New York City, and among the few in the country to be accredited by the American Association of Museums. Admission is $7.50 per person, and free for BCM members and children under one year of age.

The Bronx Zoo

2300 Southern Boulevard at 185th Street
718-367-1010
www.bronxzoo.com

At the Bronx Zoo, the largest in the United States, animals roam in large, natural settings. The Sky Ferry takes visitors through the park—a nice rest for a tired toddler and his exhausted parent. Visit the children's area, a petting zoo where youngsters can pet and feed some smaller animals and go on rides. Admission is $15 for adults and $13 for seniors and $11 for children ages three to twelve. Children under three are free and Wednesdays are free for everyone. Admission to the children's zoo is an additional fee.

The Children's Museum of Manhattan

212 West 83rd Street
bet. Broadway and Amsterdam Avenue
212-721-1223
www.cmom.org

This interactive museum allows young children to explore, touch, and investigate its various exhibits. Its size has doubled since our first edition, and the museum offers more than ever before for children of all ages. The Creative Corner is an early childhood center (for ages four and under) where children can paint, color, and play with educational toys in a specially designed kids' room. Exhibits change yearly, but you will always find something geared toward the under two set here. Story hours, puppet shows, and other activities are offered throughout the museum. It also offers terrific birthday parties that are popular for two- and three-year-olds. Admission is $10 for adults and children over one; children under one are free; seniors 65 and over are $7. Strollers or carriages must be folded up and checked at the door. On the first Friday of every month admission is free from 5 p.m. to 8 p.m.; hosted by Target.

The Children's Museum of the Arts

182 Lafayette Street
bet. Broome and Grand streets
212-274-0986
www.cmany.org

You can spend an entire afternoon at this hands-on museum, which offers exhibits as well as activities for children. You and your child can do arts and crafts, make a poster for Dad, or create a T-shirt design. Slides, climbing equipment, and a dress-up corner are also available. Two- and three-year-olds love this museum. Admission is $10 per person ages 1 to 65. Every Thursday from 4 to 6 p.m. is "pay as you wish."

❖ Jewish Children's Museum

792 Eastern Parkway near Kingston Avenue
Brooklyn
718-467-0600
www.jcm.museum

A place of learning and wonder, the Jewish Children's Museum is a unique institution where children and their parents—from all segments of the community—can explore Jewish history and heritage in a stimulating and interactive environment. General admission for the public is $10 per person, child or adult. Admission for children under the age of two is free.

❖ Museum of the Moving Image

35th Avenue at 36th Street
Queens
718-784-4520
www.movingimage.us

The Museum of the Moving Image offers hands-on interactive exhibits, classic video arcade games, movie screenings, birthday parties, a moving pictures workshop, a stop-motion animation workshop, after-school programs, and special memberships like "Red Carpet Kids" that hosts fun screenings of family-friendly films. Admission is $7 and free for children under eight years old.

❖ Metropolitan Museum of Art

1000 Fifth Avenue at 82nd Street
212-535-7710
www.metmuseum.org

There are times you just need a good place to take a sleeping baby while you stroll around by yourself or with a friend. And even when your toddler is awake, the Met does have some open spaces, such as the reflecting garden, where the little one can roam. Strollers are not allowed on Sundays, but the museum will provide you with a backpack for your child when you check your stroller. We found that our toddlers were good for about an hour. Suggested donations are $20 for adults, $15 for seniors 65+, and $10 for students; admission is free for children under twelve years old.

❖ New York Aquarium in Coney Island

602 Surf Avenue at West 8th Street
Brooklyn
718-265-4740
www.nyaquarium.com

Programs for caregivers and little ones, summer camps, and after-school workshops for school-age children offer hands-on discovery and interactive learning. Older visitors can take behind-the-scenes tours at the aquarium, help keepers take care of the animals, and conduct their own science experiments. All programs require advance reservations. General admission for adults is $13, children from ages three to twelve are $9, and seniors are $10. Children under three are free. Fridays after 3 p.m. is "pay as you wish."

The New Victory Theater

The New 42nd Street/The New Victory Theater
229 West 42nd Street, 10th Floor
bet. Seventh and Eighth avenues
646-223-3067
email: amui@new42.org
www.newvictory.org

New York City's first and only full-time theater dedicated to young people, the New Victory is committed to creating ever-widening avenues of opportunity for young people, their families, and teachers to grow professionally and personally through the arts.

Scandinavia House

58 Park Avenue
bet. 37th and 38th streets
212-879-9779
email: info@amscan.org
www.amscan.org

Scandinavia House and its Heimbold Family Children's Center offers regular programs and activities for children and families. Scandinavia House provides a cultural link between the U.S. and five Nordic countries. It's definitely worth checking out.

concerts, shows, and special events

When your child is between two and three years old, he may be ready to enjoy one of the city's many shows, concerts, or special events that are produced especially for children. Watch for:

* **Performances of The Big Apple Circus** (at Damrosch Park behind Lincoln Center from October through December), Sesame Street Live (at The Theater at Madison Square Garden), the Madison Square Garden Ice Shows (throughout the winter), and The Wiggles, Dora, Diego, Kai-lan, the Backyardigans, Wonder Pets, and more at various times during the year. Call Ticketmaster or Telecharge for ticket prices and purchases. Check out www.newyorkkids.timeout.com for the most current event listings.

* Children's theater shows are offered throughout the year by **The Puppet Company** (212-741-1646), Puppetworks (718-965-3391), TADA! (212-252-1619), The Paper Bag Players (212-633-0390), and Tribeca Performing Arts Center (212-220-1460). Call for prices, schedules, and information; some shows are for children ages three and over.

* **The Lolli Pops Concert Series** introduces children to classical music and the orchestra at hour-long concerts. Produced by The Little Orchestra Society (212-971-9500), the concerts are wonderful for children ages three to five.

❋ *The Swedish Cottage Marionette Theater* produces children's classics at the theater in Central Park at West 81st Street (212-988-9093). Kid favorites here have included Cinderella, Rumpelstiltskin, and Gulliver's Travels. Tickets are $5 for children, $8 for adults. Call ahead for reservations.

❋ *New York Theatre Ballet's* "Once Upon a Ballet" Family Series at the Florence Gould Hall (212-355-6160) is ballet made for children. Though the offerings change each year, The Nutcracker is always included in the package.

after-school
activities

Preschoolers are tremendously curious about the world and have a great capacity to learn. Today many children ages three and younger are enrolled in programs designed to expand creativity, enhance social skills, and improve fitness. They might take violin lessons, attempt computer games, or plunge into the muddy delights of clay. Many toddlers enjoy tumbling or the challenge of martial arts classes, while others study languages, take ballet, and learn to swim.

Never before have there been so many choices for your child. But a word of caution: beware of overscheduling. Every city baby, no matter how bright, needs some free time to play with friends or simply to be alone.

Choosing a Program

The hardest part of choosing a program is determining the best, most wonderful activity for your child when there are so many great options available. It's easy to become overzealous in your approach to your child's happiness and well-being, but you have to keep your perspective. Remember to be light-hearted about your child's free time. You're not sending him off to become a neurosurgeon or master violinist, but exposing him to activities that may or may not become large parts of his life. Finding a program ultimately should be a child-directed process. Rebecca tried ballet, gymnastics, soccer, and modern dance before falling in love with ice-skating; she skated for three years and went back to dance as a preteen. Alexander tried acting, soccer, and tae kwon do, among other activities, and still hasn't settled on one "thing." Ideally, you want your child to experiment and learn, and have a great time, too!

Most classes are offered once a week on a year-long, semester-long, or per-class basis. A more intensive class, like a violin class, might meet twice a week. Our kids have enjoyed taking up to three or four classes per week, but don't push; you don't want to force anything, or you'll end up making a chore out of what should be a fun, passion-driven experience. In this chapter you'll find classes in art, dance, music, pottery, and theater, as well as a number of sports and personal enrichment programs, language and computer classes, and other programs like chess.

Whatever you choose, be sure to take convenience into account. We recommend choosing classes within ten blocks of your home.

Here are a few more things to think about when choosing a class or program:

- How long has the school/gym/academy been in business?
- How large are classes?
- How many teachers/coaches are there?
- Must you commit to a full year, by the semester, or by the class?

To make the process as easy as possible for you, we have listed classes in every subject appropriate for your city baby. Our kids and our friends' kids have tried many of these programs with happy results. But be sure to check out each program carefully yourself. Notice how the afternoon is structured, and how the teachers interact with the children.

You can also contact the Parent's League (at 212-737-7385) for more information on after-school activities available throughout the city. Good luck—and remember to have fun!

one-stop shopping: after-school institutions

Our "after-school institutions" really are one-stop shopping meccas, offering a multitude of programs for children of all ages—everything from art, music, gymnastics, and cooking, to science and Jewish culture. As your child gets older, he can even join a swim team or basketball league. These all-purpose after-school institutions make your life easy (always a plus for city moms), providing everything your child could need. The following are the best of these super schools with programs for children up to three years old.

74th Street Magic

510 East 74th Street
bet. York and the East River
212-737-2989
www.74magic.com

74th Street Magic offers classes in music, art, gymnastics, cooking, science, and preschool alternatives, as well as Summer Days Camp and customized birthday parties. Sharing a building with Epiphany Community Nursery School, children will find state-of-the-art classrooms, a baby gym, a fully equipped gym for adults, a terrific party room, and an outdoor rooftop playground. 74th Street Magic gears their programs to help children gain confidence, independence, and knowledge while cultivating their curiosity and talents.

Asphalt Green

555 East 90th Street at York Avenue
212-369-8890
www.asphaltgreen.com

This huge, modern fitness complex has an extensive Youth Aquatics program for children eighteen months and up; the instructor ratio is five to one. There is also a variety of gymnastics, indoor/outdoor soccer, and basketball classes, as well as instruction in karate and chess. It has one of the best pools in the city for learning to swim.

Chelsea Piers

Pier 62, 23rd Street and Twelfth Avenue
212-336-6500
www.chelseapiers.com

This enormous sports complex has it all: huge two-level gym, an entire track, a sand volleyball court, a climbing wall, a three-level driving range, twin hockey rinks, soccer fields, roller hockey rink—you name it. Tumbling classes are offered for children ages three and up.

Discovery Programs

Elaine Winter, Director
251 West 100th Street at West End Avenue
212-749-8717
email: info@discoveryprograms.com
email: elaine@discoveryprograms.com
www.discoveryprograms.com
Ages: 6 months to 14 years

The Discovery Programs have been an Upper West Side staple forever. They offer a range of interesting, creative classes for children from toddlers to age seven. The Young Leonardos class brings together artistic creativity and scientific problem solving by exploring the outside world, while the Young Explorers class learns about cultures throughout the world. Tae kwon do, parenting, gym, art, music, dance, Spanish, story time, separation, gymnastics, sports, and acting classes are also offered. Siblings are eligible for 10 percent off enrollment.

Gymtime Rhythm and Glues

1520 York Avenue at East 80th Street
212-861-7732
www.gymtime.net
Gymtime Rhythm and Glues is a recreational and educational facility for children ages six months to twelve years old that offers movement, educational and recreational gymnastics, sports, tae kwon do, cooking, music, art, and a preschool alternative.

Jewish Community Center

334 Amsterdam Avenue at 76th Street
646-505-4444
www.jccmanhattan.org
Age: newborn to adult
The after-school programs here are abundant and include everything from swimming, art, pottery, music, dance, gymnastics, and more. After-school sports are also popular here, and kids can play soccer, basketball, and more, depending on the season.

92nd Street Y

1395 Lexington Avenue at 92nd Street
212-996-1100
www.92ndsty.org
Here classes include tennis, circus arts, chess, cooking, computers, science, soccer, tae kwon do, gymnastics, swimming, music (including guitar and piano instruction), and dance (including ballet, Isadora for Children, and modern dance classes). Art classes include Learning from the Masters, in which kids create original artwork based on the media and techniques of famous artists; and A Course of a Different Color, in which children explore their ideas, dreams, and fantasies through mask making, book making, clay sculpting, painting, collage, and more. Kelly and Alexander have taken many classes here over the years.

Rhinelander Children's Center

350 East 88th Street
bet. First and Second avenues
212-876-0500
www.rhinelandercenter.org
In Rhinelander's After School Arts & Smarts club, kindergartners and first-graders take part in the KinderClub, exploring art, music, and computers, and engaging in dramatic play, dance, outdoor play, and cooking. In The After School Visual & Performing Arts Program, kids explore health, fitness, and science among other activities. Homework time with teachers is available after school. Pickup from most neighborhood schools is available and holiday programs are also offered.

Tony Dapolito Recreation Center

1 Clarkson Street at Seventh Avenue South

212-242-5228

Ages: 4 and up

Downtown families swear by the Carmine Street Recreation Center as a terrific, inexpensive place for kids from pre-K and up and it is actually run by the City! Its after-school program is only $5 per day, and it also has sports leagues (soccer, T-ball, baseball), which involve a nominal fee. It has both an outdoor pool (open from the Thursday before July Fourth weekend until the Friday before public schools open) and an indoor pool that is open all year and is free for children under thirteen.

the arts

Art

Art Muse (formerly Museum Adventures NYC)

646-678-4497

www.artmuseny.com

Age: 3 and 1/2 to 12 years

Mother of three Natasha Schlesinger started Art Muse a few years ago when she wanted to combine her passion for art with her love of kids. Her classes take moms and kids to a variety of museums and galleries all over the city to view art and do hands-on projects that coordinate with a theme. Natasha's classes are fantastic—she is incredibly knowledgeable and makes each class fun for moms and kids. She also offers moms-only classes during school hours.

Arts in Action

212-864-4883

email: artsinactionvap@aol.com

www.artsinactionvap.org

Arts in Action offers after-school and weekend fine art classes for children, day and evening classes for adults and children, private lessons, and more.

Hi Art!

917-318-9499

www.hiartkids.com

Hi Art! is an ambitious ten-week series of workshops designed to introduce children ages two to fifteen to "real" art in highly imaginative and creative ways. Classes are held in galleries and museums throughout the city as well as in a mid-town studio, where children study opera, ballet, theater, and symphonies, and engage in ongoing art projects designed to help them understand how actual artists work. Each class series is centered around a contemporary musical work. For older children, advanced painting, life drawing, and sculpture classes are also offered.

Little Shop of Crafts

431 East 73rd Street

bet. First and York avenues

212-717-6636

711 Amsterdam Avenue at 94th Street

212-531-CRAFTS

www.littleshopny.com

Little Shop of Crafts offers craft classes, workshops, and parties, featuring popular crafts like pottery, plasterworks, mosaics, beading, stuffed animal creation, T-shirt design, and more. They also host adult gatherings of many sorts. See website for more information.

Portrait Bug Snap n' Scrap

2466 Broadway at 91st Street
212-600-4457
www.portraitbug.com

With any $10 craft purchase moms get to go free to events like breakfast clubs, scrapbooking, Monday night football, ladies' night out, and more. They offer adult classes in scrapbooking, sewing, photography, and many other craft-oriented tasks. For kids ages five to twelve, they offer specialized after-school arts and crafts classes, and for infants and babies, they hold a baby sign-language class and Mommy and Me craft classes. In addition, Portrait Bug hosts parties and private classes upon request.

Dance

The Ailey School

405 West 55th Street at Ninth Avenue
212-405-9143

The official school of the Alvin Ailey American Dance Theater offers a First Steps program for children ages three to six. Ballet is taught in graded levels, and classes incorporate other forms of dance (Dunham, Graham-based modern, Horton, and Limon techniques; West African, Spanish, and East Indian dance, mime, and floor gymnastics for boys) as children progress through the curriculum.

American Youth Dance Theater

428 East 75th Street
bet. First and York avenues
212-717-5419
www.americanyouthdancetheater.com

Kids ages two and older learn ballet and creative dance, tap, and jazz. We didn't discover this theater until Rebecca was a preteen, but it is a wonderful program that offers hip-hop and Broadway dance classes for older kids as well. Class sizes are kept small to ensure individual attention and a strong student-teacher-parent relationship.

Ballet Academy East

1651 Third Avenue, 3rd Floor
bet. 92nd and 93rd streets
212-410-9140
email: info@baenyc.com
Age: 2 years to adult

Ballet Academy East offers Mommy and Me classes for children two years to two and half, and pre-ballet, drama, and tap classes for kids three and up. The classes here are very structured and excellent. It is a must for all East Side budding ballerinas.

The Bridge for Dance

2726 Broadway at 104th Street, 3rd floor
212-749-1165
www.bridgefordance.com

Children ages three and up learn expressive movement, while ages six and up begin studying ballet, tap, and pre-jazz, pre-pointe, hip-hop, and musical theater.

Broadway Dance Center

221 West 57th Street at Broadway
212-582-9304, ext. 25
www.bwydance.com
Broadway Dance Center offers children ages three to fourteen fun, creative, and challenging classes in ballet, tap, jazz, hip-hop, creative movement, pre-dance, voice, acting, and theater performance. It also has a youth performance company, A.I.M., or Arts in Motion, providing an opportunity for young dancers to perform in the community. Past students at the Broadway Dance Center have performed in Miss Saigon, Annie Get Your Gun, Lion King, and other Broadway plays.

Chinese Folk Dance Company

New York Chinese Cultural Center
390 Broadway, 2nd Floor, bet. Walker and White streets
212-334-3764
In this Chinatown cultural center, children ages three and older can study Chinese language, Chinese dance, Chinese acrobatics, Chinese opera, and Chinese painting. All nationalities are welcome.

Dance for Children

Murray Street Studio
19 Murray Street
bet. Broadway and Church Street
212-608-7681
www.murraystreetdance.com
Children ages three and older explore the basic vocabulary of movement in the Creative Movement class, exercising their imaginations through ideas, images, and stories. Pre-ballet classes are offered for four- and five-year-olds, modern ballet for kids ages five and up, and choreography workshops for kids ages eight and up.

Djoniba Dance and Drum Center

37 East 18th Street, 7th Floor
bet. Broadway and Park Avenue South
212-477-3464
www.djoniba.com
Children ages three to sixteen can take classes in African dance, African drums, Capoeira, and ballet at this downtown studio.

Greenwich House Music School

46 Barrow Street
bet. Bleecker and Bedford streets
212-242-4770
www.gharts.org
Greenwich House Music School has been providing high-quality, affordable music education since 1902. Children ages two and older can choose from classes in music, art, ballet, and musical theater.

In Grandma's Attic

See website for locations throughout NYC.
212-726-2362
email: grandma@ingrandmasattic.com
www.ingrandmasattic.com
This is a fantasy-based creative dance program for children ages two to twelve. In Budding Ballerina (two to three years) children dance to nursery rhymes and favorite stories; in Fairies and Fantasy (four to six years) children revisit

favorite fairy tales and learn new tales and stories. Pamela and Rebecca adored this class.

Judy Lasko Modern Dance at Symphony Space
2537 Broadway at 95th Street
212-864-3143
This school offers modern dance classes for children ages three and up. Judy Lasko has been teaching for forty-five years, and is both a dancer and Orff music teacher.

Kids Co-Motion
Rebecca Kelly Ballet/Kids Co-Motion
579 Broadway, 4B
bet. Prince Street and Houston
280 Rector Place
37 West 26th Street, east of Sixth Avenue
212-431-8489
Rebecca Kelly is a choreographer with much experience teaching children's movement classes. Her whole child developmental approach results in an integrated, creative movement and dynamic dance program for every age. The toddler classes are kept small for a hands-on approach. Kids Co-Motion offers creative movement, dance basics, ballet, and modern dance classes for kids ages 4 and up.

Kinderdance
212-579-5270
email: kinderdancenyc@aol.com
Kinderdance is a developmental dance, movement and fitness program for children ages two to eight. Classes are a combination of warm-up, motor skills, ballet, gymnastics, creative move-

ment, and tap dance. This is a popular program taught in thirty different preschools throughout the city. You can also call about getting Kinderdance into your own child's school.

The Lucy Moses School for Music and Dance
129 West 67th Street
bet. Broadway and Amsterdam Avenue
212-501-3360
www.lucymosesschool.org
Founded in 1952, Lucy Moses School is one of the country's most renowned and respected community arts schools with programs in music, dance, and theater for children ages eighteen months and up. More than just a school, LMS feels like a community, specializing in making the arts fun and accessible with a wide range of classes, performance opportunities, and private lessons.

Manhattan Ballet School
149 East 72nd Street
bet. Lexington and Third avenues
212-535-6556
www.manhattanballetschool.org
At this forty-year-old neighborhood school children are taught classical ballet in a traditional manner. Children from ages three and up study creative movement and pre-ballet.

Perichild Program
132 Fourth Avenue, 2nd Floor,
bet. 13th and 12th streets
212-505-0886
www.peridance.com

Located at the Peridance Center, the Perichild Program offers technique classes in ballet, modern, jazz, tap, hip-hop, salsa, African dance, and samurai sword training (!) for children ages eighteen months and up.

The School for Education in Dance and the Related Arts

16 East 11th Street
bet. University Place and Fifth Avenue
212-254-3194
Taught in schools, day-care centers, and libraries throughout the city, this is an interrelated arts program that includes movement, music, theater games for self-esteem, exposure to visual quality arts, and tumbling as it applies to dance—all combined in each class. The purpose is to deal with the creative process at the earliest possible moment of a child's development, for lifetime use. If this program is not available in your child's school, you can call to discuss ways to bring it in.

Shake, Rhythm and Roll

West Side Dance Project
260 West 36th Street, 3rd Floor
bet. Seventh and Eighth avenues
212-563-6781
www.westsidedanceproject.com
The West Side Dance Project offers dance and music education programs for children ages five and up. Classes are offered in instrumental music (on all instruments), music introduction, voice, creative movement, classical ballet, modern jazz, and tap. Classes are also held at an Upper West Side location.

Steps on Broadway

2121 Broadway at 74th Street
212-874-2410
www.stepsnyc.com
Age: 2.5 to adult
Like Ballet Academy East on the East Side, Steps is the West Side place to get your little ballerina started. Girls (or boys) start with Little Steps and can move up to pre-dance, pre-tap, or pre-ballet classes. The program here is very structured and serious. It is a real treat to watch the older kids and adult classes here, too.

Drama

Broadway Little Stars at St. Jean's Community Center

184 East 76th Street
bet. Lexington and Third avenues
212-717-0703
www.applauseny.com
These fabulous classes are fun for toddlers and are the next step after music classes. Broadway Little Stars (ages three to six) provides an interactive learning experience that will encourage your child to participate in a class setting, while playing theatrical games, singing songs, and learning to dance. Your child will be so absorbed in the class they won't even know you are outside the room.

The Drama Zone

220 East 86th Street
bet. Second and Third avenues
917-690-0789
www.dramazonenyc.com

Age: 4 months to adult

The Drama Zone offers classes in art, dance, music, or drama for babies as young as four months to kids ages thirteen and up. It offers morning classes for the youngest babies and after-school classes for kids three and up. Classes for toddlers include Let's Pretend, MusicZone, DanceZone, and DramaZone. Drama Zone also has summer camp programs and dramatic birthday parties. Call or check website for class times and schedules.

Music

⁘ Bloomingdale School of Music

323 West 108th Street
bet. Broadway and Riverside Drive
212-663-6021
www.bsmny.org
Bloomingdale School of Music offers a variety of children's classes, including, keyboard, guitar, violin, recorder, chamber music, and Musical Adventures and More Musical Adventures, in which kids develop music skills through song, creative movement, listening, and playing.

⁘ Campbell Music Studio

305 West End Avenue at 74th Street
436 East 69th Street
bet. First and York avenues
212-496-0105
www.campbellmusicstudio.com
Felicia and Jeffrey Campbell have been teaching music to children for more than twenty-five years. Music classes for children ages eighteen months and up include live music, singing,

piano, movement, solfege, stories, notation, and original songs (Felicia writes them all).

⁘ Church Street School for Music and Art

74 Warren Street at West Broadway
212-571-7290
www.churchstreetschool.org
This school offers a variety of classes in music and art for children ages sixteen months and older. Classes are offered in everything from music and movement to visual art, with an emphasis on the process of making art in a relaxed setting. A children's chorus, private lessons, and music therapy are also available.

⁘ Diller-Quaile School of Music

24 East 95th Street
bet. Madison and Fifth avenues
212-369-1484
www.diller-quaile.org
Diller-Quaile is a New York institution. Through their Early Childhood program, this family-based school offers a number of music classes for children from two to seven years, including Music and Movement, Dalcroze Eurythmics, Story Dramatization, Chorus, and Meet the Instrument. Classes meet for a full year. A forty-five-minute Rug Concert is given once a month, on Friday afternoons and Saturday mornings, for children both enrolled and not enrolled in school; concerts introduce children to all the instruments of the orchestra, plus additional instruments (a tabla player comes once a year), and all kinds of singing voices. The concerts also involve singing, movement, and the opportunity

for audience members to play rhythm instruments. Private and group lessons are offered for piano and violin for infants and up.

This is one of the most established music schools in New York City.

❋ Family Music Center

See website for multiple locations throughout Manhattan.

212-864-2476

Colleen Itzen was the first Kindermusik teacher in Manhattan, and still offers the program to children ages newborn to seven years. In these music and movement classes children enjoy singing, rhyming, instrument playing, dancing, and composing. Private instruction on the piano is also available.

❋ The French-American Conservatory of Music

154 West 57th Street, Suite 136

Carnegie Hall, at Seventh Avenue

212-246-7378

www.facmusic.org

The French-American Conservatory of Music, located in the historic Carnegie Hall studios, offers Kindermusik® classes for children ages three years and up, as well as private instrumental and vocal instruction for ages four and older.

❋ Greenwich House Music School

46 Barrow Street

bet. Bleecker and Bedford streets

212-242-4770

www.gharts.org

GHMS has been providing music lessons, staging concerts, and reading for the community since 1905. There are classes for children as young as three.

❋ Mary Ann Hall's Music for Children

2 East 90th Street

bet. Fifth and Madison avenues

877-YES-MUSIC

These creative classes for toddlers to thirteen-year-olds weave music in and out of poetry, books, dance, drama, and art. Kelly has taken many classes here with Alexander and Angela and always finds the classes warm and upbeat.

❋ Mozart for Children

15 Gramercy Park on 20th Street

212-942-2743

www.mozartforchildren.com

Debbie Surowicz's popular classes introduce children, ages one and a half to seven, to classical music through singing, rhythmic instruments, and choreographed dances. Classes include live music and visits from various musicians. Private mini-group classes are also available at your own location.

❋ Music For Aardvarks at the Sandra Cameron Dance Center

199 Lafayette Street at Broome Street

See website for participating venues.

718-858-1741

www.musicforaardvarks.com

Ages: 6 months to 5 years

The program incorporates a wide variety of musical activities that include singing, dancing, playing instruments, and musical story-telling and puppet play.

The School for Strings

419 West 54th Street
bet. Ninth and Tenth avenues
212-315-0915
www.schoolforstrings.org

This Suzuki-based school teaches violin, cello, and piano to children ages sixteen months and up. Beginners take a full course of study, which includes a weekly individual lesson, musicianship class, group class, and parent class (in which parents learn the rudiments of the child's instrument). After the first year, parents are no longer required to take classes, but are expected to remain actively involved in the child's instruction. As children advance, study of orchestra and, eventually, chamber music is incorporated into their routine. The School for Strings is also one of the leading teacher-training schools for violin, cello, and piano in the United States.

Songs for Seeds

See website for a list of participating venues.
212-737-7385
www.appleseedsnyc.com/songsforseeds.html

Songs for Seeds is a new music class that is all the rage in New York City. The class encourages kids to sing and play instruments (from drums and guitars to pianos and accordions) with a live, three-piece band, as well as dance and move as much as possible. Kids "travel" around the world experiencing the music and languages of a new country every week. The band creates well-known nursery rhymes through art and song, does magic tricks as a way to practice numbers and counting, and spins the "animal wheel" to reinforce animal names and sounds. Classes are currently being held at Apple Seeds (see pages 166 and 180) in Chelsea.

Third Street Music School Settlement

235 East 11th Street
bet. Second and Third avenues
212-777-3240
www.thirdstreetmusicschool.org

This school was founded in 1894 as a settlement house for anyone interested in art and music, regardless of talent or ability to pay. In addition to being a fully licensed preschool with an arts focus, the school also offers a variety of music classes in voice, and various instruments and forms of performance (chamber music, ensemble, etc.) for children ages eighteen months and up. Some dance and art classes are also offered.

Turtle Bay Music School

244 East 52nd Street
bet. Second and Third avenues
212-753-8811
www.tbms.org

Turtle Bay, founded in 1925, is a full-service music school that offers private music classes in all instruments for children ages eighteen months and older. This warm and friendly school is ideal for midtown families.

World Travelers

See website for locations throughout Manhattan.
917-538-5049
www.theworldtravelers.com
Ages: 4 to 10 years
Children imaginatively "travel" to different countries around the world through songs, stories, games, crafts, costumes, and dance. Their parent-friendly policy lets parents choose from spontaneous drop-in, single session, or a seasonal series.

Pottery

Craft Studio

1657 3rd Avenue at East 93rd Street
212-831-6626
email: craftstudio@verizon.net
www.craftstudionyc.com
This is a happy place with a small toy store in front and paint your own pottery in the back. It is a popular spot for birthday parties.

Greenwich House Pottery

16 Jones Street
bet. Bleecker and West Fourth streets
212-242-4106
email: pottery@greenwichhouse.org
www.greenwichhouse.org
This long-established school offers classes exclusively for children, and also classes in which children ages two and a half to five collaborate with parents or caregivers to create imaginative clay works.

La Mano Pottery

237 West 18th Street
bet. Seventh and Eighth avenues
212-627-9450
www.lamanopottery.com
Kids ages five and up create their own pottery pieces while learning hand building, how to make mosaics, and how to use the pottery wheel.

Make

1566 Second Avenue
bet. 81st and 82nd streets
212-570-6868
506 Amsterdam Avenue
bet. 84th and 85th streets
212-579-5575
FAO Schwarz
767 5th Avenue at 58th Street, 2nd Floor
212-644-9400
email: info@makemeaning.com
www.makemeaning.com
Make, formerly known as Our Name is Mud, has served New York City for over twelve years as the premier do-it-yourself creative ceramics studio. They offer a wide array of ceramic pieces to appeal to aspiring artists of all ages. Make offers a $12 unlimited day Paint Pass and pottery ranges from $3 on up. The new membership program costs $36 for free paint time all year.

Supermud Pottery Studio

2744 Broadway, 2nd Floor
bet. 105th and 106th streets
212-865-9190
www.supermudpotterystudio.com
Children are guided through the entire process

of making a piece, from working the clay to glazing the end product after it has been fired. There are twelve-week sessions offered for children five years and up, as well as a Mom and Tots class for kids as young as three years old.

Cooking

❊ **The Miette Culinary Studio**
109 MacDougal Street at Minetta Lane, Suite 2
212-460-9322
www.cookingwithmiette.com
Age: 4 months to 11 years
The Miette Culinary Studio has classes for children as young as four months! For the youngest babies, class offerings include an organic baby foods class while older children learn real cooking techniques and skills and use a large variety of kitchen equipment and tools. All children learn knife skills, such as chopping, mincing, and slicing. The Miette studio also offers weekend workshops (such as chocolate making) and custom birthday parties.

❊ **Minichef NYC at The Art Farm**
419 East 91st Street
bet. York and First avenues
212-727-2703
www.minichefnyc.com
ages: 2 to 8 years
Minichef NYC helps kids develop a love of cooking through the guided preparation of nutritious and age-appropriate meals.

sports

Gymnastics
Gymnastics is a popular after-school activity. If your child is an avid gymnast, many of these facilities also have teams.

❊ **Asphalt Green**
555 East 90th Street
bet. York and East End avenues
212-369-8890
www.asphaltgreen.com

❊ **Chelsea Piers**
Pier 62, 23rd Street at Twelfth Avenue
212-336-6500
www.chelseapiers.com

❊ **Columbus Gym**
606 Columbus Avenue
bet. 89th and 90th streets
212-721-0090
www.columbuspreschoolandgym.com

❊ **Gymtime Gymnastics**
1520 York Avenue at 80th Street
212-861-7732
www.gymtime.net

❊ **Jodi's Gym**
244 East 84th Street
bet. Second and Third avenues
212-772-7633
www.jodisgym.com

Life Sport Gymnastics

West Park Presbyterian Church
165 West 86th Street at Amsterdam Avenue
212-769-3131
Rudy Van Daele has been teaching gymnastics for over twenty years. Classes are small with only seven to eight students per instructor, and include activities on mats, trampolines, beams, and horses. Children are encouraged to try whatever interests them, from cartwheels to flips and more. Yoga classes are also offered.

NYC Elite

100 Avenue of the Americas
bet. Watts and Grand streets
212-334-3628
421 East 91st Street
bet. York and First avenues
212-289-8737
www.nycelite.com
NYC Elite holds gymnastics classes and training for children ages nine months to eighteen years. For older kids, they also have competitive teams and Super Saturday Fun Nights.

Sokol New York

420 East 71st Street
bet. First and York avenues
212-861-8206
www.sokolnewyork.org

Tumble Town Gymnastics

Baruch College Early Learning Center
104 East 19th Street at Park Avenue South
212-387-1420

Wendy Hilliard Foundation

Rhythmic Gymnastics NY
792 Columbus Avenue at 100th Street,
Suite 17T
212-316-0315
email: info@whfny.org
www.whfny.org

Sports Training

The Baseball Center NYC

202 West 74th Street
bet. Broadway and Amsterdam Avenue
212-877-7171
www.thebaseballcenternyc.com
Age: 2 to 12 years
The Baseball Center NYC (formerly Frozen Ropes) offers baseball and softball programs for kids as young as one year old. The Baseball Center instructors teach the kids all aspects of baseball and softball including: hitting, pitching, fielding, catching, throwing, base running, confidence, visualization, breathing, focus and concentration, and goal setting. Pamela's son Benjamin has taken classes here for years and loves the small class size and individualized attention.

Lil Sluggers

See website for multiple locations throughout Manhattan.
866-321-8221
www.lilsluggersnyc.com
Ages: 2 to 7 years
Lil Sluggers is a sports-based child develop-

ment program that introduces boys and girls to the game of baseball in a fun, positive way.

❊ On Deck

See website for multiple locations throughout Manhattan.

646-808-4926

www.ondeckny.com

On Deck offers specifically designed baseball training and classes for children ages two to fourteen years.

❊ Super Soccer Stars

212-877-7171

www.supersoccerstars.com

Age: 30 months to 12 years

Super Soccer Stars is all the rage with the five-and-under set. Super Soccer Stars features skilled coaches who work with small groups of boys and girls to develop self-confidence and teamwork in a fun, non-competitive environment. It is a great after-school sports program that is held at dozens of locations around the city. Check the website for locations and class schedules.

Swimming

These locations offer individual and group lessons. A special favorite here is Take Me to the Water; many New Yorkers have taught their children to swim through this program.

❊ Asphalt Green

555 East 90th Street

bet. York and East End avenues

212-369-8890 for catalog

www.asphaltgreen.com

This huge, modern fitness complex has an extensive Youth Aquatics program for children eighteen months and up; the instructor ratio is seven to one for kids five years and older, and five to one for younger.

❊ New York Health and Racquet Club

60 West 23rd Street

bet. Fifth and Sixth avenues

212-989-2300

Private swim classes offered.

❊ Take Me to the Water

See website for multiple locations throughout NYC, Long Island, and New Jersey.

212-828-1756

www.takemetothewater.com

Yoga

As yoga gains popularity with moms and dads, kids want to join in the fun, too. Here are some studios that offer yoga for kids.

❊ B.K.S. Iyengar Yoga Association

150 West 22nd Street, 11th Floor

bet. Sixth and Seventh avenues

212-691-9642

❊ Karma Kids Yoga

104 West 14th Street, 2nd Floor

646-638-1444

www.karmakidsyoga.com

personal enrichment programs

Computers

Futurekids Computer Learning Center

1628 First Avenue

bet. 84th and 85th streets

212-717-0110

www.futurekidsnyc.com

At Futurekids Computer Learning Center, children ages three to fifteen learn the latest technology. Children are introduced to animation, graphics, operating systems, word processing, the Internet, and more—all incorporated with themes and subjects kids love.

Language

Big Apple Kids

221 West 82nd Street at Broadway

212-579-0301

email: info@bigapplekidsnyc.com

www.bigapplekids.com

Age: 6 months and up

Big Apple Kids offers French and Spanish language classes for babies (six months and older) and children in a playful and comfortable setting. These are playgroups in which French and Spanish are spoken with moms and caregivers.

China Institute in America

125 East 65th Street

bet. Park and Lexington avenues

212-744-8181, ext. 142

www.chinainstitute.org

Children ages three to ten gain familiarity with Chinese language and culture through active classroom instruction. Songs, games, and art add to the linguistic and cultural experience.

French Institute

22 East 60th Street, 3rd floor

646-388-6612

email: languagecenter@fiaf.org

La Croisette French Language Center offers three separate programs in which children learn French through a range of fun, creative activities. In the regular classes, children ages two and a half to nine learn through songs, poems, creative projects, stories, games, and educational videos, while in the Art/French class kids ages five to seven focus on painting, collage, printing, stencils, and more. A Puppetry at La Croisette class centers around puppet making, puppet "discussions," and a small puppet show kids put on for parents—all in French, of course!

La Escuelita

302 West 91st Street at West End Avenue

212-877-1100

www.laescuelitanyc.org

Age: 2 to 9 years

La Escuelita was founded in 2002 by two parents, both professional educators, who wanted bilingual play and preschool experiences for their children. Their mission is to promote bilingualism in children from a very young age. Their programs include both a Bilingual Preschool for children ages two to five years old, and an after-school program that's for children ages five and up.

❊ *Language Workshop for Children*

888 Lexington Avenue at 66th Street
See website for multiple locations throughout
NYC, Long Island, and Westchester.
800-731-0830; 212-396-0830
www.languageworkshopforchildren.com
Children ages three to ten learn French, Spanish, or Italian in an active environment, filled with songs, play, sports, gymnastics, cuisine, and dance.

kid-friendly
restaurants

Yes, dining out with your new baby or toddler can be an enjoyable experience; the choice of restaurant is critical and must meet your needs. They are as follows:

When your child is still an infant, under one year, you want a restaurant that provides stroller or carriage space and a staff that doesn't mind babies.

When your child is a toddler, an understanding staff is even more important since your youngster may knock over a glass of water, rip up the sugar packets, or throw flowers on the floor. Also, the restaurant should provide adequate booster seats and quick service (so you can be in and out of the restaurant in an hour).

Certainly, if you have favorite neighborhood spots with food you already love, you can always look around to see if children are dining there and whether there is adequate space next to tables for a stroller holding a sleeping infant.

But what do you do when you are in an unfamiliar neighborhood? For the technologically advanced, check out the following app on your iPhone for help:

⁑ iKidNY

www.ikidny.com

NYC's very first iPhone app for parents allows you to use your iPhone to find the closest kid-friendly restaurants, subways with elevators, changing tables, indoor play spaces, recreation centers, museums, playgrounds, parks, and more!

For the old-fashioned folk, look for kid-friendly clues: paper rather than cloth table covering, crayons, children's menus, booster seats, high chairs, and interesting sights such as fish tanks, rock pools, gardens, shopping areas, and the like. New York's ethnic restaurants can be wonderful for children. The owners usually like kids, waiters will bring them something to eat right away, and they can be flexible about menu offerings. Coffee shops are good, too, but not necessarily during a frantic lunch hour.

But what about the food? We are not restaurant critics, but we do know what we like where family dining is concerned. Good food for everyone is integral to the dining experience. Out of two zillion options, we are including our favorites for you to dine with your family. The Internet can also be a useful tool when you are feeling indecisive. Check out the following sites for specific kid-friendly reviews and comments, plus dining suggestions:

⁑ www.menupages.com

⁑ www.urbanspoon.com

⁑ www.eats.com

⁑ www.chowhound.com

⁑ www.opentable.com

Before you go out, consider your child's ability to sit still and eat in a somewhat mannerly fashion. Some days it might be better to stay home and order in.

Upper East Side

⁑ Barking Dog Luncheonette

1453 York Avenue at 77th Street
212-861-3600
1678 Third Avenue at 94th Street
212-831-1800

These are cozy spots with cozy food like meat loaf, pot roast, mashed potatoes, and all-day breakfast stuff. The decor is comfortable, too, with a dog motif.

Big Daddy's

1596 Second Avenue at East 83rd Street

212-717-2020

239 Park Avenue South bet. 19th and
20th streets

212-477-1500

www.bigdaddysnyc.com

Big Daddy's is an excellent place to take the kids. Enjoy your burger, fries, and shake while listening to music from the '80s surrounded by colorful lights and lots of pictures on the walls.

California Pizza Kitchen

201 East 60th Street

bet. Second and Third avenues

212-755-7773

With all of the great New York pizza in this city, who would have thought that California Pizza Kitchen would be so popular? It is Rebecca and Benjamin's first choice for a fun family lunch. People like California Pizza Kitchen for its unique style of pizza and for its tremendous variety of toppings. Proximity to Dylan's Candy Bar doesn't hurt either. The restaurant is kid friendly and offers yummy pizzas and pastas for the little ones, as well as high chairs and crayons.

China Fun

1221 Second Avenue at 64th Street

212-752-0810

246 Columbus Avenue at 71st Street

212-580-1516

www.chinafun-ny.com

These restaurants are big and noisy and just our style, with inexpensive, generous portions that kids love. In fact, we know a couple of kids hooked on the steamed vegetable dumplings.

Fetch

1649 Third Avenue at East 93rd Street

212-289-2700

www.fetchbarandgrill.com

Pamela's family loves Fetch for Sunday lunch. The restaurant offers a reasonably priced menu filled with standbys such as burgers, omelettes, and salads.

Hi Life Bar and Grill

1503 Second Avenue at 78th Street

212-628-5433

477 Amsterdam Avenue at 83rd Street

212-787-7199

www.hi-life.com

Yummy bar food and burgers—and sushi, too! It is reasonably priced, and the wait staff is friendly. Take advantage of the kid-appealing early-bird specials every weeknight until seven. Don't forget the fries—they're fabulous!

Il Vagabondo

351 East 62nd Street

bet. First and Second avenues

212-832-9221

www.ilvagabondo.com

Haven't been here for a while? Remember the bocce court? Kids love it, of course. They don't have to concentrate on eating but can look at an actual ball rolling on a floor really made of dirt . . . in a restaurant! This restaurant is crowded and loud, with Italian fare everybody likes.

Lili's Noodle Shop and Grill

1500 Third Avenue
bet. 84th and 85th streets
212-639-1313
200 West 57th Street at Sixth Avenue
212-586-5333
www.lilisnoodle.com

Lili's is a favorite with Pamela's kids who are picky when it comes to Chinese food. Lili's food is always delicious and fresh—the chicken and broccoli is a winner. It offers all of the food kids like, such as dumplings, spare ribs, and noodles, too. Lili's also has bubble tea drinks, which can keep kids occupied at the table for the entire meal.

Nick's

1814 Second Avenue
bet. 93rd and 94th streets
212-987-5700
email: info@nicksnyc.com
www.nicksnyc.com

Nick's has some of the most delicious thin-crust pizza on the East Side. It is a friendly restaurant, too, with yummy pastas and salads. Much of the food is served family style, so it is a great place to go with a crowd. Kids will love the pizza and pasta and you will, too. The back room is a great place for a birthday party.

Pintaile's Pizza

26 East 91st Street at Madison Avenue
212-722-1967
1573 York Avenue at 81st Street
212-396-3479

Incredibly delicious pizza made from organic dough with whole-wheat options and an overwhelming array of toppings to choose from. Not a lot of room to sit down, but terrific for ordering in for a birthday party.

Serendipity 3

225 East 60th Street
bet. Second and Third avenues
212-838-3531
www.serendipity3.com

A classic. Your child's not a New York kid until he's had a foot-long hot dog (which he'll never finish) and a frozen hot chocolate (which you will finish quite easily). There is lots of great stuff to look at here, from the offerings near the front door to the giant clock and colorful stained glass lampshades. It's also fun to walk up and down the spiral staircase. No strollers or carriages!

Tony's Di Napoli

1606 Second Avenue at 83rd Street
212-861-8686
147 West 43rd Street at Broadway
212-221-0100
www.tonysnyc.com

This spacious Italian restaurant is a favorite of East Side families, with enormous portions served family style. Strollers are not permitted at the tables, so bring a car seat. Families should come early for best service.

Upper West Side

✳ Alice's Tea Cup

103 West 73rd Street at Columbus Avenue
212-799-3006
156 East 64th Street at Lexington Avenue
212-486-9200
220 East 81st Street bet. Second and Third
avenues
212-734-4TEA
www.alicesteacup.com

These charming spots are the perfect place for your first mother/daughter tea or lunch with some moms and babies. With its Alice in Wonderland theme, there is plenty to look at in the shop area in the front of the stores. In the restaurant, you'll find scones, soups, sandwiches, and a full morning or afternoon tea—served on eclectic china. The children's menu includes sandwiches of granny smith apple slices and peanut butter or Nutella, grilled cheese, homemade Graham crackers, and pureed baby food. Pamela's friend Vicky had her daughter's birthday party in the back room at Alice's and it was terrific.

✳ Artie's Delicatessen

2290 Broadway at 83rd Street
212-579-5959

Artie's is a good old-fashioned deli with lots of classic choices, big portions, and fairly decent prices. Pamela's family is obsessed with the pickles from here and travel from the East Side often to sample the delicious matzoh ball soup and hot dogs.

✳ Café con Leche

424 Amsterdam Avenue at 80th Street
212-595-7000
726 Amsterdam Avenue at 95th Street
212-678-7000
www.cafeconlechenyc.com

Authentic Cuban and Dominican food for the slightly adventurous kids—the fried plantains are usually their favorite. Brunch menu features standby items like pancakes and French toast.

✳ Cafe Lalo

201 West 83rd Street
bet. Amsterdam and Broadway
212-496-6031
www.cafelalo.com

What do you get when you combine French decor, ceiling fans, light jazz, and celebrity encounters? Cafe Lalo, of course. Most New Yorkers who hang here are big fans of the foamy cappuccino, the selection of over one hundred gourmet desserts, and the sandwiches and salads. This cafe is great for a pre- or post-movie bite.

✳ Dean's Restaurant and Pizzeria

215 West 85th Street at Broadway
212-875-1100
349 Greenwich Street at Harrison Street
212-966-3200
801 Second Avenue at East 43rd Street
212-878-9600
www.deansnyc.com

A family-style, delicious pizza restaurant that is always packed with kids.

Dinosaur BBQ

646 West 131st Street at Broadway

212-694-1777

www.dinosaurbarbque.com

Loud and casual, fun, delicious, hearty…and dinosaur tattoos! Dinosaur BBQ offers some of the most delicious BBQ in New York City. Great treat for your pre– or post–Fairway shopping

Fairway Cafe

2127 Broadway at 74th Street

212-595-1888, ext. 145

www.fairwaymarket.com

Upstairs from the market (there is an elevator) you will find the Fairway Cafe. Breakfast is served here all day, or kids can opt for burgers, soup, veggie platters, or sandwiches. Fairway Cafe is mommy central—especially during the week. Pamela is a big fan of the omelettes here and her kids love the milkshakes, which are huge! Booster seats and high chairs available.

Firehouse

522 Columbus Avenue at 85th Street

212-787-3473

www.therestaurantgroup.com

www.firehousetavern.com

This is a great place to take your kids: the Firehouse menu has burgers, fries, chips, guacamole for grown-ups and kids' pizza (plus five different styles of pizza for adults). Firehouse has always been popular with the post-college crowd for its inexpensive chicken wings and beer, but before the twenty-somethings arrive, families rule.

Fred's

476 Amsterdam Avenue at 83rd Street

212-579-3076

www.fredsnyc.com

While there is no kids' menu here, kids love Fred's because of its dog theme. There are photos of dogs all over the walls and plenty to look at for younger kids. Kids dig the hamburgers and French fries here, as well as the pasta and chicken. The weekend brunch menus feature French toast, pancakes, and eggs, which are good options ,too. High chairs are available.

Gabriela's

688 Columbus Avenue at 93rd Street

212-961-9600

www.gabrielas.com

It's big, bustling, open all the time from breakfast until dinner so you can eat at odd hours, and the place is filled with kids of all ages. Authentic Mexican fare (downright cheap) from tacos to quesadillas, enchiladas, and rice and beans for the kids, to more exotic house specialties for you. Be extra early for dinner, or you'll wait.

Good Enough to Eat

483 Amsterdam Ave at 83rd Street

212-496-0163

www.goodenoughtoeat.com

Good Enough to Eat offers comfort food for kids, including kid favorites like macaroni and cheese, pizza, and desserts.

Josephina

1900 Broadway, #1

bet. 63rd and 64th streets

212-799-1000

www.jospehinanyc.com

If you're near Lincoln Center and if you're in the mood for healthy, organic California-style eating, this is the place. It's airy, roomy, and kids like it.

Pinch and S'Mac

474 Columbus Avenue

bet. West 83rd and 84th streets

646-438-9494

www.pinchandsmac.com

A delicious new collaboration from the owners of S'Mac that offers pizza by the inch ("Pinch") alongside the comfort food standby, S'Mac, and its gourmet varieties of mac and cheese. See Sarita's Mac and Cheese (page 152) for more information.

Popover Cafe

551 Amsterdam Avenue at 87th Street

212-595-8555

www.popovercafe.com

Children love the teddy bears that live all around this restaurant; kids can "adopt" one while you enjoy the wonderful food. Freshly baked popovers with strawberry butter are the main attraction here, and well worth waiting for.

Ruby Foo's

1626 Broadway at 49th Street

212-489-5600

www.brguestrestaurants.com

While Ruby Foo's does not have a kids' menu

per se, kids really enjoy the decor and vibe here. The restaurant is theatrical and boisterous with delicious Pan-Asian cuisine. Even picky eaters will like the noodles, rice and spare ribs, and dumplings all served family style.

Sambuca

20 West 72nd Street

bet. Central Park West and Columbus Avenue

212-787-5656

www.sambucanyc.com

This dinner-only restaurant offers all the traditional Italian dishes, such as penne pasta, ravioli, and chicken and veal parmigiana, so it's not difficult to find something here you and your kids will like. While there is no kids' pizza, there are plenty of good pasta dishes and classic Italian ice creams and desserts to please any toddler. Moreover, Sambuca is reasonably priced and offers takeout and delivery for Upper West Siders in this neighborhood.

Shake Shack

366 Columbus Avenue at 77th Street

646-747-8770

Madison Square Park at Madison and East 23rd Street

212-889-6600

Coming soon to East 86th Street

www.shakeshack.com

Shake Shack boasts the best burgers in the city, the most delicious shakes, frozen custard, beer, wine, and more! While a bit more pricey than the fast-food chains, this place will surely leave you and your child with numerous menu options to crave afterwards.

West 79th Street Boat Basin Café

79th Street at the Hudson River

212-496-5524

www.boatbasincafe.com

The Boat Basin Café is a huge outdoor bar/grill located off the Hudson River. While it fills up with the single folk Thursday, Friday, and Saturday evenings around 8 p.m., it's perfect for families during off-hours. The Boat Basin Café serves typical bar food, great drinks, and offers gorgeous views of the river.

Midtown East and West

Benihana

47 West 56th Street

bet. Fifth and Sixth avenues

212-581-0930

www.benihana.com

Kids adore Benihana. Watching the chefs cook at your table provides hours of entertainment. Even the pickiest eaters will enjoy the delicious steak, chicken, and shrimp here. The chefs are usually pretty friendly and put on quite a show with slicing, dicing, and tossing the food. Benihana is a popular spot for kids' birthday parties.

Broadway Diner

590 Lexington Avenue at 52nd Street

212-486-8838

This upscale diner is better than most but remains easy on the pocket. The food is typical American fare, including sandwiches, salads, grilled burgers, eggs, and pancakes. This is a good choice if you're in a hurry; you'll have no problem getting in and out in less than an hour.

Ellen's Stardust Diner

1650 Broadway at 51st Street

212-956-5151

www.ellensstardustdiner.com

This fifties-style diner features milkshakes, burgers, chicken, and tuna melts, as well as some Mexican dishes and an assortment of salads. The waiters sing and entertain; the kids will enjoy it as much as you will.

La Bonne Soupe

48 West 55th Street

bet. Fifth and Sixth avenues

212-586-7650

www.labonnesoupe.com

La Bonne Soupe is a family-friendly French bistro with a reasonably priced, straightforward menu for you and your kids. Its close proximity to FAO Schwarz (see page 255) and Rockefeller Center make it a great choice for visitors in the area. La Bonne Soupe has several prix-fixed menu choices for you and your child that range from $10 to $20.

Prime Burger

5 East 51st Street

bet. Fifth and Madison avenues

212-759-4729

www.primeburger.com

Another great choice location-wise if you are visiting Radio City Music Hall, Rockefeller Center, or The American Girl Store, Prime Burger offers good burgers at reasonable prices. It's also a good choice for breakfast in the neighborhood.

Serafina

See website for a list of locations throughout Manhattan.

www.serafinarestaurant.com

Serafina offers a kids' menu ($10) of totally locally grown, organic foods. Serafina offers delicious pizza, pasta, and salads and is always filled with families.

Supermac

348 Seventh Avenue

bet. West 29th and 30th streets

212-760-1900

www.supermacnyc.com

Supermac provides your favorite comfort food, mac and cheese, with a creative twist.

Virgil's Real BBQ

152 West 44th Street

bet. Sixth and Seventh avenues

212-921-9494

www.virgilsbbq.com

This pleasing home-style BBQ joint in Times Square is a perfect fit for kids who like to eat with their hands.

Chelsea/Flatiron

Chat 'n' Chew

10 East 16th Street

bet. Union Square West and Fifth Avenue

212-243-1616

www.chatnchewny.com

It feels like you're in a tiny town in the South in the 1950s, but you could only find a place like this in New York. There's plenty to look at in this crowded restaurant, from antique advertising signs to old jukeboxes. If you can take it, there are great deep-fried dishes, too. Chat 'n' Chew is best for booster-seat kids.

Galaxy Global Eatery

15 Irving Place at East 15th Street

212-777-3631

www.galaxyglobaleatery.com

Take a sci-fi theme for the kids, creative, healthy fare for the adults, and add slightly loud music, and you get a great place to take kids who like to make a lot of noise.

West Village

Arturo's Pizzeria

106 West Houston Street at Thompson Street

212-677-3820

Here's a neighborhood place with a low-key atmosphere that is friendly for families. Their specialty, brick oven pizza, is delicious, and the service is quick. Arturo's also serves all types of salads, pastas, and chicken dishes.

Cowgirl Hall of Fame

519 Hudson Street at West 10th Street

212-633-1133

www.cowgirlnyc.com

Lil' partners from all over come to see the Western memorabilia in this cool little shop that stocks everything from sheriff badges to squirt gun holsters, bandanas, and rawhide vests. The food appeals, too, with a perfectly messy Frito pie (a bag of chips split open, topped with chili) and a baked potato dessert (vanilla ice cream rolled in powdered cocoa and topped with "sour cream," actually whipped cream that sits on a hot fudge pond).

East Village

❋ Sarita's Mac and Cheese (S'MAC)

345 East 12th Street
bet. First and Second avenues
212-358-7912
www.smacnyc.com

This place is tiny, so go early to avoid a wait. The impact of their mac and cheese is well worth it. For more information on Sarita's newest venture, Pinch, see page 149.

SOHO

❋ Balthazar

80 Spring Street
bet. Crosby Street and Broadway
212-965-1414
www.balthazarny.com

Balthazar serves traditional bistro meals from breakfast through late-night supper. A high noise level plus menu items like Nutella on a baguette make for a perfect spot to take the kids. It's also a favorite of celebrities—a possible bonus for you and your children!

❋ Peanut Butter & Co.

240 Sullivan Street at West 3rd Street
212-677-3995
www.ilovepeanutbutter.com

Peanut Butter & Co. is a fun place to go with the peanut butter lover in your family. It doesn't serve

mere out-of-a-jar peanut butter here, of course. This peanut butter is ground fresh daily and is served on fresh bread with a tremendous variety of options on top. The peanut butter comes in six varieties: creamy, crunchy, spicy, cinnamon raisin, chocolate chip, and white chocolate.

Lower East Side

❋ Hummus Place

See website for locations throughout Manhattan.
www.hummusplace.com

Hummus Place is quick and inexpensive, yummy, filling, and best of all, chic.

Central Village/NOHO

❋ Lombardi's

32 Spring Street at Mott Street
212-941-7994
email: info@firstpizza.com
www.lombardispizza.com

Inexpensive and authentic New York City coal-oven pizza. Cash only.

❋ Noho Star

330 Lafayette Street at Bleecker Street
212-925-0070
www.nohostar.com

A standard for some Manhattanites, this restaurant has a casual and comfortable atmosphere that easily accommodates kids. You'll find interesting Chinese and Thai food here, as well as kid favorites like pasta, burgers, salad, and chicken.

Tribeca

Bubby's

120 Hudson Street at North Moore Street

212-219-0666

www.bubbys.com

The menu at this kid-friendly restaurant is standard diner fare but better, with a gourmet twist. Bubby's is best known for its delicious breakfasts; it's a popular brunch spot on weekends.

Moomah

161 Hudson Street at Laight Street

212-226-0345

email: info@moomah.com

www.moomah.com

Jon Stewart's wife opened a kid-friendly cafe that she describes as a place of sweet whimsy, wonder, and warmth. Moomah is part creative play space, cozy cafe, living classroom, quiet hideaway, art oasis, and neighborhood meeting spot.

The Odeon

145 West Broadway

bet. Duane and Thomas streets

212-233-0507

www.theodeonrestaurant.com

Popular with celebrities for years, this restaurant has gained a following among downtown families. It is a cozy spot, with great food and good people watching. Don't skip the fries! The Odeon gives out crayons, too.

The Chains

Some days you will just need a reliable restaurant where you can have a decent meal with the kids.

Special menus, reasonable prices, and high chairs are all to be expected at local and national chains. Popular national chains include Pizzeria Uno and T.G.I. Friday's.

Carmine's

2450 Broadway at 91st Street

212-362-2200

200 West 44th Street

bet. Broadway and Eighth Avenue

212-221-3800

Popular, family-style southern Italian food is the specialty here. Carmine's is bustling, fun, and noisy but the wait can be long. If you go with at least six people, you can make a reservation (and you'll be able to sample more dishes).

Dallas BBQ

See website for multiple locations throughout Manhattan.

www.dallasbbq.com

Inexpensive, big portions of kid favorites from ribs to burgers and corn on the cob make this a great standby.

EJ's Luncheonette

1271 Third Avenue at 73rd Street

212-472-0600

447 Amsterdam Avenue

bet. 81st and 82nd streets

212-873-3444

432 Sixth Avenue

bet. 9th and 10th streets

212-473-5555

Tons of families come for the children's menu featuring everything from PB&J to scrambled eggs. Breakfast is served all day long, an interesting concept. (We call it brinner.) Lines are long for weekend brunch.

Jackson Hole Burgers

See website for multiple locations throughout Manhattan.

www.jacksonholeburgers.com

This traditional burger joint has every kind of burger and topping you could ever want, as well as great fries, salads, omelettes, Tex-Mex stuff, and fantastic chocolate cake and sundaes. Kids love it!

John's Pizzeria

260 West 44th Street

bet. Broadway and Eighth Avenue

212-391-7560

408 East 64th Street bet. First and York avenues

212-935-2895

278 Bleecker Street

bet. Sixth and Seventh avenues

212-243-1680

www.johnspizzerianyc.com

Some New York parents we know swear these thin-crust pies from a wood-burning oven are the best in the city. The service is fast; there's pasta for the rare child that does not eat pizza; there's plenty of room around the tables; and it's noisy, so your child won't stand out among the loud voices of all the other children. Another plus: your child can watch the chefs prepare your pizza.

Johnny Rocket's

930 Third Ave at 56th Street

212-813-0003

www.johnnyrockets.com

A classic burger joint with juke boxes and a fun waitstaff to help keep your kids distracted, complete with an inexpensive full kids' menu for those under ten. This burger joint is especially great for parties.

La Cocina

217 West 85th Street

bet. Broadway and Amsterdam Avenue

212-874-0770

430 Third Avenue at 30th Street

646-424-9035

714 Ninth Avenue bet. 48th and 49th streets

212-957-8719

www.lacocinanyc.com

La Cocina features moderately priced but quite generous single tacos, burritos, enchiladas, and more, including large, well-deserved margaritas for the adults. There's plenty of room around the tables. Kids get to choose a marble to take home for their collections.

Ollie's Noodle Shop & Grille

411 West 42nd Street at Ninth Avenue

212-921-5988

1991 Broadway near 68th Street

212-595-8181

Early every evening, Ollie's is filled with children who love the soups, noodles—from soft to crispy; from hot to cold—and all the other classic Hong Kong–style dishes. Huge portions, moderate prices, and the fastest service a parent could ever hope to find are all huge plusses.

✳ *Patsy's*

See website for multiple locations throughout Manhattan.

www.patsyspizzeriany.com

Families love Patsy's and for good reason. The pizza is delicious, the service fast, and the prices reasonable. With seven locations around Manhattan, there is surely a Patsy's near you. They don't take reservations, and waits can be long, so go early if you are bringing hungry kids along. They don't have a kids' menu, but pizza and pasta do the trick.

✳ *Two Boots Pizzeria*

See website for multiple locations throughout Manhattan.

www.twoboots.com

The "boots" of Italy and Louisiana kick in for great pizza with creative toppings. Great decor, lots to look at, and a great party atmosphere that's enhanced by lively music.

Theme Restaurants

The West Fifties now offer big blaring restaurants of all varieties and gimmicks that are sure to attract visitors. Amid the tourists, you won't find a whole lot of New York parents popping in (waiting in line is more like it) as their first choice for dining. However, you may find yourself in that neighborhood or planning a birthday party, and these places do come up in conversation. So here goes:

✳ *Hard Rock Cafe*

1501 Broadway at 44th Street

212-343-3355

www.hardrock.com

✳ *Jekyll & Hyde*

91 Seventh Avenue South

bet. West Fourth and Barrow streets

212-989-7701

www.jekyllpub.com

✳ *Mars 2112*

1633 Broadway at 51st Street

212-582-2112

www.mars2112.com

Creatures from all planets are welcome at this Times Square restaurant. This restaurant's theme, celebrating all things from the Red Planet, is wacky and fun. It serves the standard kids' fare, such as hamburgers and chicken fingers, but also has adult entrees, such as salmon, for parents. Dancing martians and other aliens will keep your little ones entertained while you dine. Mars 2112 has an arcade and a gift shop.

✳ *Mickey Mantle's*

42 Central Park South

bet. Fifth and Sixth avenues

212-688-7777

www.mickeymantles.com

✳ *Planet Hollywood*

1540 Broadway at West 45th Street

212-333-7827

www.planethollywood.com

Outdoor Treats

For some delicious treats while you're on the go, check out the following food trucks. If you're super savvy, you can grab a snack and then sit down at a nearby park or bench to enjoy the food and the people watching. For updates on location schedule, please call or visit the following websites or Twitter feeds.

The Cup Cake Stop

718-702-2825
email: info@cupcakestop.com
twitter.com/cupcakeSTOP
www.cupcakestop.com

The Dessert Truck

6 Clinton Street (permanent location)
email: mail@desserttruck.com
twitter.com/desserttruck
www.desserttruck.com

The Treats Truck

212-691-5226
email: info@treatstruck.com
twitter.com/theTreatsTruck
www.treatstruck.com

Coffee Bars

It is amazing that we once lived without double iced-mocha lattes. Even more important, that hit of caffeine, administered at opportune moments during the day, does a lot for a mother who has been called into action during the wee hours. Here are some places to swill coffee, accompanied by babies and toddlers.

Grey Dog Coffee

90 University Place
bet. 11th and 12th streets
212-414-4739
33 Carmine Street
bet. Bedford and Bleecker streets
212-462-0041
www.thegreydog.com

Once Upon A Tart

135 Sullivan Street
bet. Prince and Houston streets
212-387-8869
www.onceuponatart.com

Starbucks*

See website for multiple locations throughout NYC.
www.starbucks.com
Atmosphere and ample space at Starbucks make it a good choice for a group of stroller-clad moms. You can sit for hours and chat over a coffee. (That is, if your munchkin will allow it.) And, if you're hungry, Starbucks offers a nice selection of breakfast foods all day, plus prepared sandwiches for lunch. We couldn't live without their tall skinny vanilla lattes. In fact, we wrote the bulk of City Baby at various Starbucks around town!

Tisserie SoHo

96 Thompson Street
bet. Spring and Prince streets
646-613-8650

a few words on bathrooms...

We can't even begin to tell you how important this topic is. Once you begin to venture into the world with your child, you'll soon realize the challenge of finding a decent bathroom in the city. New York can frustrate even the most formidable city moms searching for a clean place to change a diaper. To aid you in this important mission, here are some good bathrooms in a variety of neighborhoods. Keep them in mind in case you suddenly find yourself in a bathroom bind. We've noted the best places for diaper changing and nursing; all bathrooms include a handicapped stall unless otherwise noted.

❋ *Barnes & Noble*

See website for multiple locations throughout NYC.

www.barnesandnoble.com

All the Barnes & Noble stores have bathrooms, and the stores with a Junior section have an oversized stall with a changing station inside.

❋ *Starbucks*

See website for multiple locations throughout NYC.

www.starbucks.com

All Starbucks have large bathrooms; most locations have a diaper deck inside.

See the lists below for some of the nicest spots in town, but remember any hotel will suffice! If you are desperate, McDonald's and Burger King have bathrooms, but they are rarely the cleanest. We suggest scoping out your neighborhood for kid-friendly restaurants that will let you use their bathrooms when needed. This will come in handy for potty training, too!

East Side

If you're anywhere in midtown on the East Side, you're near a number of department stores that provide comfortable, clean bathrooms. Barneys (Madison Avenue at 61st Street), Bergdorf Goodman (Fifth Avenue at 57th Street), Bloomingdale's (Third Avenue at 59th Street), Bendel's (Fifth Avenue at 54th Street), Lord & Taylor (Fifth Avenue at 39th Street), and Saks Fifth Avenue (Fifth Avenue at 50th Street) all have bathrooms with enough stalls so that there's usually not a line; all include diaper changing areas and/or couches or chairs nearby or in the stalls that are suitable for diaper changing or for nursing.

Here are some other facilities you'll want to know about:

❋ *FAO Schwarz*

767 Fifth Avenue at 58th Street

212-644-9400

Location: second floor

❋ *The Hotel Pierre*

2 East 61st Street

bet. Madison and Fifth avenues

212-838-8000

Location: main floor

❋ *The New York Palace Hotel**

455 Madison Avenue at 50th Street

212-888-7000

Location: second floor (take stairs up one flight
or the elevator)

❄ *The Regency Hotel*
540 Park Avenue at 60th Street
800-233-2356
Location: main floor lobby

❄ *Tiffany & Company**
727 Fifth Avenue at 57th Street
212-755-8000
Location: mezzanine

❄ *Trump Tower*
725 Fifth Avenue at 56th Street
212-832-2000
Location: downstairs at the towers

❄ *The Waldorf-Astoria*
301 Park Avenue at 50th Street
212-355-3000
Location: main floor lobby

West Side

❄ *Macy's*
151 West 34th Street at Herald Square
212-695-4400
Locations: cellar, second, sixth,
and seventh floors

❄ *Manhattan Mall*
100 West 32nd Street at Sixth Avenue
212-465-0500
Locations: second, fourth, sixth,
and seventh floors

❄ *New York Hilton*
1335 Sixth Avenue at 53rd Street
212-586-7000
Location: second floor on
the 54th Street side of hotel

❄ *Time Warner Center*
10 Columbus Circle at 59th Street
212-823-6300
Location: downstairs in Whole Foods or
upstairs in Borders

Downtown

❄ *ABC Carpet & Home*
888 Broadway at 19th Street
212-473-3000
Location: second and fourth floors

❄ *Bed, Bath & Beyond*
620 Avenue of the Americas at 18th Street
212-255-3550
Location: main floor

❄ *SoHo Grand Hotel*
310 West Broadway
bet. Grand and Canal streets
212-965-3000
Location: main floor

❄ *South Street Seaport
(The Fulton Market)*
12 Fulton Street
212-748-8786 (general information)
Location: mezzanine

Tribeca Grand Hotel

2 Avenue of the Americas bet. White and
Walker streets
212-965-3114
Location: lower level past the concierge desk

World Financial Center

The Winter Garden, 220 Vesey Street
212-945-0505
Location: main floor

the big firsts

A baby is to celebrate! First you mark the new arrival with a printed birth announcement, something special, of course, but where do you find exactly the right thing? In the ensuing months, as you watch your baby grow, there will be many joyful and singular moments to celebrate. We call them "the big firsts." For each, New York can provide an expert who will help you make the most of these once-in-a-lifetime occasions. This chapter lists what we've discovered to be the best stationers for buying ready-made or personalized birth announcements; the most fun and unusual party places; the absolute best bakeries for ordering that first—and second, and third—birthday cake; the most skillful and entertaining hair cutters; the most reliable shoe stores; and the most artful photographers for that important first portrait.

Of course, you will be taking hundreds of your own photos as your child grows. For Rebecca and Alexander, we always had a camera at hand to record such things as haircuts and parties. But with the second and third child, we found it was easy to overlook either photographing or videotaping their big firsts. To make sure you never miss a special moment, do what lots of moms do: keep a disposable camera or Flip video camera in your stroller.

You will be amazed at how fast your baby grows. Just when you are wondering when your baby will ever have enough hair to warrant a real haircut, it will be time to consider another important first: preschool. This is a rite of passage in New York, or anywhere, and we conclude with a few suggestions on how to start exploring the options.

birth announcements

Even in this day of email and websites, printed birth announcements are still the most popular way to get the word out about the new addition to your family.

There are several options available. You can purchase ready-made cards at a stationery or party store and fill in your new baby's name, weight, size, and birth date.

Most parents we know order pre-printed cards. Another alternative, economical too, is to buy plain cards and print announcements from your computer at home. If you have a digital camera, you can even print a snapshot of your little bundle of joy on the card, or use one of the photo websites such as Shutterfly.com or Kodakgallery.com where you can download your photo and get cards made with a few clicks of a button. Kelly did this the second time around, believing that everyone who knew her well already knew about Angela's arrival, and that it was unnecessary to spend hundreds of dollars on birth announcements.

It's a good idea to choose your announcements a month or so in advance of your due date. If you are ordering from a store or website, plan on two weeks for printing. Get your envelopes early, and address them in advance. Then, after the baby is born, call the shop with all the details, such as height, weight, sex, and date and time of birth.

New York stationers have everything you could possibly want, and they will ship your selection directly to you. Below, we list the best. These are also great sources for special birthday party invitations for the years to come.

Alpine

30 East 33rd Street

bet. Park Avenue South and Madison Avenue

212-989-4198

www.alpinecreativegroup.com

Alpine puts an emphasis on quality and creativity. In addition to a large selection of stationery lines, their on-site printing capabilities, including letterpress, engraving, and foil stamping, allow for fast lead times. They will even print on balloons! Prices vary based on level of customization.

Blacker & Kooby

1204 Madison Avenue at 88th Street

212-369-8308

www.blackerandkooby.invitations.com

With more than seventy companies to choose from, the selection at Blacker & Kooby is outstanding. It ranges from well-known lines like Crane's, Regency, Grosvenor, and William Arthur, to smaller, more creative ones like Blue Mug and Stacy Claire Boyd. At this Carnegie Hill spot, an order for 100 baby announcements starts around $200.

Ceci New York

130 West 23rd Street, 2nd Floor

bet. Sixth and Seventh avenues

212-989-0695

email: info@cecinewyork.com

www.cecinewyork.com

As seen in The Knot and Brides magazine, Ceci makes unique custom-designed birth announcements and more.

Crane & Co. Paper Makers

59 West 49th Street at Rockefeller Plaza

212-582-6829

www.crane.com

Crane has been making beautiful stationery for over two centuries. You'll find their own brand, as well as designers such as Kate Spade and Martha Stewart. In addition to birth announcements you can also find great children's stationery and birthday party invitations. One hundred birth announcements start in the mid $200's.

Hudson Street Papers

149 Orchard Street

bet. Stanton and Rivington streets

212-229-1064

Hudson Street Papers is a legendary West Village shop (now located on the Lower East Side) where parents can create the announcements of their dreams. In addition to name-brand cards like William Arthur, it offers a choice of 450 varieties made from their unique in-store computerized lettering and design system. With a turn-around time of one week, it is a terrific alternative to more traditional cards. One hundred birth announcements start at $180 to $250. This is also a great shop to find fun and creative gifts.

Kate's Paperie

See website for multiple locations throughout NYC as well as Connecticut.

www.katespaperie.com

These crème de la crème of paper stores carry an outstanding selection of baby announcements, including unusual and hard-to-find manufacturers, such as Sweet Pea, Indelible Ink, Blue Mug, and Stacy Claire Boyd. Working with an experienced staff person, customers can also design their own cards and choose from dozens of papers and type styles. Announcements can then be printed by letterpress if so desired. An order of 100 cards starts at $200. Kate's hands-on approach and the store's very welcoming atmosphere make new moms feel right at home.

❈ Laura Beth's Baby Collection

321 East 75th Street
bet. First and Second avenues
212-717-2559
www.uppereast.com/laurabeths.html
Laura Beth, a former buyer in the Baby Department at Barneys New York, meets one-on-one with stylish moms-to-be to help them select their birth announcements as well as linens and accessories. She offers high-end cards, both whimsical and classic, at prices 20 percent below retail—or 100 cards for $150. Lines include Stacy Claire Boyd and more.

❈ Lauren Wittels

Excellent Paper Place
235 West 76th Street
212-580-0921; 703-832-2193 (fax)
email: lauren@excellentpaper.com
www.excellentpaper.com
Excellent Paper offers all of the latest and greatest options in baby announcements and stationery. Check out the offerings online, or call for an appointment to view the extensive card lines. It also offers 20 percent off retail prices on all

orders. Designers include Stacy Claire Boyd, Robyn Miller, Caspari, Pipo, and more.

❈ Lincoln Stationers

43 West 33rd Street at Broadway, 3rd Floor
212-664-0780; 800-298-PENS
www.lincolnstationers.com
Lincoln Stationers is a wonderful resource. It carries all major brands, or you can create your own card with the staff.

❈ Madison Signatures

743 Madison Avenue at 64th Street
800-783-9590
www.madisonsignatures.com
Madison Signatures has a wide variety of papers, fonts, engraving, and imprinting options—for birth announcements and great party invitations. They offer customization in foreign languages, and can print your announcement on almost anything if traditional paper isn't your style. Madison Signatures also has an incredible selection of pens.

❈ Papyrus Cards & Stationery

See website for locations throughout NYC.
www.papyrusonline.com
Papyrus is an upscale chain of fine papers and cards, with lines like William Arthur, Crane's, Stacy Claire Boyd, Cross-My-Heart, and Carlson Craft. An order of 100 announcements costs between $240 and $500, and is usually shipped to the customer within seven to ten days. Papyrus can be found in malls around the tri-state area. This is also a great place to find special gift items.

Squiggly Bee Ltd.

email: info@squigglybee.com

www.squigglybee.com

Squiggly Bee offers new moms a creative way to remember their child's first moments. They have gift sets of bibs, onesies, hats, and more that allow you to document your child's growth month by month, creating a lasting photographic memory.

Tiffany & Co.

727 Fifth Avenue at 57th Street

212-755-8000

www.tiffany.com

Tiffany & Co. has a large stationery department offering both the Tiffany brand and some Crane's lines. The Tiffany cards are simple, elegant, engraved, and pricey. The average cost for 100 announcements is more than $500. It also has contemporary lines of cards that are a bit more fun (and less expensive).

Venture Stationers

1156 Madison Avenue at 85th Street

212-288-7235

www.ventureonmadison.com

One of the most popular East Side shops for stationery and announcements, Venture carries a large selection of manufacturers, including Stacy Claire Boyd, Sweet Pea, Crane's, Lalli, and Regency. The price for 100 announcements starts at $200. Venture is also a great place to pick up a quick birthday gift. Pamela often shops here and loves their selection of cards, paper and gifts.

Websites For Birth Announcements

- www.tinyprints.com
- www.storkavenue.com
- www.vanillaprintdesign.com
- www.invitationbox.com

birthday parties

Many parents love extravagant birthday parties, especially their child's first one. When your baby hits the magic age of one, the birthday party is mostly for Mom, Dad, grandparents, and friends. A cake and a few balloons will make most one-year-olds very happy, and you'll get great photos of your baby mushing up the icing.

We like the idea of having the first birthday at home, but this may not be possible if you have a big family, many friends, and a small apartment. Happily, New York is full of places that organize parties for one-year-olds. Keep this list handy for future reference—two- through six-year-olds can have even more fun at a party place.

Most of these sites will host a party seven days a week. Many offer catering services that supply everything down to the cake and party favors, though all will let you bring your own. Prices are noted, but this is New York, so they may change over time. Call ahead. The Parent's League at 115 East 82nd Street (212-737-7385) has more party information; however, you must be a member ($90 annual fee) to use their files. Many of the listings that follow are great for older kids' birthdays, too. We've hosted and attended many second, third, fourth, and even seventh birthdays at several of the places we list here.

Birthday Party Invitations

Websites have become the most popular form of invitation giving and receiving. You can customize almost any part of the invitation and add any photos, text, and images you want—with many sites charging little to nothing. Photo-sharing websites such as Shutterfly.com and Snapfish.com are great because your photos are already in their system, and they offer step-by-step directions, ensuring that even the most computer-illiterate mom can create an invitation to be proud of. Newly launched Pingg.com combines digital and print—offering the best of both worlds. You can create a personalized invitation and email for free, or have them print, stamp, and mail each one for a small fee. Some other sites to check out are (and some of these are great for birth announcements, too):

- www.evite.com
- www.sendomatic.com
- www.mypunchbowl.com
- www.smilebox.com
- www.plumparty.com
- www.paperlesspost.com

The Five Best Places to Have a Two-year-old's Party

1. Your home, if you have room, or a common space in your apartment building.
2. Any place with Broadway Babies or Little Maestros
3. River Run Playground (season permitting)
4. Kidville New York
5. Children's Museum of Manhattan (212-721-1234)

Party Places and Entertainment

❊ Apple Seeds

10 West 25th Street
bet. Fifth and Sixth avenues
212-792-7590
www.appleseedsnyc.com

Apple seeds features activities for children ages newborn to five, and is a great option for your child's first birthday. You can choose from themes such as music, sports, princesses and pirates costumes, building (as well as breaking and fixing), and cooking. The on-site party planner will also work with you to individualize any party package. A Basic Birthday package includes free play and guided activities in the sports gym, as well as activities and food in the party room for $890 for the first ten children, $25 for each additional child (birthday child is always free). You can also rent the entire playground after-hours (for a higher fee) for an Ultimate Playground Party on weekends at 4:30 p.m.

❊ Chelsea Piers Gymnastics*

Pier 62, 23rd Street at Twelfth Avenue
212-336-6777
www.chelseapiers.com

Little ones, ages six months to three years, spend thirty minutes in a party room and an additional hour or more in the baby gym, where they can crawl, explore, play in a ball pit, and be entertained by an instructor. For $350, ten kids can play for one and a half hours ($15 for each additional child, per hour). Older children, ages three and four, have a more advanced gymnastics experience in which they play on rope swings and a trampoline. Chelsea Piers also offers theme Barbie or Batman party packages. For older kids, Chelsea Piers offers parties of all types, including bowling, ice-skating, roller-blading, and basketball. Catering is additional. The bowling parties are a lot of fun— Kelly can attest to this.

⁂ Citibabes

52 Mercer Street at Broome Street, 3rd Floor
800-697-0107
www.citibabes.com
Citibabes offers a variety of birthday party options, at both locations as well as in your own home. The Signature Party (75 minutes is $800 for twelve children) allows you to choose from themes including Pirates & Princess, Plane's, Trains & Automobiles, and Under the Sea – and includes children's food and cake, decorations, toys, two party facilitators and your choice of room. You can arrange a Custom party for additional costs for features such as adult catering, gift bags, the Citibabes band, a magic show and more. If you're looking of a less-expensive alternative, try an Off-Peak Party (starting at $550 for twelve children) offered on select holidays, days and times.

⁂ Cowgirl

519 Hudson Street at West 10th Street
212-633-1133
www.cowgirlnyc.com
Cowgirl Restaurant is a great, budget-friendly, theme-party alternative. You can choose from two dude-ranch-themed private party lounges, the Western Lounge or the Cowgirl Portrait Library. Parties start at $13.50 per child, which

includes chicken fingers or quesadillas with fries, a selection of drinks, and birthday cake with ice cream. You can add on extras such as piñatas, cowboy hats and goodie bags, or arrange arts and crafts time for the little ones ($6–$8 extra per child). Don't miss the "Frito Pie" which is the best!

⁂ The Craft Studio

1657 Third Avenue at 92nd Street
212-831-6626
www.craftstudionyc.com
The Craft Studio is one of our favorite birthday party spots. The staff is superb and the craft choices for parties are endless. You can choose from a wide array of parties, including pottery painting, cookie decorating, gingerbread houses, chocolate houses, decorating picture frames, and much more. The parties are held in the back room, where there is fun music and games are played when the little ones are done with their projects. Parties are designed for children ages three and up, with prices beginning at around $700 for the first ten children. The Craft Studio also offers To-Go Parties now!

⁂ Eli's Vinegar Factory*

431 East 91st Street at York Avenue
212-987-0885, ext. 4
www.elizabar.com
Eli's Vinegar Factory offers a wide variety of party options in their own setting on the second floor of the store. Spacious and comfortable, this is a terrific place to hold large birthday parties for any age. The basic party package costs $25 per child (with a minimum of

twenty-five kids), and another $300 for staffing ($150 additional staffing fee for parties with thirty-five children or over). Clearly this is not a bargain, but we've never tasted better food at a birthday party! This price includes a two-hour party, tables and chairs, balloons, snacks, juice, and two kid entrees—with options like chicken fingers, mini pizzas, and PB&J. Eli's does not provide entertainment, but you are free to hire your own entertainers and have them perform in the space. For an additional charge, Eli's will host a pizza-making party or a cookies-and-cake-decorating party. Eli's offers a full adult catering menu as well, so if you'd like to offer food for adults, they can do it all. The party space is available Monday through Friday 11 a.m.–6 p.m.

✳ Funworks for Kids

201 East 83rd Street at 3rd Avenue
917-432-1820

Funworks offers a safe and fun place for children (ages one to three) to explore and play with toys and games. A two-hour party costs $300, and you provide food and refreshments. Parties can only be held on Saturdays.

✳ Gymtime*

1520 York Avenue at 80th Street
212-861-7732
www.gymtime.net

Partygoers can play in the padded big or mini-gym spaces. Kids enjoy tumbling and crawling in the gym spaces, and participating in activities involving a trampoline, a parachute, a ball pit, and bubbles. There are also circle songs. Helium balloons are provided, along with coffee and tea for adults. Kids can choose from five themes: Sports, Gymnastics, Tae Kwon Do, Fabulous Foodies, or a Combination of two. The space is available Friday, Saturday, and Sunday during the school year, and Monday and Wednesday in the summer. The "Basic Party" costs $750 for ten children ($23.50 for each additional child up to twenty, and $33.50 for each additional child up to a maximum of forty) for one and a half hours. An "All Inclusive" option is also available, starting at $850 for ten children.

✳ Jodi's Gym*

244 East 84th Street bet. Second and
Third avenues
212-772-7633
www.jodisgym.com

Jodi's Gym is very popular among the two through four crowd. This bright and spacious facility provides a young child with gym equipment all scaled down to just the right size. Birthday party kids play for forty-five minutes with an obstacle course, air mattress, balance beams, bars, mats, slides, parachutes, bubbles, and much more. After playing, the kids then have thirty minutes for cake and ice cream. Jodi's will also arrange everything from goodie bags and temporary tattoos, to balloons and a drop-in by your child's favorite cartoon character. A party for ten children costs $525 ($16 for each additional child). Food packages are available. Jodi's is available Monday through Friday in the summer, and Monday, Friday, Saturday, and Sunday during the school year.

Kidville

See website for multiple locations throughout Manhattan.

212-772-8435

email: birthdays.ues@kidville.com

www.kidville.com

Kidville offers birthday party at most of their locations. The basic party starts at $895 and includes ten children plus the birthday boy or girl. The parties are always lively and include a theme of your choice. The price includes: a ninety-minute party, birthday invitations, pizza and juice, birthday cake, party favors, balloons and paper goods and a Kidville art table.

Linda Kaye's Birthday Bakers Party Makers

195 East 76th Street

bet. Third and Lexington avenues

212-288-7112

www.partymakers.com

Linda Kaye offers children's birthday parties at a most unique location, The Central Park Wildlife Center. For children ages one to four, she offers two themes: Animal Alphabet Safari, where children learn about animals through the alphabet. The cost for ten children is $660 to $750 for one and a half to two hours, respectively. Linda Kaye offers an extensive party selection for older children as well, both at the zoo and at the Museum of Natural History. Linda's famous Bake-A-Cake Parties (held at the Birthday bakers Magic Cottage–address above—should not be forgotten! The Party-In-Our-Home Package includes a professional baker and assistant, invitations, chef hats and aprons for all children, baking diplomas, balloons, and snacks—costing $875 for twelve. Party-In-Your-Home costs $695 for twelve children and includes everything you'd find at an Our-Home party, minus the snacks.

Moon Soup

1059 Second Avenue

bet. 55th and 56th streets

212-319-3222

www.moonsoup.net

Moon Soup offers a warm and friendly atmosphere for parties as unique as your child! The Full-Service Party Package includes two hours of play, decorations, food, entertainment, and cake (prices range from $595 to $1,195). You can also go for the Just-The-Space Party Deal, which is offers two hours of playtime and kids eating tables, while parents provide food, drinks, decorations, paper goods and other entertainment for $295. All parties are designed for children ages six months to five years old.

92nd Street Y

1395 Lexington Avenue at 92nd Street

212-425-5710

www.92y.org

The Y offers great party options for children from age two and up. There are a variety of sports and an indoor pool for the older kids, and use of the two-level Gym Maze climbing/crawling structure with a spiral slide, ball pool, air bounce, and spider net for the little ones. The Y provides staff, invitations and party favors, parents provide food and decorations. Call for pricing details.

New York Kid's Club

See website for multiple locations throughout NYC.

www.nykidsclub.com

New York Kids Club's party packages include personalized invitations, pizza, cake, and party favors. For $895 (for up to ten children, and $18 for each additional child) you can host a ninety-minute theme party for your artist, gymnast, or chef-in-training. Families registered for a class receive a $50 discount.

Party Poopers*

100 Greenwich Street at Rector Street

212-274-9955

www.partypoopers.com

Party Poopers creates zany and original theme parties at its various locations throughout the city (pirate-themed parties on the Peking at the South Street Seaport are among the most popular). It has a large selection of costumed characters to choose from, as well as magicians, clowns, storytellers, puppeteers, and other entertainers. Prices start at $500 for one character at your own location for half an hour, and go up to $3,000 and more for full-service party packages at its place that include costumes, dancing, snacks, soda and juice, balloons, and paper goods. Kids can also have fun with a closet full of costumes, a tiny castle, toys, a moonwalk, and face painting. Pamela has used them for some of Benjamin's birthday parties with great success.

The Poppyseed Pre-Nursery

424 West End Avenue at 81st Street

212-877-7614

Poppyseed provides parties for babies, toddlers, two-year-olds, and three-year-olds—all centered around singing, dancing, movement, and play. Arts-and-crafts activities are also available. Prices start at $500 for twelve children. Be sure to book at least one month in advance (it's required)!

74th Street Magic*

510 East 74th Street

bet. York Avenue and the East River

212-737-2989

www.74magic.com

74th Street Magic has a big and beautiful indoor play space, and holds parties on Friday, Saturday, and Sunday. Toddlers spend one hour in the baby gym with a supervisor/teacher who helps them with the equipment, swing, and ball pit, and then another thirty minutes in the party room. The basic package costs $675 for twelve children (time can be extended to two hours for an extra $200, and additional children are $20 each), and includes invitations and thank-you cards, activity staff, a balloon for each child, and ice for beverages. The deluxe party features the same as above, with the addition of all necessary paper goods for adults and children, pizza and juice for children, and soda for adults ($825 for the basic package; $1,125 for two hours and $30 for each additional child).

If you're having a party at home and want to hire entertainment, check these out:

❋ *Arnie Kolodner* (best for three and up; most popular with the four- to six-year-old crowd, with wonderful Cinderella and Peter Pan parties—in addition to a whole selection of Birthday Fairy Tale Magic Shows!), Rebecca's favorite birthday parties included Arnie and seeing him pull a white dove out of a hat never failed to amaze us! 212-582-2633 or www.arniemagic.com.

❋ *Bobby DooWah** (music with instruments and dancing or a puppet show; fabulous for first and second birthdays! A favorite of Pamela's and Kelly's—between the two of us, we've used him five or six times), 914-838-4527 or through 212-772-7633 (Jodi's Gym). Bobby charges $275 for 30 minutes, $375 for 45 minutes. www.bobbydoowah.com.

❋ *Clown Magic Party Entertainment* has any kind of entertainment you can possibly imagine for your child's birthday. It features clowns, costumed characters, magicians, face painters, balloon sculptors, puppet shows, pony rides, petting zoos, storytellers, and sing-alongs. 212-544-8153 or www.clownmagicnyc.com.

❋ *Confetti Clowns*
917-579-0867
www.confetticlowns.com
Specializing in princess, fairy, and superhero parties with face painting, balloon art, magic, games, and cotton candy.

❋ *Face Painting and Balloons*
718-318-0110; 917-969-5473
email: FacePainterWithBalloons@verizon.net
www.FacePainterWithBalloons.com

❋ *Hollywood Pop Gallery*
(all kinds of costumed characters),
212-777-2238
www.hollywoodpop.com
Hollywoodpop brings theme parties to the next level. Children can choose from themes such as exotic animals, a petting zoo, a Wonka party, magic, and more.

❋ *Jam With Jamie*
305-321-3192
www.jamwithjamie.com
Jamie specializes in guitar, combining music and movement for children's parties. She also teaches local music classes and performs at the Literally Alive Children's Theater. $175 for forty-five minutes.

❋ *Kent Axell*
207-458-3115
www.kentaxellmagic.com
Kent offers an array of magic, juggling, comedy, and balloon sculpting for kids ages four and up. Prices are $250 for thirty to forty-five minutes in Manhattan. Kent has years of experience performing at children's shows and will tailor his show to fit your specific requests.

Little Maestros

Ronni Soled, Party Coordinator

212-744-3194

www.littlemaestros.com

Add parties to the list of Little Maestros credentials. It does birthday parties as well as all "special event" parties for ages one to six. The parties are forty-five-minute performances and can be anything from one teacher (with guitar) to "full band." Prices vary accordingly for these fun-filled parties.

Looney Louie

212-533-7491

www.looneylouie.com

Looney Louie offers magic and slapstick comedy, including juggling and balloon twisting for children ages three to ten. The birthday boy or girl becomes the star of his or her own show, and is even given a special gift from Louie himself. He also offers parties in Spanish and French. Prices start at $200 for a forty-five-minute show with balloon animal time afterwards.

Madeleine the Magician

516-733-0373

www.madeleinethemagician.com

Madeleine is a popular figure on the kids birthday party circuit. She is a lot of fun for kids and adults and has some creative and fun magic tricks that kids love.

Magical Marion

917-922-9880

A costumed character provides music and entertainment for your child's party.

Marcia the Musical Moose

212-567-0682; 914-358-8163

www.marciathemusicalmoose.com

Costumed moose character, puppet show, and sing-along; Marcia did the second birthday for Alexander, Kelly's son, with great success.

Mario the Magician

917-605-0662

www.mariothemagician.com

Mario uses his background in education to create an uplifting and interactive show for children ages two and up. He uses toys, rings, ropes, balls, coins, and silk scarves in addition to many other handmade props. Mario also offers an add-on balloon animal session. Price is $300 for thirty to forty minutes.

Monkey Monkey Music

212-673-6472

www.monkeymonkeymusic.com

Meredith LeVande dazzles children ages one to six with her peppy tunes, props, instruments, and even bubbles. Prices start at $275 for one hour.

New York Sketches

646-452-9946

www.nysketches.com

This all-purpose birthday party entertainment company can provide invitations, party favors, and a plethora of entertainers for your soiree. Entertainers include balloon artists, face painting, magicians, and costumed characters.

❈ Only Perfect Parties
212-869-6988
www.nycparties.com
Choose from a variety of theme characters and fun shows.

❈ Party Kids
646-489-6447
From fantasy tea parties and glamorous makeup and dancing parties to celebrations starring Mary Poppins, Elmo, Spider-Man, clowns, magic, and face art and balloon art, Party Kids has it all.

❈ Party Safari
203-249-8878
www.partysafarionline.com
Party Safari provides an exotic animal show for birthday parties, schools, camps, and day cares.

❈ Send in the Clowns*
718-353-8446 (ask for Gary)
www.sendintheclowns.com
Variety of theme characters and shows; Kelly has used Gary for years and has had Barney, Baby Bop and BJ, Batman and Robin, and the Power Rangers come visit her!

❈ Silly Billy
212-645-1299
www.sillybillymagic.com

Magic, comedy and fun; he's a legend among kids ages four to seven.

Party Favors

❈ HomeFront Kids
202 East 29th Street, 3rd Floor
bet. Second and Third avenues
212-545-1447, ext. 1302
This store carries a large selection of educational toys that make special party favors. The staff is very knowledgeable and will help you find age-appropriate items to fit your theme and budget. They will also personalize and wrap them in cellophane at no extra charge and deliver them for free in Manhattan.

❈ Cozy's Cuts for Kids
See website for multiple locations in Mahattan.
212-744-1716
www.cozycutsforkids.com
Yes, Cozy's is the spot for your child's first haircut (see page 254) but it is also a great place to pick up party favors. They offer tons of items that are perfect for parties of all ages.

There are plenty of places online that offer party favors, and here are some of the best:

- ❈ www.partypalooza.com
- ❈ www.partybagstogo.com
- ❈ www.smalltoys.com
- ❈ www.birthdayinabox.com
- ❈ www.orientaltrading.com
- ❈ www.birthdayexpress.com
- ❈ www.pearlriver.com

Central Park Parties

Central Park offers a myriad of party opportunities and is reasonably priced! Hurray! Here you are only limited by your imagination. To begin, for parties of more than twenty people, you need a permit from the City Parks and Recreation Department (212-360-8111 or www.nyc.gov/parks). A permit costs $25, payable to the city by credit card through their website. All permits require at least twenty-one to thirty days for processing. Central Park parties have to be planned with a rain date or a backup (indoor) plan in case of inclement weather. That aside, plan for lots of outdoor games, such as circle time for younger kids, hot potato, freeze dance (bring your iPod speakers), or have a friend (or Bobby DooWah) play guitar. Any entertainers you would hire for indoors—clowns, costumed characters, and so on—can be hired for outdoors as well.

Pamela's friend Esther planned a softball party for her son's sixth birthday, and it was a huge success. She got a permit for a softball field, provided each child with a team T-shirt, and had a real game.

Some popular party locations in Central Park include:

‡ *The Great Lawn*
   mid-park, between 79th and 86th streets

‡ *Sheep Meadow*
   mid-park, between 66th and 69th streets

‡ *Strawberry Fields*
   west side, between 71st and 74th streets

‡ *Any playground with a picnic table*

In addition to Central Park, NYC has several smaller parks that make great venues for birthday parties, many of which are serviced by their own nonprofit conservancies:

‡ *Battery Park City*
   1 World Financial Center
   212-267-9700
   www.batteryparkcity.org/kids

‡ *East River Park*
   Along the East River, from 12th Street down to Battery Park
   www.nycgovparks.org/parks/eastriverpark

‡ *Riverside Park*
   Along the Hudson River from 59th to 158th streets
   212-408-0209
   www.riversideparkfund.org

Make sure to mark your area with balloons, streamers, etc. (The Balloon Man is a great resource; Kelly has used him for years, and he will deliver everywhere. Call Harvey at 212-268-3900). Bring lots of blankets, paper tablecloths, and napkins. A folding table for food and cake is a good idea, too.

If you want a more organized party in the park, the Central Park Carousel is a lot of fun for kids age two to five. Call 212-736-8700 (or go online at www.centralparkcarousel.com) to book a party there. Parties start at $21.95 (Mondays–Fridays) or $27.95 (weekends) per child (minimum of twelve children) and include four carousel rides per child, plus one hour in the picnic area. The carousel staff supplies paper goods, hot dogs or pizza, and juice, plus a small party favor and a helium balloon for each child. All you need to bring is the birthday cake. For an additional fee, you can also request a face painter, clown, magician, or costumed characters for $230 per forty-five minutes. Extra party time is $145 for each additional half hour. Parties are held April through November, seven days a week, weather permitting.

Balloons and Decorations

❖ Balloon Bouquets of New York

457 West 43rd Street at Tenth Avenue
212-265-5252
www.balloonbouquetsnyc.com
This balloon decorating service can provide anything from a bunch of plain, loose latex balloons to elaborate Mylar bouquets and large-scale decorations like centerpieces, arches, and banners. If you prefer, you can rent a helium tank and do it yourself. One dozen latex balloons cost $28. Free delivery from Monday through Saturday; $10 to deliver on Sunday.

❖ Balloon Saloon

133 West Broadway at Duane Street
212-227-3838
www.balloonsaloon.com
This full-fledged party-supply store, which sells paper goods, favors, and piñatas, also sells balloons in all shapes and sizes. In addition to the basic loose latex balloons and Mylar bouquets they do elaborate party decorations. Twenty-five latex balloons cost $50. Delivery below 60th Street is free and costs $5 above 60th Street. It also rents helium tanks for do-it-yourselfers.

❖ Birthday Express

800-424-7843
www.birthdayexpress.com
This catalog/Internet company sells all sorts of paper goods, decorations, favors, balloons, piñatas, party crafts and activities, costumes, and cake-baking supplies for children's birthday parties. Its themed party kits, which cost around $25, have everything you need to throw a party for eight children including invitations, tableware, table cover, and balloons. Deluxe versions for $30 to $40 and "ultimate" versions for $130 and up include extras like decorations, candles, favors, piñata, and thank-yous.

❖ Party City

38 West 14th Street
bet. Fifth and Sixth Avenues
212-271-7310
www.partycity.com
This huge chain store is worth traveling to and has tons of party supplies for every occasion at bargain-basement prices.

❖ State News

1243 Third Avenue bet. 71st and 72nd streets
212-879-8076
151 Amsterdam Avenue bet. 67th and
68th streets
212-787-6450
112 East 86th Street bet. Lexington and
Park avenues
212-831-8010
These stationery stores have some of the biggest selections of party paper goods and tableware in the city, including over eighty children's birthday

party patterns. They also have a nice selection of Mylar balloons, invitations/thank-you notes, favors, and cake/cookie baking and decorating supplies. Pamela was thrilled when they opened in her neighborhood, and it is the go-to spot for cards and the best Halloween costumes and decorations.

Birthday Cookies and Cakes

Everybody has a bakery in the neighborhood that makes perfectly fine, even fabulous birthday cakes. Explore your neighborhood, and be sure to ask other moms where they get cakes. Heck, you can probably get a cake from the supermarket complete with your baby's name and ubiquitous frosting flowers (truthfully in our opinion, there is nothing as delicious as a supermarket cake). But for your child's first birthday, you may want to go all out. We've listed some makers of outstanding (though sometimes outrageously priced) birthday cakes, and clued you in on which ones will incorporate themes such as Superman, ballerinas, or Peter Rabbit. Don't panic, though. For Angela's first birthday (Kelly's second child), she had an Entenmann's chocolate cake at home with big brother Alexander, and she was perfectly happy! Entenmann's can be quite good when they're fresh, and for $3.99, who's complaining?

❖ BeautifulCookies.com

866-FUN-GIFT; 212-386-4438

www.beautifulcookies.com

These adorable hand-decorated cookies are great to serve at a party or to use as favors. Choose from dozens of designs on the website or provide the company with a photo, and it will

scan it on in edible ink. The cookie-decorating kits make great kids' birthday and holiday gifts. Pamela just used them to make the most adorable cookies for her niece's baby naming.

❖ Cakes 'N' Shapes, Ltd.

403 West 39th Street

bet. Ninth and Tenth avenues

212-629-5512

For $150 and up, Edie Connolly can create a unique cake in the character or design of your choice. She can sculpt everything from a ballerina to a teddy bear, Batman, or Superman. Give her a favorite picture, and she will scan it onto a cake. A simple round cake for twenty-five costs $100+. For Rebecca's Cinderella party, she designed a 3-D cake with Cinderella's gown as the cake, and a Barbie doll as Cinderella. Order at least one week in advance. Pamela recently had Edie make a Football cake for Benjamin and it was delicious as ever. Delivery available.

❖ CBK Cookies of New York*

226 East 83rd Street

bet. Second and Third avenues

212-794-3383

www.cbkcookies.com

You can order chocolate or vanilla single-sheet or double-layer cakes in various styles, including cakes baked in the shape of a character of your choice. A basic decorated cake that serves approximately twenty people costs $100+, and specially decorated ones are $150+. These cakes are so special, CBK makes only two a day, so order at least two weeks in advance. It makes wonderful cupcakes and cookies, too, in every shape and style. Delivery is extra. By appointment only. For years Kelly has used CBK for birthdays, baby showers, and Halloween parties.

Creative Cakes

400 East 74th Street
bet. First and York avenues
212-794-9811

Creative Cakes hand-sculpts 3-D cakes to look like a fire truck, barnyard, basketball court, or anything you can imagine. Its smallest cake serves twenty-five people and ranges from $300 to $325. Make sure to call two to three weeks ahead to place your order. Delivery costs $50. By appointment only.

Crumbs

See website for multiple locations in NYC, New Jersey, Connecticut, and Long Island
www.crumbs.com

Crumbs bakeries (with more than ten locations in Manhattan) offer to make your own cupcake or cookie parties (to go). The bakery supplies cookies with edible color markers or cupcakes with choices of frosting, sprinkles, and edible cake toppers. These provide a fun alternative to birthday cakes and an activity for partygoers, too. If you just want to buy cupcakes as part of your birthday celebration, the cupcakes here are delicious and come in creative varieties such as Oreo cookie and Snickers.

Cupcake Cafe*

522 Ninth Avenue at 39th Street
212-465-1530
www.cupcakecafe.com

Cupcake Cafe is one of our favorites! A round cake serving twelve to twenty people with flowers and an inscription costs around $70. A theme cake with Big Bird or Barney, serving twenty-five people, is $100 and up. Call two to three days in advance to pick up a cake Monday through Saturday; call Thursday for a cake to be ready on Sunday. Delivery is about $25. No credit cards; cash, money order, or company check only.

Dean & Deluca

See website for multiple locations throughout NYC.
www.deananddeluca.com

Dean & Deluca's chocolate cake is phenomenal. A layer cake that serves approximately twenty-five people starts at $50. Order two days ahead—although some moms have been lucky enough to walk in and find one already made. D&D also carries fantastic cupcakes as well as adorable large character cookies. Delivery is free in the neighborhood with $25 minimum.

Flour Girl

Call to schedule a private appointment.
212-595-9505
www.flourgirl.com

Flour Girl makes adorable cakes decorated with cookies instead of icing. It can make a cake to coordinate with any party theme and can even match your invitation or a photograph. Cakes cost $6 per portion and include a cookie for each person. The minimum size is for twenty people. Ten- to fourteen-day lead time is required. It will deliver cakes of $200 or more for $40 per hour.

Grace's Market Place

1237 Third Avenue at 71st Street
212-737-0600
www.gracesmarketplace.com
Grace's has a wide selection, including carrot and chocolate mousse cakes. Some are beautifully decorated with flowers and scrolls of dark chocolate. A cake serving twelve people costs $40 and up. You can stop by Grace's on the spur of the moment and find a cake, perhaps its delicious $25 American Beauty chocolate cake. Can you tell we like chocolate? This cake is one of our favorite chocolate cakes in New York City. It can be customized with three days' notice. Delivery is $4 within eight blocks.

Lafayette Bakery

26 Greenwich Avenue
bet. Tenth and Charles streets
212-242-7580
email: anycbakery@aol.com
Lafayette Bakery will customize a cake with a simple design for an extra $5 to $15 over the regular price of $69 for a cake serving twenty-five. Its cakes have fruit, custard, or mousse fillings, and they can be topped with whipped cream or a variety of icings. Order a week in advance. No delivery, but open seven days a week.

Magnolia Bakery*

401 Bleecker Street at 11th Street
212-462-2572
200 Columbus Avenue at 69th Street
212-744-8101
1240 Avenue of the Americas at 49th Street
212-767-1123
www.magnoliabakery.com
Specializing in old-fashioned, homemade cakes, Magnolia Bakery offers delicious yellow or chocolate half-sheet cakes. A cake serves twenty-five to thirty-five. Magnolia won't custom-make a cake, but with a day's notice, it will personalize one. Call one to two weeks in advance. Pamela's family adores the cupcakes here, which are some of the best in NYC. These are a favorite with kids and adults alike, so nobody will be disappointed with Magnolia cupcakes at their birthday party. No delivery.

Make My Cake

121 St. Nicholas Avenue at 116th Street
212-932-0833
www.makemycake.com
Make My Cake is a full-service bakery specializing in wedding, shower, and birthday cakes.

My Most Favorite Food Company

120 West 45th Street
bet. Sixth Avenue and Broadway
212-997-5032; 212-997-5130
www.mymostfavorite.com
Well-known for delicious kosher food and desserts, My Most Favorite Food Company sells a two-layer round cake (chocolate or vanilla) that serves twenty-five people and costs

$75. A beautifully decorated kids' theme cake is about $95. Call three to four days in advance. Delivery is $12.

The Perfect Cake

42-25B Vernon Boulevard
Long Island City
718-606-2144
www.perfectcake.com

The Perfect Cake will custom-design a birthday cake in the shape of your child's favorite character, animal, sport, hobby, or object. There is no limit to what this creative bakery can do. A 10-inch cake for fifteen to twenty people starts at $150. Pick a design from the website or have the bakery create something just for you. Not only are these cakes beautiful, but they are delicious, too.

Soutine*

104 West 70th Street
bet. Columbus and Amsterdam avenues
212-496-1450
www.soutine.com

Pamela buys wonderful cakes at this tiny bake shop. A two-layer round cake serving twenty people costs $45, and a cake with special decoration costs an additional $10 to $15. You can customize designs and flavors. Through a computer graphics program, kids can design their own cake online and Soutine will make the cake of your child's dreams. Order one to two days in advance. Delivery costs $15 to $20 in Manhattan. Cupcakes are also available, made to order with sprinkles.

Sylvia Weinstock Cakes

273 Church Street
bet. White and Franklin streets
212-925-6698
www.sylviaweinstockcakes.com

Known in New York as "the cake lady," Sylvia creates masterpieces that range from castles for birthdays to fantasies for brides. She is known around the world for her wedding cakes. Her concoctions start at about $350 for a cake that will serve thirty-five people. Give at least three weeks' notice. Delivery within Manhattan is $50; outside depends on mileage.

Veniero Pasticceria

342 East 11th Street
bet. First and Second avenues
212-674-7264

Famous not just for fantastic cannoli, it also makes light and creamy cakes for kids. A round cake that serves up to thirty people costs $50. Bring in a postcard-size picture of anything you want on the cake, and it'll be copied for an additional $20. Order two days in advance. Delivery is $10 in Manhattan.

William Greenberg Desserts

1100 Madison Avenue
bet. 82nd and 83rd streets
212-861-1340

Another baker well known for elaborate designs and decorations, Greenberg's produces a beautiful baby carriage cake for baby showers. It made President Clinton's fiftieth-birthday American flag cake. A two-layer round cake serving twenty-five costs $130 to $150; decorated cakes go up to $265. Call at least two days in advance; longer for more elaborate creations. Delivery with one day advanced notice.

With many birthday cakes under our belt, we've discovered there is nothing better than an ice-cream cake from Häagen-Dazs or Carvel, especially in the spring and summer months. These cakes are usually two layers of chocolate and vanilla ice cream with cookie crunch and icing on the sides and tops. These bring us back to our own childhood birthdays, and you can never discount nostalgia as a good reason to buy one; your kids will love it as much as you did. If you call in advance, you can choose your child's favorite ice cream flavors.

There are Häagen-Dazs stores throughout the city, so they are ideal places to pick up a quick birthday cake. Cakes range in prices—cakes that serve twenty to twenty-five people are around $50 to $70, depending on the decoration. Here are two Häagen-Dazs locations:

187 Columbus Avenue
bet. 68th and 69th streets
212-787-0265

33 Barrow Street bet. Seventh Avenue
and Bleecker Street
212-727-2152

There is only one Carvel location in the city, but many supermarkets carry the cakes, which are relatively inexpensive. For approximately twenty-five people, an ice-cream cake will cost around $43.

1501 Broadway bet. 43rd and 44th streets
www.carvelicecream.com

haircuts

Many New York moms take their babies to their own hair salon or attempt to give that first trim themselves. But we think you'll want to try one of these shops that specialize in children's haircutting. Little kids are notoriously bad at sitting still, and most of these places offer fun distractions like Dora, Barney, or Sesame Street videos to watch, and toy cars for your child to sit in. You might even come away with a first haircut diploma, a lock of hair, or a balloon. Bring some toys from home so your child won't badger you to buy one of the pricey toys for sale in some of these salons.

Appleseeds
10 West 25th Street at Fifth Avenue
212-792-7590
www.appleseedsnyc.com
A salon that is uniquely designed, kid friendly, comfortable, clean, and fun. They provide professional cuts and styling for kids (as well as adult trims, styling, and touch-ups). Appointments are available from 10:00 a.m. until 5:30 p.m. on Tuesdays, Wednesdays, and Thursdays. Children's cuts are $28 ($25 for members). Twin Discount: When both twins get their hair cut, Twin "B" receives 50 percent off.

Astor Place Hair Designers
2 Astor Place bet. 8th Street and Broadway
212-475-9854
email: email@astorplacehairstylist.com
www.astorplacehairnyc.com
Nothing special here for children: no cars to sit in or balloons, just a cheap haircut, good peo-

ple watching, and a friendly downtown staff. A kid's cut is about $15.

Cozy's Cuts for Kids*

1125 Madison Avenue at 84th Street
1416 Second Avenue at 74th Street
448 Amsterdam Avenue at 81st Street
212-585-COZY
email: customercare@cozycutsforkids.com
www.cozyscutsforkids.com
Cozy's Cuts is "the" uptown place to get your child's haircut. It offers a fun environment for babies as well as older kids with their cool trucks to sit in which double as styling chairs. In addition, their hair-care products called So Cozy smell yummy and really work. The 74th Street location also offers mini-manicures and the same great glamarama birthday parties.

Doodle Doo's

543 Hudson Street near Perry Street
212-627-3667
Owner Dana Rywelski is a former nanny with a master's degree in education, a (perfectly coiffed) one-year-old son, and an intimate knowledge of the families around the West Village.

The Hair's Castle

1470 York Avenue at 78th Street
212-744-2177
Built by Broadway set designers, The Hair's Castle offers lots of brightly colored diversions, including a gigantic pocket watch on the wall with a tortoise and a hare as hands. Each station is equipped with a television and VCR, and

Sony PlayStation or Nintendo 64. A child's haircut is $25+. Appointments are recommended.

Jennifer Bilek

Get Conveniently Coiffed
917-548-3643
email: getcoiffed@rcn.com
www.getcoiffed.com
If you want an alternative to the frenetic kiddy salon, Jennifer Bilek will come to your home to cut your child's hair (and the whole family's!) for about the same price as the salons. Her services also include haircutting house calls for adults, "glamour" parties for girls, and hair and makeup for weddings and special occasions. Haircut house calls start at $55.00 (child) with a family discount for two or more children.

Kids Cuts

201 East 29th Street at Third Avenue, 3rd Floor
212-684-5252
email: info@kidscutsny.com
www.kidscutsny.com
This store provides a great experience for your child's first haircut. While the haircutter snips away, your child can watch movies and sit in a miniature car. After the cut, you receive a certificate with a lock of your child's hair for your album, as well as a pinwheel for the little one. Kids Cuts also has a boutique that sells toys for both entertainment and educational purposes. This boutique tends to be pricey, so the pinwheel may have to suffice as a post-cut treat.

✣ Kidville

163 East 84th Street

212-772-8435

www.kidvilleny.com

Named "Best of" by New York magazine, Kidville operates large, upscale facilities, catering to young children and their families. Kidville also features an indoor playground, a retail boutique, the Kidville salon, and will host birthday parties for children up to age nine.

✣ Paul Molé Barber Shop

1031 Lexington Avenue at 74th Street

212-535-8461

email: information@paulmole.com

www.paulmole.com

Paul Molé has been around "forever" but has kept up with the times. Your child can watch a video, eat a lollipop, and go home with a toy. Children sit in an old-fashioned kid-size barbershop chair and will receive a special certificate for their first haircut.

✣ SuperCuts

See website for multiple locations in NYC.

800-SUPERCUT

www.supercuts.com

All the salons in this chain cut infants' and toddlers' hair, and award a diploma for the first haircut. Salons are clean and designed to provide quick, easy-in/easy-out service. Haircuts for toddlers cost around $18. Appointments aren't required but, if you wish, you can make one with your favorite stylist.

shoes

Buying your child's first walking shoes is an exciting and important task. Because your one- or two-year-old can't tell you whether the shoes are comfortable, watch carefully as she is being fitted. If it seems difficult to get the shoes on and off, they are probably too small. Shoes should generally last at least two months: if they seem small three weeks after you bought them, go back and have them checked.

The salesperson at the shoe store should measure your child's foot while he is standing, toes uncurled. Ask about the width of your child's foot and don't buy a shoe that narrows greatly at the toes. Also, look for a soft, flexible sole. A soft sole is necessary for the first year. After that, when your child is really walking and running, you can buy any shoe except slip-on penny loafers. Your youngster won't develop the gripping action that a slip-on shoe requires until he is four or five.

✣ Collections/Stride Rite*

1542 Third Avenue at 87th Street

212-249-0551

www.striderite.com

This big, bright store has areas carved out for different age groups. It carries brands like Stride Rite, Nike, Reebok, LA Gear, Elefanten, and a wide variety of styles. Prices are among the best around, and the staff is generally quite knowledgeable about little feet. This store gets a star because it stands behind what it sells, exchanges mistakes readily, and has great sales!

✣ Harry's Shoes

2299 Broadway at 83rd Street

212-874-2035

www.harrys-shoes.com

An Upper West Side fixture, Harry's carries a wide selection of American and European brands, including Stride Rite, Elefanten, Jumping Jacks, Shoo Be Doo, Nike, Reebok, New Balance, and Enzo. This place can get very crowded, especially on the weekends and after school.

Ibiza Kidz

61 Fourth Avenue at East 9th Street
212-228-7990
www.ibizakidz.com

This small downtown store is part shoe store, part toy store, and part clothing store. It carries a large line of shoes with brands such as Aster, Baby Botte, Elefanten, Mod 8, Superga, and Venettini. In the toy section you can find educational toys, Gund and Russ plush toys, and much more. This comfortable neighborhood store has great service and a very loyal customer following. There are good seasonal sales at the end of summer and winter.

Kin Kidz

2472 Frederick Douglass Boulevard
bet. West 132nd and 133rd streets
212-368-5224

Kin Kidz, located in Harlem, offers a wide variety of shoes and boots for kids from toddlers through high school students. The store also stocks assorted accessories, including seasonal hats, as well as a selection of toys.

Lester's

1534 Second Avenue at 80th Street
212-734-9292

www.lestersnyc.com

This Manhattan branch of the Brooklyn chain has an impressive shoe department tucked behind the clothing. Lester's is a discount store carrying a good selection of European and American brands; there's a wide variety of styles, and friendly, knowledgeable service, too!

Lilliput Soho Kids

240 Lafayette Street at Spring Street
212-965-9201
email: info@lilliputsoho.com
www.lilliputsoho.com

This charming little boutique offers lovely, colorful, well-made clothing, party shoes, and sundries for children.

Little Eric Shoes on Madison*

1118 Madison Avenue at 83rd Street
212-717-1513

A wide selection of shoes for children ages six months to seven years. Brands include Nike, Keds, Converse, and Kangaroos, with styles from sneakers to high-end imported designer shoes. The Little Eric store brand makes up the majority of its stock and is excellent and very fashionable. This is a child-friendly store, with plenty of space and toys to keep children busy as they are fitted. It has a loyal following but a limited selection of shoes for wide feet.

The Little Stinkers Shoe Company

280 East 10th Street bet. First Avenue and Avenue A
212-253-0282
www.thelittlestinkersshoeco.com

Little Stinkers is all about value: solid shoes that are fun but won't break the bank. Shoe sizes range from pre-walkers to size 8 and brands include Vincent, Morgan and Milos, and Havanianas.

❁ *Naturino*

1184 Madison Avenue at East 87th Street
212-427-0679
1410 Second Avenue at East 74th Street
212-794-0570
email: info@naturino.com
www.naturino.com
Naturino offers fabulous shoes for the fabulous small fry. Sizes here run from newborn to fourteen years (size forty), and the staff is friendly and helpful.

❁ *The Shoe Garden*

152 West 10th Street at Waverly Place
212-989-4320
email: store@shoegardennyc.com
www.shoegardennyc.com
The Shoe Garden was started by two downtown moms who wanted a great shoe store for their kids with a varied selection of shoes, boots, sandals, and sneakers. At the Shoe Garden, parents will find a unique selection of footwear for all ages of kids.

❁ *Shoofly*

42 Hudson Street at Duane Street
212-406-3270
email: info@shooflynyc.com
www.shooflynyc.com
This is one of the most stylish kiddie shoe stores in the city, carrying all the high-end brands for boys and girls such as Aster, Baby Botte, and Deoso. There's also an excellent selection of purses, hats, barrettes, and other accessories. It has extra-special shoes for girls; it was Rebecca's favorite shop when she was little. Try to shop during the week; weekends are quite busy.

❁ *Tip Top Kids**

155 West 72nd Street bet. Amsterdam and Columbus avenues
212-787-4960
800-WALKING, ext. 22
www.tiptopshoes.com
This store is nicely laid out, with plenty of space for walking around and trying on shoes. The staff is friendly and helpful, and kids are kept occupied by a supply of toys and movies. Tip Top has shoes for every occasion, with prices ranging from $20 to $80. Popular brands include Stride Rite, Monroe Kids, Nike, and New Balance.

photographs

It doesn't take long for your drawers to become stuffed with photos taken of your adorable baby by you and your relatives, or all the room taken up on your hard drive with digital downloads. But there's a reason why you've left your photos languishing in a drawer. When you want a picture to put in that beautiful silver frame you got as a baby gift, it's time to go to a professional. A real photographer can work in your home, the park, or her studio, and can include parents or grandparents in the shots, as well as props such as stuffed animals, antique toys, costumes, and more.

If you don't know a photographer, here are some places to start. These are fairly traditional professionals who are experienced in photographing children (it's an art, truly). Ask to see their portfolios, and if you don't see the kind of work you want, ask your friends for some recommendations. Also, look for photo credits in parenting magazines. There's a good chance the photographers live in New York. Since prices vary greatly from one photographer to another, it is best to call or check their websites for current pricing. Also, be sure to ask if they offer any first-time deals. You would be surprised at how many photographers offer special packages . . . so just ask!

❊ A Perfect Portrait

Principal Photographer: Nancy Ribeck
476 Broome Street, Suite 6A
bet. Wooster and Greene streets
212-534-3433
email: nsrac@nyc.rr.com
www.nanchanpartners.com
Nancy Ribeck's studio photography is classically lit but casually designed. This combination gives her portraits the beauty of traditional portraiture mixed with a contemporary look. Photos are taken at the studio at 476 Broome Street, or at a location of your choice for an extra fee. Sessions last two or three hours. Print photos are an additional fee.

❊ Barry Burns

260 West 36th Street, 2nd Floor
bet. Seventh and Eighth avenues
212-713-0100
email: bb311photo@aol.com

www.barryburnsphotography.com
Barry Burns captures the spontaneity of the moment. Family portraits can also be made in color or black-and-white film. Most work is done in his studio in the heart of the theater district, but an outside location is possible for a negotiable additional fee.

❊ Alice Garik photography

718-499-1456
www.alicegarik.com
Alice Garik takes beautiful photographs and is best known for her work with brides and grooms and babies. Her photographs have an artistic quality to them that is striking and elegant. Alice takes time getting to know her subjects and prints her work in both black-and-white and color.

❊ Brian Kao

646-552-8965; 201-583-1003
email: brian@captureyourself.com
www.captureyourself.com
Brian Kao is a photographer with a portfolio of artistic baby and family portraits. He features nature in a lot of his themes, and provides a creative edge for your child's photos. Contact Brian for prices.

❊ Diana Berrent Photography

917-292-0151
145 West 79th Street, #2B
bet. Amsterdam and Columbus avenues
email: diana@dianaberrent.com
www.dianaberrent.com
Leading family portrait photographer and

native New Yorker, Diana Berrent works both outdoors and in her studio to create one-of-a-kind works of art you will treasure for a lifetime. Diana's honest style of portraiture captures the moments you want to preserve for your children's children. With a spare style that focuses on your child's quick smile, sparkling eyes, and captivating spirit, Diana has created a unique approach to portraiture that is both modern and timeless. Diana has been a featured favorite at many Babybites (www.babybites.net) NYC events.

Donna Padowitz

917-626-6492

www.donnapadowitz.com

Donna has been featured on Good Morning America, the Rachael Ray Show, and is currently listed in *Time Out New York Kids* as a children's photographer favorite.

Fromex

182 East 86th Street

bet. Third and Lexington avenues

212-369-4821

Tucked in the back of this average-looking "one hour" photo place is a photo studio with a photographer on staff. Fromex offers many packages that range in price but are on the inexpensive side. It's best to call ahead for an appointment, but walk-ins are possible. We both have had good results with Fromex.

Gail Sherman

88 Central Park West at 69th Street

212-877-7210

email: gail@gailsherman.com

Gail Sherman's work is dramatic. Her photographs are printed in black and white, then hand-colored with oil paints. Her photographs are works of art, not just "pictures."

Heidi Green Photography

212-545-5304

email: info@heidigreen.com

www.heidigreen.com

Heidi's work has been featured in *Time Out New York Kids*, *The New York Daily News*, *Gotham* magazine and she is a regular photographer for *New York Family* magazine. Check out her fun webpage for more details.

Jami Beere Photography

646-505-5636; 917-903-4212

email: jamibeere@yahoo.com

www.jamibeere.com

Jami is a talented photographer who is well-known for her exquisite children's portraits. She is expensive, but many parents believe she's worth it because of the beautiful work she does. Once the client chooses the image she wants, Jami hand-prints it. Prices vary with size of the print.

Jennifer Lee Photography

40 West 72nd Street, Suite 53

bet. Central Park West and Columbus Avenue

212-799–1501

www.jenniferleephotography.com

Jennifer Lee has been photographing kids for over ten years including Pamela's own. As a mother of two children, she appreciates photography's unique ability to freeze the moments that matter the most. Her goal is to create images that are natural and reflect your child's personality—images that will immediately evoke a memory of a certain stage or age and make those moments eternal. Most of Jennifer's portrait work is still done in film, which makes her unique. She photographs children all over the city: at their homes, in the park, at their favorite locale or at her conveniently located Upper West Side studio. She also shoots families on the beaches of Long Island, New Jersey, and Cape Cod. Session fees start at $325. Jennifer Lee also designs unique custom stationery, birth announcements, invitations and cards for all occasions, using her photographs as the inspiration.

❊ Jordan Elyse Photography
26 West 17th Street, Suite 801
bet. Fifth and Sixth avenues
646-519-6080
email: info@jordanelyse.com
www.jordanelyse.com
Photographer Jordan Rosner specializes in birth announcements (with your baby's picture on them), holiday cards, and great photo shoots of your baby alone or with the whole family. Contact Jordan for her price list or check out her comprehensive website.

❊ Karen Michele
350 West 50th Street
bet. Eighth and Ninth avenues
212-355-7576
www.karenmichele.com
Karen Michele will design a backdrop for your

photo shoot using colorful balloons or anything else you want. She operates from a full retouching production facility, where she personally works with on-film retouching for each portrait. Her photos can be seen in the children's section of select Barnes & Noble stores. Parents make a selection from approximately thirty proofs. By appointment only.

❊ Kate Burton Photography
86 Union Street at Columbus Street
Brooklyn
email: kate@kateburton.com
www.kateburton.com
Kate Burton has been photographing children for over eight years in New York City. Her work has been featured in the *New York Times* and *Time Out New York*, and is frequently displayed in children's stores such as Shoofly, Little Eric, and Bu & The Duck. Kate Burton shoots in her own full-service studio, but will also go on location to the park or your home. Sitting fees range between $600 and $800, depending on location. A number of Pamela's friends have used Kate, and all of them attest that Kate does beautiful work and is a pleasure to work with.

❊ Kate Engelbrecht Photography
55 Washington Street at Front Street
Brooklyn
718-858-5165
email: kate.engelbrecht@gmail.com
www.kephoto.net
While her studio is located in Brooklyn, this documentary-style photographer will come to Manhattan to photograph your children at

home or in the park. Her specialty is the family docu-portrait, a still photo essay that captures individual personalities and tells an honest and intimate story. Kate's sitting fee starts at $500 and includes the proofs.

Leshem Loft

888-790-9066; 917-608-7818
email: info@LeshemLoft.com
www.leshemloft.com

Providing fine art family portraiture and a boutique, Leshem Loft is an event space (baby showers, christenings, baby namings), shop, and photo studio all rolled into one. This 2,000-square-foot Flatiron space features exposed brick walls, 16-foot ceilings, and a gallery of photographer Yaron Leshem's portraits. Yaron is a brilliant, award-winning photographer who also snaps gorgeous pregnancy photos.

Loreto Caceres

516-457-7559
email: info@loretocaceres.com
www.loretocaceresphotography.com

Loreto brings a contemporary fine-art approach to her work by entering your child's world so she can focus on their true personality rather than forced expressions, making picture taking a stress-free process. She can shoot at any location.

Lucille Khornak

425 East 58th Street at First Avenue, Suite 45D
212-593-0933
email: lucille@theportraitspecialist.com
www.theportraitspecialist.com

Lucille has been a prominent photographer for

over twenty years and has established many lasting relationships with the families she has photographed. One of Pamela's friends has used her for years and always has the best holiday card on the block.

Marci Clark Photography

917-301-6259
email: marcilacenere@me.com
www.marciclarkphotography.com

Marci, a new mom herself, knows how to get babies and kids to cooperate for photos! She creates custom settings specifically designed to fit you and your family's needs.

Nancy Pindrus Photography

21 West 68th Street, 3F
bet. Central Park West and Columbus Avenue
212-724-4681
email: pindrus@earthlink.net
www.pindrusphotography.com

Nancy has been a professional photographer for twenty-five years. She is both patient and accommodating. Her basic prices start around $350. She works from her studio. Other locations, such as Central Park, are negotiable.

Nina Drapacz

500 East 85th Street at York Avenue, Suite 14C
212-772-7814
email: ninaspictures@aol.com
www.fotonina.com

Nina Drapacz apprenticed with Richard Avedon, has been working for over fifteen years in Manhattan, and specializes in hand-colored black-and-white photos. She does fabulous work and is extremely accommodating and patient. Pamela's friend Marty used her twice for family photos. Nina will do studio or outdoor shoots.

✳ Paloma Sendrey

917-428-2843; 718-432-2365
email:paluki@optonline.net
www.palomasendrey.com
Paloma Sendrey shoots beautiful family and maternity photographs in sepia, black and white, and color. A full session lasts ninety minutes to two hours, resulting in two rolls of film at a cost of around $400. She also shoots photo "playdates" in Central Park and will shoot holiday cards in thirty-minute sessions.

✳ Rachel Klein*

917-414-5485
email: rachel@rachelkleinphotography.com
www.rachelkleinphotography.com
Rachel Klein is a New York City photographer who specializes in black-and-white family portraits. A typical sitting with Rachel resembles a play date in the park or at home. Rachel photographs families in familiar settings with natural light only. It is this formula that makes her work distinct. Rachel is a pleasure to work with and is extremely easy-going and flexible.

✳ Sarah Merians Photography & Company

104 Fifth Avenue at 16th Street, 4th Floor
212-633-0502
email: info@sarahmerians.com
www.sarahmerians.com
Sarah Merians Photography has been photo-graphing children and families for fifteen years. She employs thirteen child-experienced photographers, so the company can easily accommodate your family's schedule. The starting price for an in-studio photo shoot is approximately $300, which includes two rolls of film—color and/or black and white. Sarah Merians will also shoot on location. Prices vary according to the locale you choose. Pamela used them to photograph her wedding, with wonderful results.

✳ Treasure Portraits

See website for multiple locations throughout NYC and New Jersey.
Contact: Joe Accardo at 973-366-0550
email: treasureportraits.46@gmail.com
www.treasureportraits.com
There is no session fee for this service! All photograph sizes are available, from standard-size wallets to 24 x 30-inch prints. Mounting, composite format, and wooden plaque lamination are also available.

a word on preschools

As you begin to check out preschools—sometime between your child's first and second birthday—you will probably be subject to intermittent panic attacks. You'll hear rumors that this or that school is "hot" this year. You'll be baffled by the complexity of the admissions process. You'll feel as though you're trying to get an eighteen-year-old into Harvard, not a two-year-old into a sweet little place where she'll play and eat crackers and drink juice. Try to relax. Things will work out.

Here are some basic facts to keep in mind as you and your child march toward preschool:

- Many children begin preschool at age three or three and a half years old; others begin as early as two years and four months old. Schools decide on cutoff ages for admission and often change these arbitrarily—a one-year-old born before March 15 can apply for admission for the following September; the next year, perhaps, a child born before March 31 can apply. Schools hold tight to their birth date policies, and there are few exceptions.

- There are many excellent preschools in New York. Pick up a copy of the Manhattan Directory of Private Nursery Schools by Linda Faulhaber. This book describes all the private preschools in New York by neighborhood, with pertinent information from phone numbers to cutoff dates. Or look through the New York Independent Schools Directory, published by the Independent Schools Admission Association of Greater New York (and available through the Parents League). But remember, there are excellent schools that are not members of the Parents League, and are therefore not listed in the League guidebook.

- As you begin your search, look for a school in your neighborhood, if possible. Try to keep your travel distance to about ten blocks. Otherwise, you'll spend all your time getting there, when the school time itself is only two or three hours a day twice a week for children under three. Three-year-olds may go every day, and they'd rather spend their time at school than traveling to it.

- Talk to friends about their experiences with preschools. Make arrangements to visit the schools you're interested in; tours usually take place from October through January. You must call the day after Labor Day to make an appointment for a tour and/or request an application. Some schools will not schedule a tour until they receive a completed application; others supply applications only after you have toured the school.

- Apply promptly. Schools have been known to stop sending applications by the second week of September, when they have already received enough applicants to fill their classes three times over. Apply to six to eight schools. If you have a first choice, indicate it in a letter to the director of admissions of that particular school. It also helps greatly if you know families that attend the school you're most interested in. If possible, have them write or call for you.

Your child will almost surely find a place in a preschool you like, and you will almost surely wonder a year from now what all the fuss was about.

Note: Each spring the 92nd Street Y offers a workshop called "Planning Your Child's Early School Years," conducted by Sally Tannen. The Parents League at 115 East 82nd Street (psadvisory@parentsleague.org) runs one-on-one advisory sessions for school and summer programs; it will give you the names and phone numbers of parents at various preschools who have agreed to talk to interested prospective parents. You can also find this and other information at the website: www.parentsleague.org.

There are a few professionals who specialize in helping parents through the nursery school and (in some cases) the ongoing school process. They will meet with families to discuss their needs and will try to steer them toward schools that will be a good fit. Of course, there are no guarantees for admission. Some recommendations:

* *Nina Bauer, M.A.*
  Ivy Wise Kids
  212-262-4100
  email: info@ivywise.com
  www.ivywise.com
  Ivy Wise Kids helps parents with the admissions process from nursery school to college. Check out their extensive website for some good tips, or call for more information.

* *Private Education Advisory Service (PEAS)*
  917-301-6354; 917-476-9544
  email: info@nypeas.com
  www.nypeas.com
  Jennifer Brozost and Vimmi Shroff have first-hand knowledge of the admission process. They both have master's degrees in education and have worked on the admission teams at the top New York City private schools for the past fifteen years! PEAS helps to guide families through the whole process, from filling out applications to identifying the right school for their child.

maternity clothing

Whatever clothing your lifestyle demands, you can find it in New York's maternity stores. From Veronique Delachaux for sophisticated French clothing, to American Apparel for great comfy basics to office wear at Destination Maternity, or the hippest Madison Avenue has to offer at Rosie Pope, these stores have everything you need to stay comfortable and look great.

We shopped every maternity store in New York and tried on dozens of items. We tested oversize and large-cut non-maternity wear by well-known designers such as Eileen Fisher and Victoria's Secret. We discovered which designers make maternity lines and which stores carry them.

If you're not much of a shopper or if you're sticking to a budget, the Belly Basics Pregnancy Survival Kit can be a staple of your wardrobe from day one of your pregnancy. The kit includes boot-cut leggings, a skirt, a long-sleeved tunic, and a baby-doll dress, all of which are made of cotton and Lycra and come in three colors. You can mix and match the pieces or wear them with non-maternity clothes. Kits are available online at www.bellybasics.com and various stores around NYC; some pieces are sold separately. Pamela bought the leggings when she was pregnant with Benjamin and found them so comfortable she practically lived in them.

This chapter describes the New York maternity scene—its focus, style, quality of merchandise, price range, and level of service. Most of these stores hold their sales in January and July.

shopping tips

Before you shop, here's some advice from two women who have learned a lot by trial and error.

❊ Hold off on buying maternity clothes for as long as you can. Remember, nine months is a long time, and you'll need new and different things as you grow bigger.

❊ In the first and second trimester, shop in regular clothing stores for larger sizes and items with elastic waists. The Gap, Old Navy, and Victoria's Secret often offer inexpensive, machine-washable items with elastic waists. Buy one or two sizes larger than you usually do.

❊ Don't buy shoes in your first trimester; your feet will probably expand. Kelly had to buy two more pairs of shoes in her eighth month because she had only one pair that fit her.

❊ Buy fabrics you are used to and comfortable with. If you never wear polyester or rayon, there's no need to start now. Stick to cotton or other natural fabrics that breathe, such as heavyweight cotton blend suits you can wear when you go to a business meeting or out to dinner.

❊ Buy new bras, pantyhose, and maternity panties. You may go up as many as three cup sizes during your pregnancy, and bras with good support are essential. (Can you imagine going from an A to a D? We can.) Maternity pantyhose by Hue and underwear by Japanese Weekend are two of our favorites.

❊ For the last two months, invest in a maternity support belt, sold at every maternity store. The belt is a large, thick band of elastic that closes with Velcro under your belly to help hold it up. You will be able to walk more comfortably and for longer periods of time.

- A pretty vest is an easy way to dress up an oxford shirt and a skirt or pair of leggings. Kelly loved to wear an oversized black turtleneck with black pants and a bright vest.
- Look in your husband's closet. A man's oxford shirt over a long elasticized skirt or leggings provides comfort and a clean, crisp look. Kelly bought some men's sweaters and shirts during her winter pregnancy—now her husband Carlo wears them.
- Don't be afraid to wear fitted clothes. As more and more fashion models become pregnant, it's become the trend to wear form-fitting tops and dresses! Feel sexy and be pregnant at the same time. Belly Dance Maternity and Capucine specialize in that sophisticated pregnancy look.
- Pregnant women are more fashionable than ever these days. If the thought of traditional maternity clothes makes you shiver, Dynasty Tailors (212-679-1075) can turn your own wardrobe into a maternity wardrobe by adding elastic triangles or panels to any items of your own clothing you wish.

the stores

A Pea in the Pod*

at Macy's at 34th Street
151 Broadway at 34th Street
212-695-4400
www.apeainthepod.com
Return Policy: Exchange and store credit only.
This is a top-of-the-line maternity store. It carries its own exclusive line and also commissions suits, dresses, and weekend wear by a variety of designers. The sales people are helpful and are

Top Eight Alternatives to Maternity Stores

1. Your husband's shirts and sweaters
2. A friend's maternity clothes
3. Eileen Fisher stores
4. Jumpers and waistless dresses in Victoria's Secret catalogs are perfect and affordable, with clothes at $59 or less
5. The Belly Basics Pregnancy Survival Kit
6. Leggings and sweaters
7. Anything from American Apparel
8. Secondhand stores

trained to fit you with the maternity and nursing bras you'll need. Prices run in the $175 to $225 range for most designer pieces. Denim jeans are $175; leggings $15; and bras range from $36 and up.

A Second Chance

1109 Lexington Avenue
bet. 77th and 78th streets, 2nd Floor
212-744-6041
www.asecondchanceresale.com
Return Policy: All sales are final.
A Second Chance offers previously owned clothing for resale. Prices are about one quarter of the cost of a new item, and most of the pieces are in good shape. Although maternity wear is only a small segment of the inventory, the store stocks many basics you might be looking for. A Second Chance is hit or miss, so you'll probably have to go more than once.

American Apparel

See website for multiple locations throughout NYC.

www.americanapparel.net

Return policy: Lenient in store; clothing purchased online cannot be exchanged in stores.

Boy, does Pamela wish this chain had been around when she was pregnant! Rebecca and Benjamin love American Apparel, and after spending much time shopping there, Pamela realized it is the perfect destination for expectant moms. The clothing is monochromatic and mostly unisex, so it is supereasy to mix and match colors and styles. The clothing is cut generously, and their leggings are reasonable and durable. The oversize cardigans are perfect and will last through your whole pregnancy.

Belly Dance Maternity

548 Hudson Street

bet. Charles and Perry streets

212-645-3640

www.bellydancematernity.com

Return policy: Store credit.

This West Village shop carries hip, fashionable maternity clothing. They carry clothing by some of our favorite vendors such as Paige, Michael Stars, and J Brand. Whatever you don't find in the store, you will find on their excellent website.

Capucine

20 Harrison Street

bet. Greenwich and Hudson streets

212-219-4030

www.capucinemaman.com

Return policy: Store credit.

This boutique looks tiny but carries chic maternity clothes with many labels from France. The shop also stocks adorable infant clothing.

Destination Maternity

28 East 57th Street at Park Avenue

212-588-0220

www.destinationmaternity.com

Return policy: Refund with receipt.

Destination Maternity is a mecca for expectant moms. It is a combination store housing two of the most comprehensive maternity stores: A Pea in The Pod and Motherhood Maternity. It also features the maternity spa Edamame and an in-house studio offering a multitude of yoga classes and parent education seminars.

Eileen Fisher

See website for several locations throughout NYC.

www.eileenfisher.com

Return Policy: Money is refunded within two weeks of purchase with a receipt; after two weeks, a store credit is issued.

Eileen Fisher sells a range of wonderful full-cut separates, including elasticized pants with full legs, loose tunic-type sweaters, roomy skirts, vests, and empire-waist dresses. Most of it is machine washable. This is not a maternity store, but the clothing is perfect for your first or second trimester.

H&M

435 Seventh Avenue

bet. 33rd and 34th streets

212-643-6955

150 East 86th Street

bet. Third and Lexington avenues

See website for multiple locations throughout NYC, New Jersey, Conneticutt, and Pennsylvania.

www.hm.com

Return policy: Lenient.

These H&M locations have maternity departments that are worth checking out. H&M carries its own private-label maternity line called MAMA. Maternity styles range from trendy and casual to office attire; prices are moderate.

❈ Motherhood Maternity at Destination Maternity

28 East 57th Street at Park Avenue

212-588-0220; 800-4MOM2BE (catalog)

www.motherhood.com

Return Policy: Store credit only.

Motherhood Maternity has recently changed its line and reduced its prices, and now carries trendy, inexpensive maternity clothes, many of which are 100-percent rayon. Most suits and dresses cost less than $80. Jeans range from $15 to $35; black leggings are $13 and up. Motherhood offers an extensive website that is easy to navigate.

❈ Old Navy

150 West 34th Street at Seventh Avenue

212-594-0049

610 Sixth Avenue at West 18th Street

212-645-0663

www.oldnavy.com

See website for multiple locations throughout NYC, New Jersey, Conneticut, and Pennsylvania.

Return Policy: Lenient.

Besides offering reasonably priced kids clothing, the Old Navy on 34th Street also carries trendy maternity styles at reasonable prices.

❈ Rosie Pope

1265 Madison Avenue at 90th Street

212-608-2036

www.rosiepopematernity.com

Return policy: Store credit.

This gorgeous boutique recently moved uptown and has some of the most beautiful maternity clothing around. Special-occasion dresses are perfect here—with many to choose from starting at under $200. Rosie Pope offers complimentary tailoring on all clothing and will even tailor your maternity clothes to fit once the baby is born.

❈ Topshop

478 Broadway at Broome Street

212-966-9555

www.topshop.com

Return policy: Refund with receipt.

Topshop came to New York City last year with much fanfare. It is a trendy British import featuring this season's best sellers at a fair price. We saw a maternity jersey tube skirt (online) that is fashionable, comfortable, and reasonably priced at only $24.

❈ Veronique Delachaux

1321 Madison Avenue at 93rd Street

212-831-7800

www.veroniquematernity.com

Return Policy: Store credit only.

Veronique Delachaux carries its own chic line of

imported French-designed maternity wear, as well as a wide range of trendy maternity clothing by designers such as Liz Lange, Juicy, Paige, and J Brand. The Parisian-styled clothing give pregnant women a tailored look, focusing on casual business attire: pants, blazers, and tops, with some special-occasion items. The sales staff is knowledgeable and helpful. Prices befit the Madison Avenue location—gorgeous knit dresses start at $300+.

Shopping Online

Nothing beats online shopping for convenience—just one click and you can outfit yourself for the next two trimesters! Here are five of the best online options:

- www.duematernity.com
- www.japaneseweekend.com
- www.bellablumaternity.com
- www.unbuttonedmaternity.com
- www.target.com

Helpful tip: Don't throw out your old maternity clothes. Save them for the next baby, or if you are certain that there are no more babies in your future, check out www.rehashclothes.com, where you can trade in your maternity clothes for post-baby clothing.

baby furniture
and accessories

Walk into any baby furniture store in this city and you'll face a sea of cribs, changing tables, and strollers. A year from now you'll be an expert on all of these items—but, for new moms, some advice is in order. This chapter tells you what you need and why you need it. We worked with the amazingly knowledgeable staff at Albee's (www.albeebaby.com) to help us sort through all of the new products on the market since our last edition. Many of the "best of" opinions are those of the folks at Albee's whom we trust implicitly.

While cost and style will influence your choice of your baby's new stroller, crib, or changing table, New York mothers-to-be must also consider space. Is your apartment a roomy two-bedroom plus dining room, or is it basically a large studio? Portability will also be a consideration. Do you have any idea how hard it is to maneuver a super-deluxe stroller in and out of a city bus or taxi?

Don't run out and buy everything at once. You'll need the crib and stroller immediately, but wait until after the baby is born for the rest. You may receive useful gifts. Also, try to borrow some things, such as bouncy seats and swings. When you are ready to shop, read through our listings. Baby "superstores" carry almost everything you will need; the information here will give you an idea of what you want before you go shopping.

Think about purchasing the Consumer Reports Guide to Baby Products as well. This guide lists basic products by manufacturer and notes the pros and cons of each. While the information can sometimes seem outdated, you will be able to see pictures of some of the products you're interested in.

If you're of a mind and pocketbook to go all out and fix up a splendid room for your little one, New York has decorators and design consultants at your service. Several interior designers who specialize in children's rooms are listed on page 217. They can help with choosing paint colors, wallpaper, and furniture, and can also contribute great space-saving ideas for city apartments. While you're planning the decor, don't forget to make sure everything is baby-safe. Check here for tips and resources.

A few last bits of advice, however. Order your furniture at least twelve weeks before your due date. Kelly ordered her crib well in advance, and Alexander still arrived first. Also, many items can be called in and ordered by phone or through the Internet. It saves time and anything that saves time helps—especially if this is your second or third child. Finally, if you are a second-time parent, be aware that many car seats and toys have been recalled in the past four years. Please call the Consumer Products Safety Commission (800-638-2772) to find out if your old infant car seat is still okay, before you use it.

the necessities
Bassinets

A bassinet is a lovely basket for a newborn to sleep in. It is usually used for about three months. It can be handy if you want your baby to sleep in your bedroom, or if a full-size crib seems too big for that tiny infant. There are a lot of styles—from bassinets with wheels to those that rock and those that lift off the stand—and some come with full bedding ensembles, including linens, coverlets, and fitted sheets. Prices generally range from $89.99 to $500, though you can pay up to $1,000 for a full, top-of-the-line bassinet set. Our favorite is the Monte bassinet, which is well priced yet stylish. The unit collapses for easy storage or travel, and the bassinet linens (available in a variety of different colors and patterns) are removable for washing.

Co-sleepers have gained in reputation and are now a more popular (and less expensive) option than bassinets: A co-sleeper attaches to an adult mattress so your child can be next to you in bed without being in your bed. The most popular model in New York is the Arm's Reach, sold for about $89.99.

Here are some of the popular brands of bassinets in New York:

* *Caribou*
* *First Years*
* *Fisher-Price*
* *Monte*
* *Kolcraft*

Cribs

There are so many choices of styles, colors, and finishes, it can be overwhelming. And, since the first edition of City Baby, new crib manufacturers have entered the marketplace—most of them high-end, offering designs, styles, and colors that reflect trends in the adult market. You can find cribs in sleigh-bed styles and distressed wood finishes, in traditional styles or sleek, modern designs, but in almost all cases, the choices you're making are purely aesthetic. Don't worry, however—there's no need to be concerned about safety issues. All cribs sold today are certified by the Juvenile Products Manufacturers Association (JPMA), which develops standards for many baby products, including

strollers/carriages, high chairs, and playpens. JPMA safety specifications require that the space between crib bars is no more than two and three-eighths inches apart.

The following list includes some of the most modern and trendy cribs on the market, some of which can be found at the largest stores, and others that can only be found at exclusive boutiques like Giggle (www.giggle.com).

* Cribs by the Netto Collection, which can be found at www.nettocollection.com.
* Cribs by designer Roberto Gil (the Offi Bebe Crib) can be found at www.modernseed.com.
* The Ouef crib, designed by a Brooklyn mother of two, is a gorgeous crib that converts to a toddler bed; www.ouef.com or 718-965-1216.
* IKEA even makes a very sleek and very affordable crib; www.ikea.com.

Here are the questions to ask when you shop for a crib:

* Do the crib's sides raise and lower? Some of these types of cribs have been recalled.
* Does the mattress raise and lower to make for easy access to the baby?
* Is the crib stable when you shake it? A loose crib frame or the sound of metal knocking against metal might indicate faulty construction or assembly.
* Does the crib include stabilizer bars, metal rods fastened to the end boards and located underneath the crib? These bars provide additional stabilization and protection for baby.

- Do the wheels have locks to prevent the crib from "walking"?
- Can the crib be converted into a youth bed (is one side completely removable)?

Just as this edition was going to press, there was a large recall of drop-side cribs, and there has been talk of manufacturers discontinuing this style. Please check with Consumer Reports (consumerreports.org) and the Juvenile Products Manufacturers Association (jpma.org) before making your purchase.

The crib you bring home should have a mattress that fits snugly (a gap of no more than one and a half inches between the mattress and the crib's sides and ends). Bumpers should be securely tied on with at least six ties or snaps. (Bumpers do not have to be used in the crib. Talk to your pediatrician about risks associated with bumpers.) Keep the crib clear of any items—mobiles, clothing, and toys—that have strings longer than seven inches. Don't set up the crib near any potential hazards in the room, such as a heater, window, or cords from blinds.

In the next column, you will find the the crib manufacturers whose products are widely available in the New York area. The choice comes down to what you like and what you can afford. Shop around: prices range from less than $200 for a Costco to more than $900 for a Bellini. (At Little Stars, we saw a line of sleek metal cribs from Bratt Decor that started at $1,000!) Ask whether the store delivers and what they charge for this service, and confirm they will assemble the crib in your home. They should.

- AP Industries
- Argington
- Bassett
- Bellini
- Bonavita
- Bratt Decor
- Costco
- Delta
- Ducduc
- Dutailier
- Legacy
- Million Dollar Baby
- Netto
- Nurseryworks
- Oeuf
- Pali
- Romina
- Stokke

Changing Tables

Parents today tend to purchase contoured pads that attach to the top of a dresser to use as a changing table. This is inexpensive and practical, with most pads costing between $19.99 and $60. Some dressers, like the Argington, come with a removable tray built into the top.

Conventional changing tables have a little pad with a small guardrail that goes all the way around the top (picture a rectangle) so your baby can't roll off. There are shelves underneath for storing diapers and wipes. However, you should never leave a baby unattended, no matter how secure your baby might seem. Popular brands for these tables include Argington, Pali, Stokke, and Sorelle, and prices are $179 and up. Most crib manufacturers also carry coordinating changing tables as part of nursery suites that also include chests and cribs. These fancier tables generally cost between $100 and $200.

Gliders

A glider or some type of nursery chair is optional, but if you have the space and the money, you may find having one helpful when you're feeding your baby or trying to get him to sleep. Dutailier gliders retail for about $399 and are practical for New York apartments. The popular sleigh glider is very compact. It comes in your choice of white or wood finishes, with different fabric patterns for the cushions. Matching ottomans are also available. A stylish and cool alternative to the glider is the upholstered nursery chair, which reclines nearly to a bed so parents can nap in the baby's room. Some popular brands are Shermag, Little Castle, and Monte Designs. These chairs range from a low-end $199 to nearly $1,000 for a custom make and model. Albee's and other baby superstores will custom-make a glider or nursery chair cover to match your decor. But beware: Alexander got trained to fall asleep while being rocked; as he got older, he expected to be rocked whenever he woke during the night. Angela did not have a glider in her room for this reason and was a better sleeper from day one.

Carriages/Strollers

Newborns and toddlers alike spend many hours in the stroller going to the park, the supermarket, or window-shopping along the avenues. New York is a walking town, and your stroller is the equivalent of a suburban minivan. Whether you choose a carriage (a bassinet like construction on wheels) or a stroller (easily collapsible) depends on your personal needs. While suburban mothers and fathers may be content with an inexpensive umbrella stroller that spends most of its time in the trunk of a car, city parents know a sturdy carriage is a must-have for babies and toddlers, especially since we use it to carry the groceries home, too.

All strollers sold today are safe (the JPMA sees to that), but not every type may be right for you. Consider what time of year your baby is due before you purchase your carriage or stroller. For winter babies, a carriage with a boot (an enclosed end) might be the best bet to keep your infant warm. For summer babies, look for a carriage with good ventilation and a sunshade. Also consider where you live. If your building has a doorman, you can usually get some help carrying a heavier stroller up the stairs and inside. If you're in a walk-up or non-doorman building, look for one that's light and portable, and practice folding it to get it down to a quick routine; you're going to be wrestling that stroller in and out of buses and cabs for a good couple of years.

Other desirable features include a stroller seat that reclines (a must for newborn to three-month-olds), plenty of storage space underneath, brakes on all four wheels, and a handle that reverses to allow the baby to face you or to face out. One of the best innovations is the popular stroller/car seat combination. This is an infant car seat that straps and snaps into a stroller base. New moms swear by this for taxi travel and city walking. Popular models include the Snap 'N' Go by Baby Trend, Century 4-in-1 Plus by Century and the Kolcraft Secura Travel System by Kolcraft. The Snap 'N' Go is by far the most popular model, with prices ranging from $100 to $180.

For umbrella strollers, the English-made Maclarens consistently have the lowest rate of returns or repairs of umbrella strollers and have withstood the test of time for parents who reuse them with their second child. It retails for $170 to $300, depending on the model.

All-terrain strollers are also very popular with parents who exercise with their babies, or who like the three-wheeled stroller look and durability. Some of the most popular brands are Mountain Buggy, Valco, Bumbleride, and City Mini (Albee's favorite!). A marathon runner we know used one of these to run with his daughter for years. For parents of twins or two small children, side-by-side or tandem strollers might be good options. Side-by-sides are great for twins or children close to the same weight, while tandem strollers are great for kids of different sizes—with larger kids in front, and smaller in back. With the explosion of multiples in New York, this is a category with lots of great options. Some of the popular double-stroller brands are the City Mini, Phil & Teds, and the I Candy.

When preparing to buy, tell the store clerk how you plan to use the carriage, and ask for a recommendation. Take the carriage for a "test drive" in the store to see whether it feels comfortable for you and your partner; check the height of the handles or bar, and make sure neither of you has to hunch over to reach it comfortably.

It is difficult to discuss strollers in New York without using the word *Bugaboo*. The Bugaboo has truly revolutionized the stroller category, turning it from practical to cool overnight. The Bugaboo is a convertible-type stroller that comes outfitted with a car seat option, and many bells and whistles. Bugaboo's are quite pricey (many are over $900) and are the status stroller, with Uppa and City Mini nipping at its heels. Type the word *Bugaboo* onto the urban-baby.com message board, and you will get a variety of strong opinions—from moms singing the stroller's praises and forming "Bugaboo groups" to moms abhorring the stroller and all that it means vis-à-vis perception and status. That being said: this is an awesome-looking stroller, very stylish, and probably the most popular stroller brand in Manhattan.

Here is a list of popular brands sold in New York:

- *Baby Jogger*
- *Bugaboo*
- *Bumbleride*
- *Chicco*
- *City Mini*
- *Combi*
- *Cybex*
- *Graco*
- *ICandy (the best-looking stroller on the lot in awesome colors)*
- *Inglesina*
- *Kolcraft*
- *Maclaren*
- *Mountain Buggy*
- *Orbit (travel-system stroller sold with car seat)*
- *Peg Perego*

- *Phil & Teds*
- *Quinny*
- *Stokke*
- *Teutonia (build your stroller to your specifications—pretty cool)*
- *Uppa*

The must-have accessory for any New York City parent with a stroller is the "foot muff," because in NYC, our strollers function as our cars and the foot muff keeps the baby warm and dry inside the stroller. The most popular brand is the JJ Cole Bundle Me, but there are others, such as Toastie Toddlers. Many of the stroller companies (Bugaboo, Maclaren, Baby Jogger) make their own foot muffs, which coordinate with their strollers.

Also, be sure to think of crafty ways to store your stroller in your newly crowded apartment. Check out StrollAway, an over-the-door solution made of steel that hangs neatly out of site (www.metrototots.com).

Car Seats

Even if you don't have a car, you must have a car seat. State law dictates that your newborn must leave the hospital in one, and while you could borrow a seat from a friend, purchasing your own will be a practical investment. If you want to hold off until after your baby is home, check out Kid Car New York (212-862-SAFE, www.kidcarny.com) for a great car-seat option. If you register for the pre-equipped car-seat car service before giving birth, your ride home from the hospital is free!

State law also dictates that babies must always ride in a car seat whenever in an automobile, not just when coming home from the hospital. City taxis must come equipped with rear seat belts to attach over the car seat, so double check before you get into a cab. If you have any questions, call the New York Coalition for Transportation Safety at 516-571-5032. That said, it's very difficult to carry both a car seat and a stroller around with you. Hence, the stroller/car seat combinations, with the removable infant car seats that strap and snap into a base. Prices for this great alternative range from $100 to $180. Some city parents just use a baby carrier for infants, and hold toddlers on their laps.

The more ungainly convertible seats can be used from birth through the toddler years and have a reclining mechanism so they are rear-facing for infants and forward for toddlers and young children. With more features and an advanced five-point tethering system, the Britax Roundabout ($200) is one of the most popular models on the market right now, along with the Graco Infant Safe seat ($109.99).

Visit www.thecarseatlady.com for accurate, up-to-date information from NHTSA-Certified Child Passenger Safety technicians and instructors about how to keep your most precious cargo safe.

Three designs of restraining straps or harnesses are available in car seats: the five-point harness, the T-shield, and the bar shield. Most experts agree that the five-point harness is the safest, but all three are sound options. The five-point harness is also the most time-consuming to put on and off, which can be annoying to impatient toddlers. The newest restraining system is called the "universal latch system." Our experts tell us that this is the new gold standard, and is good for kids up to 80 pounds! All of this will make sense once you see them in the stores.

Though convertible seats can be used from

birth, experts advise you to buy an infant-carrier car seat for babies from birth up to twenty pounds (these range in price from $99 to over $200), and the convertible car seat when the child weighs more. Infant car seats are smaller, recline better, often come with a sunshade, and are more heavily padded than the convertible. They're portable and can easily be carried in and out of the car without disturbing a sleeping baby. Remember that these seats must be rear-facing in your vehicle; toddler seats forward-facing.

Booster seats and high-back boosters are designed for kids over forty pounds—too big for convertible seats, but still too small for regular seat-belts. They have a raised, rigid base that allows children to use adult belts. Prices range from around $49.99 to $119.99.

Many new parents are concerned that their car seat is not installed properly (and for good reason, because this is often the case). The National Highway Traffic Safety Administration provides a service through www.seatcheck.org that will check that your seat has been installed correctly. For those of you who live outside of the city, or who have relatives that do, local suburban police and fire stations will also do the car-seat checks at no cost. Some of the Manhattan smaller DMV offices will also perform checks; call ahead or check online at www.nydmv.state.ny.us.

The best-selling infant car seats are:

- *Britax*
- *Chicco*
- *Combi*
- *The First Years*
- *Graco (most popular)*
- *Maxi-cosi*
- *Peg Perego*
- *Sunshine Kids*
  (converts from infant to toddler seat)

One of the best inventions we have seen since our kids were babies is the Nomie car-seat cover. This adorable, comfy car-seat cover comes off easily when it's time to be washed. Until you've seen how sticky and messy your car seat can get, you have no idea how revolutionary this product is. Go to www.nomiebaby.com to purchase online, or see which stores in your area carry them.

Baby Swings

A swing might be your lifesaver during your baby's first few months—or maybe not. This is something your child either loves or hates. (Rebecca hated it, but Alexander loved it and never made a peep when he was in it.) We recommend you borrow one from a friend or relative before making the investment. Graco, Fisher-Price, Carter's, and Costco are some of the companies that make baby swings. Prices range from $49.99 for a Costco to $129.99 for a top-of-the-line Graco.

Bouncy Seats

The bouncy seat is another potential lifesaver; in fact, we know women who would not have been able to shower for six months had they not made this investment. It's portable; you can move it from the living room to the kitchen to the bathroom so you can always see your baby and he can always see you. Plus, the newest bouncy seats are more plush than ever and have a vibrating feature that can lull a fussy baby right to sleep. (Another new innovation we don't know how we lived without!) The bouncy seat is great for feeding your baby when he's starting to eat solid food but is still too small for a high chair. Some of the funkiest bouncy seats we have seen come from Bloom. These are pricey ($199) but are fabulous looking, modern, and look truly comfy. On the less-expensive side is the ever-popular bouncy seat from Fisher-Price, which starts at $39.99. The newest brand to look out for is the Nap Nanny, which provides a quiet place for the baby to sleep.

Best-selling Bouncers:

❊ *Bloom*
❊ *Combi*
❊ *Fisher-Price*
❊ *Inglesina*
❊ *Summer*
❊ *Svan*

High Chairs

When you are buying a high chair, it is advisable to:

1. Buy a chair with a wide base to limit the chances of the chair tipping over.
2. Find a chair with a one-hand tray-release mechanism, which makes it easier to take your baby in and out.
3. Look for a wrap-around tray—easier to eat from and keep clean.
4. Find a chair with a detachable seat cushion. These chairs become dirty easily and you will want it to last more than a year.

Most high-chair accidents occur (usually with children under one year) when a child has not been strapped in properly and tumbles out. Don't rely on the chair's tray to keep your baby enclosed; use the safety belt and never leave your baby unattended.

Before buying a high chair, decide if you want wood or metal and vinyl. Wooden high chairs are beautiful, but they don't collapse—so they are not ideal for those with limited apartment space. Also they require the use of both hands to take the tray off. Some models require you to flip the tray over the baby's head. If you're not careful, this can be a dangerous maneuver.

Right now, the most popular and functional high chairs on the market are perfect for New York City apartments. They fold easily and can be put away and stored when you need more space. Some of the popular styles are Anka, Bloom Nano (these are gorgeous and modern), Inglesina M'Home, and Valco Baby (an Albee Baby personal recommendation).

Our favorite high chair on the market is the Peg Perego Prima Pappa (starting at $200)—with seven height adjustments and four recline positions, a thickly padded seat, a wrap-around tray, and a wide-wheeled base, this high chair is ideal. High-chair prices start at around $79 for a Graco.

First Years' Reclining Three Stage Feeding Seat is a great alternative to a high chair because, like a booster seat, it straps onto a regular chair (at $30, it's also an inexpensive alternative). This seat has three recline positions for each stage of early childhood: newborn, infant, and toddler. To adjust, you simply press two buttons and slide the seat. This product is ideal for traveling, as well as smaller apartments where space is limited.

Finally, we must repeat: Never leave your baby unattended (without being strapped) in a high chair, even for a few seconds!

Here are some of the best and most popular brands:

- Anka
- Bloom
- Chicco
- Graco
- Peg Perego
- Stokke
- Svan

Booster Seats/Hook-On Seats

You may want to buy a portable chair to use when you take your baby or toddler to a restaurant or other place where no high chair is available.

Hook-on seats have a short life. (Rebecca couldn't sit comfortably in one after she was nine months old.) Also, if the seat is hooked incorrectly onto the table, or if the child can detach the seat from under the table with his foot, these seats can cause accidents. If you do use a hook-on seat, always place a chair under it. Manufacturers include Graco, Chicco, Mutsy, and Phil & Teds (great looking and quite popular) with prices starting at $49.99+, but Consumer Reports does not recommend using hook-on seats at all; the hazards are just too serious.

We have found booster seats to be safer and more practical than hook-ons. They can be used for children up to preschool age, and our favorite, the Safety 1st ($30), can be easily folded. Put this on a chair in your kitchen and you may be able to live without an expensive high chair! Other popular brands include First Years, and Summer, with prices $25+.

Playpens/Portable Cribs

Playpens are a great place to park your baby when you need five minutes to yourself to shower, answer the door, talk on the phone, or make dinner. Some babies might amuse themselves in the playpen for up to thirty minutes at a time, but not all children like them. Kelly used a playpen for months with Alexander and yet Angela wouldn't stay ten minutes without screaming her head off. Playpens are also big and difficult to store and transport, so you might want to go for the portable crib instead. It can function as a playpen, but it's smaller and can easily be put away. Portable cribs have a thin mattress and sheets, so they can be used as a crib when you're traveling. Many of the playpens and cribs are fundamentally the same, but each brand offers different additional features. When shopping for a playpen, be sure to compare different brands to find the best features for your specific needs. Prices range from $69.99+ for the Graco Pack 'n Play, to $175 for Arm's Reach Concepts' dual playpen/bassinet. Popular brands include:

- Arm's Reach Concepts
- Chicco
- Combi
- Graco Pack 'n Play*

Bathtubs/Bath Seats

At first, bathe your tiny baby in the kitchen or bathroom sink. When he's a little bigger and you'd prefer to use the bathtub, you may want to buy a special baby tub that fits into the big tub. Most baby tubs are similar; they come either with or without a sponge insert, some also have a handy built-in hammock. The sponge tends to get a mildew odor, is hard to wring out, and takes days to dry—so we opt for without. The two bathtub brands that are most widely available are Summer and Fisher-Price. All of the tubs function quite similarly, and range in price from $17.99 to $29.99.

When your baby is old enough to sit up on his own, he's ready for a bath seat. The Aqua Baby bath seat ($24.99) is a ring that attaches to your bathtub with suction cups. It is roomy enough to hold a two-year-old. We have both been happy with Safety 1st. Once she can sit up on her own, your baby will also enjoy the inflatable Ocean Friends Snug Tub ($19.99). It looks like a mini pool and is lots of fun for older babies (over six months).

Baby Carriers

You see these pouchlike, soft cloth carriers strapped onto the fronts of mothers and fathers everywhere. They're often referred to as "bjorns" or "slings" for the companies that invented them. Baby Bjorn has traditionally been the most popular of the infant carriers. A friend gave Pamela her old Baby Bjorn when Benjamin was born, and she used it every day.

This is typically an item that you'll use for only a short time. Kelly purchased one and then had a nine-and-a-half pound baby who quickly became too heavy to carry strapped onto her shoulders. Try to borrow one from a friend and test it with your baby before purchasing to see if you're comfortable with it. Baby carriers are popular with second- or third-time moms who might have a stroller to push or other hands to hold.

Prices range from $64.99 for the best-selling Baby Bjorn to more expensive Bjorn models at $129. Another popular brand of infant carrier is Ergo Baby which ranges in price $100 and up. Phil & Teds also makes a nice-looking carrier for $79.

Baby Slings are a great way to carry your baby as it permits you to hold your baby horizontally as well as vertically (allowing baby to sleep more comfortably). My Baby Nest Baby Carrier is another great product. It is wonderful for breastfeeding because you simply pull the fabric up over baby's head and you are guarded from exposure. Balboa also makes a wonderful nursing cover and baby carrier, which comes in gorgeous patterns and colors and is a must for every nursing mother.

Backpacks

Women who use backpacks swear by them for comfort and convenience. Your baby is ready for a backpack once she can sit up on her own. Borrow one from a friend, and try it out with your baby on board before you decide to purchase your own.

The most popular brand is the Kelty backpack, which is strong and durable. Kelty is well known for its outdoor equipment and this product is just as heavy-duty. It costs slightly less than the other brands (about $79) but will last forever.

Ergo Baby and Phil & Teds also make dependable backpacks starting at about $129.

Baby Monitors

Here's how to be in one room and hear your baby crying in another. These gadgets give you plenty of different options. Some monitors are battery-operated and can be carried throughout the apartment. It is difficult to say which brand is the most functional because of varying frequencies in different areas. Baby monitors range in price and can be found for as low at $25 for the simplest model to over $200 for one with a handheld portable video camera. The most secure method in buying the right monitor is to ask other parents in your neighborhood or building, which monitors works best for them. Many New York buildings pick up "noise" from other apartments. You may hear another baby crying and think it's your own. Here are some of the most recent and popular additions to the monitor category:

※ *2.4 GHz monitors:* These offer greater range and clarity than earlier models. Options include First Years, Safety First, and Graco.

※ *Monitors with two receivers:* These are great and functional for larger living spaces because you can leave monitors in separate rooms. Graco makes a most-popular model, and both Summer and Avent have many options, too.

※ *Rechargeable Monitors:* Available from Safety First and Avent, these work much like your portable or cellular phone, except it is a direct line to your little darling.

Summer makes a few different monitors that have audio, video, and movement-detection capabil-ities. This includes an ultra-sensitive sensor pad that is placed under the baby's mattress. If the pad does not sense motion, including heartbeat and breath, for twenty seconds, an alarm sounds to alert you. It costs $189+. Beware: this can drive you crazy and keep you up at night, even when your baby is asleep.

You may have to try out a few different monitors before you settle on one product—sometimes you pick up your neighbors' conversations instead of the baby's cries.

Diaper Bags

Diaper bags used to come in two basic styles: over-the-shoulder, which zips or snaps closed, and the backpack with a drawstring opening. Along came Skip Hop a few years back and revolutionized the diaper bag category. The creators of Skip Hop came up with the brilliant idea of creating a diaper bag that would attach directly to the stroller. This eliminates having to actually carry your bag, or having to drape it over the stroller only to have it slip down a million times. Skip Hop bags are not only reasonably priced ($54 and up), they also come in every pattern and color imaginable.

Whatever diaper bag style or brand you choose, you won't believe how much stuff you have to carry for your baby. Find a roomy bag with lot of pockets (for bottles, wipes and the like) and a plas-tic lining. A changing pad is another great feature. The superstores have terrific selections. JJ Cole makes funky diaper bags starting at $59 with bright patterns and colors that are fashionable and func-tional. Peg Perego, Bugaboo, and Phil & Teds make patterns that match their carriages. Chic designers like Kenneth Cole, Donna Karan, and Kate Spade have also gotten into the act with stylish, subdued bags (mostly in basic black), available at Bellini and other upscale stores. Prices range from $39 for a Carter's diaper bag to over $300 for an Elizabeth StorkSak. Baby Bjorn and Evenflo make popular backpacks that don't even look like diaper bags.

This is another category that keeps getting better and better. Some of the newest diaper bags are trendy, functional, and great looking, too. A few other brands that are all the rage are bags by Pack Happy, Petunia Pickle Bottom, and Fleurville. A diaper bag just for dad is by Diaper Dudes and is cool enough looking for hip dads to carry around the city.

City Baby surveyed new moms attending the New York Presbyterian Hospital new mom's group to find out the baby products they couldn't live without and the best baby gifts they received. Here are the results:

- ❋ *Best baby gift:* Anything personalized, especially cashmere blankets

- ❋ *Can't live without for a newborn:* a bouncy seat

- ❋ *Favorite book to read:* Good Night Moon

- ❋ *Must-have product:* a baby swing

- ❋ *Most frequented shop for baby clothing:* BabyGap

- ❋ *Most popular stroller (by a large margin):* Bugaboo, followed by Snap 'n Go

the stores

Our baby superstores are not necessarily large in size, but we consider them super because they provide one-stop shopping. You can buy all the furniture you need (crib, changing table, dresser), as well as sheets, towels, diapers, nipples, bottles, layettes or clothing for newborns, strollers/carriages, high chairs, playpens, baby carriers/backpacks, and much, much more. You get the idea. We like them because they make your life easy. Most sell toys, too, but be aware that the selection is limited and the prices are often higher than at Toys "R" Us or other toy stores.

Some stores are ritzier than others, some more value oriented. The proximity of the store to your home should help you decide where to shop. Many expectant moms in New York visit too many stores in their quest for the perfect crib, sheets, and towels. You don't have to! Find a place that's convenient, and use it for all your needs. Patronize one store consistently, so the staff gets to know you and will go that extra mile when necessary. Also, buy in bulk. Many stores never "officially" discount, but may give you a better price if you are placing a large order. Don't be afraid to ask. And there's no harm in asking if they'll match a better price that you have seen somewhere else.

Also check out the store's delivery policy. Policies vary widely.

Superstores

- ❋ *Albee Baby**
  715 Amsterdam Avenue at 95th Street
  212-662-7337
  email: info@albeebaby.com
  www.albeebaby.com

Return Policy: Refunds with receipt.

Albee's is not glamorous—fluorescent lighting, no carpeting, and lots of chaos gives you an idea of the atmosphere—but we love it. Albee's has been around forever and the staff is friendly, knowledgeable, and down-to-earth. The store is packed full of just about everything your baby could ever need. We also appreciate their honesty. Pamela was talked out of purchasing a slew of newborn sleepers that one of the managers said the baby would outgrow in a month. (And, she was right!) Prices here are the best in the city on many items including high chairs, playpens, and strollers. Yet it's not for the faint of heart. Albee's is always busy and so fully stocked that you have to navigate carefully. It carries many brands of baby furniture and all the carriage/stroller brands. What it doesn't have in stock can be ordered for you. Albee's also sells clothing, bedding, nipples, bottles, bottle racks, carriage accessories, tapes, videos, books, bibs, cloth diapers, and diaper bags, but not formula. There is a baby registry—great for people looking to purchase gifts for a new mom.

Baby Depot

707 Sixth Avenue at 23rd Street
212-229-1300
www.babydepot.com
Return Policy: Store credit only.

Baby Depot is part of Burlington Coat Factory, a huge store at 23rd Street and Sixth Avenue. This neat and brightly lit department carries everything you'll want, including cribs, high chairs, strollers, clothes, and accessories. The prices are very good. Baby Depot carries a large selection of cribs and strollers. There is a nice selection of books and videos for babies and toddlers as well as all the nipples and bottles, bibs, cups, and spoons you could ask for. Its layette and clothing selection is great (it carries maternity clothing, too) and it has good prices on Carter's. It's best to know what you're looking for when shopping at Baby Depot, because the service can be hit or miss. Still, it's worth the trip—the prices are some of the best in town.

The Baby Show NYC

212-242-1213
email: info@thebabyshownyc.com
www.thebabyshownyc.com

Metropolitan Pavillion Events hosts a two-day showcase of the best products, speakers, information, and resources in the industry with over 50+ top-notch exhibitors.

Buy Buy Baby

270 Seventh Avenue
bet. 25th and 26th streets
917-344-1555
www.buybuybaby.com
Return Policy: Refund with receipt.

Buy Buy Baby typically is at the top of the list for new parents looking to augment their baby supplies. Buy Buy Baby offers everything from baby furniture, clothing for newborns to toddlers, and accessories, including toys, books, CDs, audio and video tapes, stuffed animals, infant seats, bassinets, playpens, high chairs, car seats, and more. Buy Buy Baby is also a great place to stock up on formula, diapers, wipes, and related items.

There are many other stores in the U.S., so it is a good place to register so that out-of-town relatives can see what you really need for your new baby. Their website is also extensive and easy to use for online shopping.

✽ Planet Kids

247 East 86th Street
bet. Second and Third avenues
212-426-2040
191 Amsterdam Avenue at 69th Street
212-362-3931
www.planetkidsny.com
Return Policy: Return within seven days, exchange within twelve; after twelve days, store credit only.

These bright, spacious stores contain everything your child needs. There are three floors filled with clothes, cribs, changing tables, car seats, strollers, and huge, colorful displays of toys and accessories. Planet Kids sells a wide range of cribs including some that are quite modern with brands like Stokke, Offi, and Oeuf. Strollers on offer at Planet Kids include all of the major brands such as Bugaboo, Uppa, Stokke, and Graco.

✽ Schneider's

41 West 25th Street
bet. Broadway and Sixth Avenue
212-228-3540
www.schneidersbaby.com
Return Policy: No refund. Store credit or exchange with receipt on new merchandise in original package, within twenty days.

Schneider's is a neighborhood store that's been serving the downtown crowd for over fifty years. This store carries nearly every brand available in strollers, cribs, gliders, high chairs, and more. They also have an excellent staff and a great registry. This well-stocked store carries a full line of accessories but no clothing.

✽ Toys "R" Us

1514 Broadway at West 44th Street
646-366-8858
www.toysrus.com
Return Policy: Refund with receipt, otherwise store credit only.

We love Toys "R" Us. It sells furniture and accessories at the best prices in town. You'll find cribs for under $200, strollers, high chairs, playpens, bottles, bibs, and waterproof bed pads, as well as diapers and formula (available by the case). While Toys "R" Us favors the mass-market labels, you can find some of the better brands such as Peg Perego and Graco, plus Costco, Evenflo, Kolcraft, and Fisher-Price. Weekdays and evenings are your best bet for shopping; these stores are mobbed on the weekends. Delivery service is available; prices depend on the size of the items to be shipped.

Specialty Stores

✽ ABC Carpet & Home

888 Broadway at 19th Street
212-473-3000
www.abchome.com
Return Policy: Refund with receipt, otherwise store credit only.

Style-conscious parents need not worry about

outfitting their little one's room. ABC Carpet & Home stocks a small but carefully chosen selection of nursery furnishings in keeping with its antique and country chic theme. The look here is sophisticated rustic, evoking the nineteenth century. You'll find everything from Victorian-inspired cast iron cribs and cradles to fashionably distressed decorative accessories. In addition to home furnishings, there is an impressive selection of high-quality baby and toddler clothing, a huge range of plush and classic toys, and children's books and stationery. This is an excellent spot to pick up gifts.

❖ Bellini

1305 Second Avenue
bet. 68th and 69th streets
212-517-9233
www.bellini.com
Return Policy: Store credit.
Customers who shop here rave about the top-of-the-line furniture and service at this Tiffany's of baby stores. The store is beautiful, with bright, muraled walls and the longest list of baby necessities we've ever seen! The staff will spend hours helping you select the perfect crib, (this is the only place in town to find a Bellini crib), and coordinating furniture, bedding, and accessories. It custom-makes bedding sets and has a library of fabrics you can choose from. Special knit items like sweaters and christening outfits are exquisite. Kelly got a wonderfully trimmed receiving blanket from Bellini with a matching diaper and bib. It says it will match prices if it can verify what another store charges.

❖ Blue Bench

979 Third Avenue at East 58th Street,
Suite 1600
212-644-6097; 212-267-1500
www.bluebenchnyc.com
Return Policy: Store credit only.
The Tribeca location closed, but fortunately Blue Bench has relocated to the D & D building. It is both open to the trade and to customers by appointment. Blue Bench features exquisite solid-wood pieces such as cribs, rocking chairs, bureaus, and desks. Most items are fashionably distressed with an heirloom quality about them. Blue Bench carries toys, books, and stuffed animals as well. Susan, one of the founders, provides a full interior decorating service, and will come to your home to take pictures and measurements to help you choose everything from colors to fabric, rugs, and curtains. The rooms are classic, making them a one-time investment.

❖ Giggle

120 Wooster Street
bet. Prince and Spring streets
212-334-5817
1033 Lexington Avenue at 74th Street
212-249-4249
www.giggle.com
Return Policy: Store credit only.
Giggle is a fabulous boutique with locations in Soho and on the Upper East Side. Shopping here is a pleasure; the accessories and furniture are beautifully displayed and easy to navigate. Specializing in all that is new, trendy, and modern, with a few of the classics, Giggle fits in per-

fectly with the upscale neighborhoods in which it resides. Prices here are high, but so are the quality and the service. The bedding here is beautiful and unique and the stores stock some crib and furniture brands that we have never seen in NYC.

Karin Alexis

490 Amsterdam Avenue
bet. 83rd and 84th streets
212-769-9550
www.karinalexis.com
Return Policy: Store credit or exchange.
An eclectic shop replacing a furniture store reflects the Upper West Side's practical, yet funky sensibility. Karin is the owner and operator of this shop specializing in clothing, accessories, and gifts for children newborn and up. She designs many of the items in her store, and they are usually boldly patterned and brightly colored. This is also a great spot for baby gifts and accessories.

Kid's Supply Co.

1343 Madison Avenue at 94th Street
212-426-1200
www.kidssupplyco.com
Return Policy: Quite restrictive; call store
for details.
Kid's Supply Co. is a small, high-end store brimming with an eclectic mix of timeless, sophisticated furniture, and unusual accessories. Befitting its tony neighborhood, Kid's Supply is quite pricey, and designs and manufactures its own line of high-quality goods. The staff will work closely with you to create the room of

your dreams. Beds convert from bunk beds to twins, and they come as day beds and trundle beds. They can be custom-finished, too. Cribs and changing tables, which convert into dressers, are available as well. Linens can be customized, and it has an especially wide selection of boys' bedding.

Pamela Scurry's Wicker Garden

1300 Madison Avenue at 92nd Street,
2nd Floor
212-410-7001
Return Policy: Store credit only.
This top-of-the-line boutique is exquisite, and the baby furniture, much of which is hand-painted, is some of the loveliest (and most expensive) in town. You'll find finishing touches, such as coordinating wastepaper baskets, diaper pails, chests, and changing tables to match a crib. It has books of linens to choose from, will custom-make anything, and carries top brands such as Blauen. This is the place for beautiful children's clothes and hand-painted furniture when you choose to go first class.

Pottery Barn Kids

1311 Second Avenue at 69th Street
212-879-4746
www.potterybarnkids.com
Return Policy: Refund with receipt.
Pamela has shopped at Pottery Barn online for years, so when an actual PB Kids store opened in Manhattan we were very excited. We have since purchased our children's beds and dressers from here, and wish we had another baby on the horizon to redecorate the nursery, too. The store is

Ten Tips for a Baby's Room

1. Good overhead lighting is key for convenience and safety.
2. A humidifier can be important in overheated New York apartments.
3. Have as many dressers, drawers, or shelves as possible—you'll need them.
4. Design the closet in the baby's room to allow for more toy than clothing space; baby clothes are tiny.
5. Baby-proof the room.
6. Have some toys placed within your baby's reach.
7. A glider or rocker can save the day (or night).
8. Curtains or shades help baby sleep.
9. If possible, leave a play space in the middle of the room.
10. Keep it simple—a busy or over-decorated room gets old quickly.

terrific, with a wide range of price points from the very reasonable to the pricey. It is easily shoppable, and it has become a destination for East Side moms, too. The store offers a scheduled story time, a play area, and more.

Room and Board

105 Wooster Street
bet. Prince and Spring streets
212-334-4343
www.roomandboard.com
Return Policy: Full refund or store credit.
Room and Board is a great four-story furniture store located in Soho. It offers functional yet stylish furniture for every room in your home. It also offers unique options for the nursery and kids' rooms. Selections include cribs, gliders, mini tables and chairs, even bedding.

The Upper Breast Side

220 West 71st Street, Suite 1
bet. Broadway and West End Avenue
212-873-2653
www.upperbreastside.com
Return Policy: Exchange only within two weeks of purchase.
This boutique for breastfeeding moms is all the rage with Upper West Siders. This is a one-of-a-kind place offering every accoutrement for breastfeeding, from bras and breast pumps to nursing pillows and more. The owner is extremely knowledgeable and committed to finding the best products for nursing. She also carries some baby accessories.

Yummy Mummy

1201 Lexington Avenue
bet. 81st and 82nd streets
212-879-8669
www.yummymummystore.com
Return Policy: Refund with receipt; store credit after 14 days.
Once you get past the cringe-inducing name, you will find a store packed with all of the supplies a new nursing mother needs. The store sells everything from bras and clothing to breast pumps and offers classes and seminars, too. The staff is helpful and advises solutions to nursing issues. The store also has a great educational video section.

Furniture, Clothing, and Donations

You will see how quickly your child outgrows everything from bassinet to rocking chairs, cribs, and clothing. Two terrific outlets to donate your gently used gear are:

❖ *Baby Buggy*

212-736-1777

www.babybuggy.com

Baby Buggy, a nonprofit organization founded by Jessica Seinfeld in 2001, is dedicated to collecting and distributing gently used and new gear, clothing, and products for infants and young children in need throughout the five boroughs of New York City. Since 2001, Baby Buggy has given hundreds of thousands of essential items to thousands of families through its network of qualified social service partners. Check its website for information about donating items.

❖ *Room to Grow*

54 West 21st Street, Suite 401

212-620-7800

www.roomtogrow.org

Started in 1988 by Julie Burns, Room to Grow is a nonprofit organization providing low-income parents with clothing, books, toys, and other baby essentials from birth to three years old. Room to Grow gladly accepts new and nearly new items.

Interior Design and Decoration

Ready to get creative? The following New York stores sell children's wallpaper and accessories to help you pull together your baby's room. Many have in-store consultants with experience or degrees in interior design. We have also listed a few interior designers and consultants who specialize in children's rooms. We have seen their work, and it is truly special.

❖ *Charm and Whimsy*

Esther Sadowsky, Allied ASID

143 Madison Avenue at 32nd Street, Suite 200

212-683-7609

email: esther@charmandwhimsy.com

www.charmandwhimsy.com

Esther has found her niche designing nurseries and children's rooms. From a small room to a suite of rooms, she will create a fun, delightful space for your child to grow up in. She can design furniture, select fabrics and carpeting, and hand-paint your chairs and benches. She can even paint a mural on your child's ceiling; the cost is based on a case-by-case appraisal. Custom, hand-painted furniture, murals, and finishes are all specialties of Charm & Whimsy. Esther designs rooms for the parents, too.

❖ *Gracious Home*

1217/1220 Third Avenue at 70th Street

212-517-6300

1992 Broadway at 67th Street

212-231-7800

Gracious Home sells beautiful coordinated borders, wallpaper, and paint. It has a children's section offering beautiful bumper sets and bedding. It carries area rugs, wastepaper baskets, lamps, and bathroom accessories. Gracious Home will make up any window treatment you desire, or coordinate an entire room. The entire selection is quite beautiful.

Janovic Plaza*

See website for locations throughout Manhattan.

212-772-1400

Janovic Plaza offers a wide selection of wallpaper, borders, paints, and window treatments, and designers there will help plan your room and coordinate everything. There's a broad selection of reasonably priced fabrics suitable for a child's room. Ask about Janovic's classes on painting and wallpapering. Pamela has used the Janovic Plaza store on West 72nd Street for borders and window treatments, with happy results.

Laura Beth's Baby Collection

321 East 75th Street bet. First and Second avenues

212-717-2559

A former buyer in the famed Baby Department at Barneys New York, Laura Beth meets one-on-one with stylish moms-to-be to help them pick out linens and accessories for the wee one's room at her chic store. She offers one-stop personal shopping for crib linens, custom bedding, and a variety of accessories for the nursery, including mobiles, frames, bookends, and more. Laura has great taste, and carries only the finest collections the baby market has to offer at prices better than retail. The new location has a great collection of nursery items for stylish moms-to-be plus a huge selection of stylish baby

announcements, thank-you notes, birthday invitations, stickers, and gift enclosures.

Robin Weiss

Paint Your World

917-751-4412

www.paint-your-world.com

Robin Weiss, founder of Paint Your World, specializes in custom-painted wall murals. She does beautiful, creative murals for children's rooms (and for other parts of the home as well). Check out her website for some samples of her work.

YoyaMart

15 Gansevoort Street at Hudson Street

212-242-5511

www.yoyamart.com

YoyaMart is a hip store designed to bring parents high-quality imported furniture and accessories. It also carries Netto cribs, Kiehl's baby products, and fun toys, too.

Best Places for Gift Items

Sometimes finding a great baby gift is tough to do—especially if you are really busy (and who isn't these days?). These are three no-fail places to get the perfect gift for your friend's new addition—or your own!

Cocoa Crayon

www.cocoacrayon.com

Cocoa Crayon is a gift business that was born out of a passion for finding hip, well-designed, useful things for kids. Creator Lisa Moss features a fabulous selection of gifts for new moms, babies, kids, and adults, too. Pamela uses Cocoa Crayon for nearly all of her baby gifts.

✻ Go To Baby

315 East 57th Street
bet. First and Second avenues
212-223-8090
www.gotobaby.com

Go To Baby's unique baby gifts and baby gift baskets are high quality and well-priced. It offers a wide selection of baby gifts including clothing, stuffed animals, books, personalized gift items, and more. Its website is easy to use and it also has a retail store that carries many of the same things.

✻ Fill-R-Up Gift Baskets

197 East 76th Street at Third Avenue
212-452-3026
www.fill-r-up.com

Fill-R-Up is a customized gift basket service and retail store located on Manhattan's Upper East Side. The company is the brainchild of Amanda Moses, who, as an event planner at a top fashion company, was often looking for gift baskets for VIP clients and events. Amanda offers great baskets for new moms, new babies, birthday parties, and more.

baby proofing

Little did you know your apartment was a danger zone. Beware if you have—as do most of us—a glass or sharp-edged coffee table, electrical outlets, lamps, lamp cords, drawers, cleaning solutions and cosmetics under sinks/vanities, or anything sitting on a table. Baby proofing your home is one of the most important tasks you'll undertake. By the time your child begins to creep and crawl, all potentially dangerous objects must be covered, secured, removed, or replaced.

Here are ways to get baby-proofing help:

- ✻ Buy a book or video such as Mr. Baby Proofer, a thirty-minute video that shows parents how to create a safe environment for newborns.
- ✻ Ask for advice at any of the baby superstores. A salesperson will talk you through what you need in order to create a safe home.
- ✻ Hire a baby-proofing expert. Howard Applebaum of Baby Proofers Plus (800-880-2191) will come to your home for a free consultation, determine what you need, prepare an estimate, and install everything. We have both used Howard, who gives seminars on child safety at local hospitals, and we highly recommend him. Another excellent baby-proofing company is All Star Baby Safety, Inc. (212-396-1995), run by Tom Treanor, who will come to your home for a consultation and price estimate for the full service. He will also travel to Long Island and Westchester if you want to baby-proof a beach or country house. Tom is a distributor of the magnetic Tot-Lok safety system and a member

of the International Association for Child Safety.

※ Also check out www.babybodyguards.com, the website of a baby-proofing service based in Brooklyn, which is also an excellent baby-proofing resource.

Many people baby-proof their own apartments. Howard Applebaum provides the following safety suggestions:

※ Poisons or toxic materials (i.e. all cleaners) should not be stored under the sink; place them high up, out of your baby's reach.

※ Attach all busy boxes, mirrors, or crib toys on the wall side of the crib, so that your baby cannot use the objects to climb out of the crib. Do not mount a wall hanging above the crib, where your child can pull it down and perhaps dislodge nails.

※ Toilet lids should be locked closed.

※ Keep all trash containers locked up and out of baby's way.

※ Remove tall lamps or coat racks or block them with furniture to ensure that your baby can't pull them over.

※ When cooking, all pot handles should be turned inward so your baby cannot reach them. Use back burners when possible.

※ Separate plants and babies. Some plants are poisonous, and a young child may eat the leaves or pull the whole plant on top of himself.

※ Hanging cords from answering machines, phones, lamps, and appliances should be out of your baby's reach.

※ Do not take pills or medication in front of children; they mimic what they see.

※ Remove all soaps, razors, and shampoos from around the edge of the bathtub.

※ Do not use tacks or staples to secure electrical cords to walls; they can fall out or be pulled out and swallowed. Use tape.

※ Discard plastic dry cleaner bags before entering the house. Babies can suffocate in them or pull off pieces and choke on them.

※ Keep emergency phone numbers, including the poison control center, near all telephones.

※ To prevent carpeting from sliding, use a foam grid padding beneath it.

※ Babies like to pull off the tips from doorstops. Place some glue inside the cap, then stick the cap back onto the doorstop.

※ Remove magnets from your refrigerator door. If they fall to the floor and break, a child may pick up the pieces and swallow them. Invest in baby magnets or plastic non-breakable ones.

※ If you have a fireplace, place a piece of carpet or foam on the whole base so your child won't bang into the brick.

※ Get a bathtub spout cover to prevent your child from hitting his head against it.

※ If you have a home gym, keep that room closed when you're not in it. Babies can get their fingers stuck in the spokes of exercise bikes, put their fingers in the gears, or pull weights onto themselves.

※ Glass panels in coffee tables can break under the weight of a child. Replace with acrylic.

※ Mobiles should be removed when a child is five to seven months old. A baby of that age can pull the mobile down or be injured if the little strings from the mobile get wrapped around his fingers.

* Cords for window blinds should be lifted high and out of reach. Babies can accidentally wrap the cords around themselves.
* Wash out cleaning fluid bottles before putting them in your recycling bin. Just a drop of cleaning fluid can cause serious injury to a baby.
* Never leave infants alone in the bathtub. Ignore telephone calls and doorbells. Babies can drown in just an inch of water. Never leave a tub with water standing in it.
* Check the underside of upholstered furniture for loose staples or sharp points.

baby and toddler clothing

If you've always thought baby clothing was the cutest thing in the world—well, you are going to love this chapter! New York stores have all the baby clothing you need, want, or have dreamt of. There's tons of adorable stuff to choose from, but don't bring all of it home at once. Babies grow very, very quickly, and the outfit that fit the last time you put it on may not even come close a few weeks later. We'll tell you about some of the best clothing shops in the city to help you save time, energy, and money.

What a difference a second child made in our shopping habits! The first time around, only the "best"—meaning most expensive—would do for our little ones. From dresses to pajamas, we spared no expense. Now, with our second children, Benjamin and Angela, we've opted for a different strategy: Buy on sale! Shop at the Gap, Children's Place, and Old Navy. Pamela swears by Greenstones 50-percent-off sales in January and June, and Kelly has been known to travel down to Baby Depot for bargain-priced turtlenecks. And Century 21 can't be beat for socks and underwear.

Luckily, you can also do some shopping online! If you know exactly what size and style you usually purchase, then skip the lines and head to your nearest computer. Just be sure to read the store's return policy before giving your credit card information, as some stores make it harder to return or exchange than others. Most stores, however, will let you return online merchandise directly in the store with receipts and tags intact. Check out:

* www.zappos.com
* www.piperlime.com
* www.amazon.com
* www.threadlesskids.com
* www.blissbybrittany.com
* www.sonnyboutique.com

shopping tips

If your shower gifts include too many outfits in three- and six-month sizes, return most of them for a credit, or exchange them for twelve- or eighteen-month sizes. Don't dawdle, either. If you put it off, you'll find the stores won't take them back or they'll have been marked down. Also, wait until all the baby gifts are in—you may not need as much as you think.

* Pay attention to a store's return policy. Most of the shops—especially the European-style boutiques, such as Jacadi and Bonpoint—are very strict when it comes to returns. Department stores tend to be the most lenient; goods can usually be brought back for cash or credit for up to one year.
* Ask about the sales. Small shops often have January and June/July special pricing events; some have quarterly sales. Department stores always seem to have sales. In some shops, you won't be able to use gift certificates on sale items.
* If you plan to shop with your little one in tow, use a baby carrier or small stroller. Some of these stores are small, crowded, and you may have to walk up a flight of stairs.
* Onesie outfits are practical. You can't have too many of these pullover, short sleeve T-shirts with bottom snaps to layer under winter clothes or to use as-is in hot weather. All the stores carry onesies, in a variety of price ranges. Buy the least expensive ones you can find and always in 100 percent cotton.

* Think cotton. It's cozy, soft, and easily washable. (Your pediatrician will probably tell you to wash your baby's clothes for the first year in the non-detergents Dreft or Ivory Snow, which do not irritate a baby's sensitive skin.)

* You'll find it convenient to have many sleeping outfits, but test several before buying a bunch to see which your baby prefers. Pamela bought half a dozen Carter's sleeping gowns with drawstring bottoms but found that Rebecca was uncomfortable with her feet restricted. She exchanged them for open sleeper bag pajamas, and Rebecca was much happier. (All sleepwear must be 100 percent polyester to be flame retardant.)

* Don't buy any infant clothes with strings around or near the neck, which can be dangerous. Most manufacturers have stopped making baby clothes with strings.

* Use clothing with snaps around the bottoms, for easy changing.

* Give some thought to how and when you'll do laundry. Your baby will go through several outfits a day. If you have a washer and dryer in your apartment and it's easy to throw in a load at odd moments, a large layette may be unnecessary. If you use a machine in your building's basement or take clothing to a neighborhood laundromat, it may be more convenient and easier on your pocketbook to stock a relatively large supply of clothing. Either way, all clothing should be machine washable.

* Buy ahead whenever possible. (Winter coats are often on sale in January.) Also, try to borrow expensive items, such as snowsuits.

* If you receive many gifts in small sizes, always exchange some for larger ones.

* Many stores have prepared an essential layette list for you—some of them incredibly long! Take such lists with a grain of salt, keeping in mind your own budget and storage space.

* Because store hours can change frequently, we suggest calling before making a trip. Most stores are open seven days a week, from 10 or 11 a.m. until 6 p.m.

Here's a practical layette:

For Baby

* 6 onesies
* 2 side-snap or side-tie shirts (until umbilical cord separates)
* 6 stretchies or coveralls, which cover your baby from neck to feet and have snaps (these in heavier material are good for sleeping)
* 4 sleep gowns or sleeper bags (Kelly favors the sleeper bags—great in cold weather and with air-conditioning)
* 2 caps
* 6 pairs of socks
* 1 snowsuit (for winter babies)
* 4 receiving blankets (to lay the baby down on and wrap her up in)
* 1 heavier waffle-weave blanket
* 3 hooded towel/washcloth sets
* 12 cloth diapers (for burping the baby)
* 4 bibs
* 1 outdoor hat (keeps winter babies warm, protects summer babies from sun)
* 1 pair cotton mittens (to prevent your baby from scratching her face)
* 1 pair outdoor mittens (for winter babies)

* baby scissors, nail clipper, non-glass thermometer, nasal aspirator, hairbrush/comb
* bath tub

For Crib

* 2 quilted mattress pads
* 2 waterproof liners
* 3 to 4 fitted crib sheets
* 6 crib bibs (to protect sheets from baby spit up)
* 1 bumper pad

Top Seven Things to Know About Baby Clothes

1. Buy your layette, but wait to buy more clothes until all the gifts are in; you might not need as much as you think.
2. All clothes should be machine washable.
3. If you receive many gifts in small sizes, always exchange some for larger sizes.
4. Use clothing with snaps around the bottom for easy changing.
5. Buy ahead when possible; winter coats, for example, are on sale in January.
6. Try to borrow expensive items like snowsuits and coats.
7. Patronize stores with liberal return policies.

the stores

From expensive designer boutiques to discount department stores, children's shops dot the retail landscape of New York. We can't even begin to explain the prices at some of these European boutiques found on Madison Avenue. (Neither of us would pay $100 for a child's T-shirt from France, but apparently someone does.) Meanwhile, Sixth Avenue, from 16th to 23rd streets, is home to terrific bargain shopping: Baby Depot in the Burlington Coat Factory, Old Navy, and Daffy's.

* ### A Time for Children
  506 Amsterdam Avenue
  bet. 84th and 85th streets
  212-580-8202
  www.atimeforchildren.org
  Return Policy: Refund within seven days.
  This Upper West Side boutique is the brainchild of philanthropist Marjorie Stern, who conceived the store and brought it to life through funding from the Big Wood Foundation. The small but well-stocked store features great clothing, books, toys, and stuffed animals for children from newborn to six years old. Store employees are teens learning all aspects of retail though the Retail Readiness training program, which aims to give kids the skills necessary to support a family without a college degree. Brands carried: Petit Bateau, Splendid, Tumbleweeds, Cotton Caboodle, and Ella Moss. One hundred percent of profits are donated to the Children's Aid Society.

Babesta

66 West Broadway
bet. Murray and Warren streets
212-608-4522
email: jcg@babesta.com
www.babesta.com
Return Policy: Full refund in fifteen days,
exchange up to forty-five days.
This trendy little store has everything to bring
your baby from infancy to age seven in true
punk-rock style. From vintage T-shirts featuring
Styx, Jimi Hendrix, and Pink Floyd, to funky
printed overalls and sleek leather jackets, you'll
be sure to find something edgy and exciting.
For $20–$25 you can create your own customized T-shirt, with the colors, iron-on
designs, and wording of your choosing. Prices
don't generally go above $200 for a single gar-
ment, and if you're there at the right time you
can sometimes find a 44 percent–off sale going
on. The store also carries a selection of CDs,
Uglydolls, and diaper bags. Babesta carries
brands like Boo Foo Woo, Mini Rodini, Pura
Vida NYC, and Kea & Joby.

BabyGap*

See website for multiple locations throughout
NYC.
www.gap.com
Return Policy: Lenient.
Who doesn't love the Gap? Nothing outrageous
here. The Gap's baby clothing is often 100 percent cotton, and in traditional colors and styles.
But the sales are great! Comfortable play clothes
hold up well after repeated washings. (Just be
prepared to see other babies at the playgroup

Prettiest (and Priciest!) Layettes in Town

La Layette
Bonpoint
Spring Flowers

wearing the exact same outfit.) With eight locations in Manhattan and over twenty in surrounding areas, babyGap is usually housed within Gap
and GapKids stores. Their Herald Square location also offers GapMaternity products.

Babylicious

51 Hudson Street
bet. Duane and Jay streets
212-406-7440
www.babylicious.com
Return Policy: Refund with a receipt,
within thirty days.
This new store offers an exciting environment
for kids and moms alike. You'll find tons of
trendy casual clothing for newborns to seven-
year-olds, with many brands using organic cot-
tons. There's also a great selection of books
(lots about NYC), unique toys, and Truffles
stuffed animals. Their gift baskets make fantastic presents for new moms and can be individu-
ally designed to fit any taste and budget. The
sale rack offers great buys all year round; be
sure not to miss the semiannual private sales
where you can find brand-new merchandise at
20 percent off. Babylicious carries brands like
Sister Sam, Mish Mish, Appaman, EGG by
Susan Lazar, Malina, and Kit + Lili.

Bambini

1088 Madison Avenue at 83rd Street
212-717-6742
Return Policy: Store credit within fourteen days.
The epitome of an Upper East Side shop, Bambini offers fine Italian clothing for children from three months to eight years old. The selection is formal and pricey; this is a good place to purchase a holiday or special occasion outfit for a boy or girl. If you wait for the twice-a-year sales you can find beautiful outfits at half off the regular prices.

Barneys

660 Madison Avenue at 61st Street
212-826-8900
www.barneys.com
Return Policy: Refund with receipt
within thirty days.
The children's department at Barneys is small but well stocked. Just as you'd expect, most of the clothes and accessories—for newborns to children age four—are stylish and expensive. The department also carries pretty linens, shoes, albums, hand-painted pillows, stuffed animals, toys, and Kate Spade diaper bags. Barney's stocks brands like Amber Hagen, Leaves of Grass, True Religion, Blume Forever, Vilebrequin, Little Marc by Marc Jacobs, Etro, Egg + Avocado, Lili Gaufrette, Kid by Phillip Lim, Juicy Couture, Kico Kids, Lacoste, Diesel, Monster Kids, and Barneys' private label.

Bloomingdale's*

1000 Third Avenue
bet. 59th and 60th streets
212-705-2000
www.bloomingdales.com
Return Policy: Lenient.
The sprawling children's department on the eighth floor has one section for layettes, newborns, and toddlers, then separate sections for girls, boys, and teens. You'll also find accessories, toys, and gifts—and end-of-season sales. We have shopped here for years. Bloomingdale's carries brands like Burberry, Juicy Couture, Ralph Lauren, Splendid Littles, Diesel, Ed Hardy, Kissy Kissy, Pumpkin Patch, and its private label, Aqua.

Bonpoint

1269 Madison Avenue at 91st Street
212-722-7720
810 Madison Avenue at 68th Street
212-879-0900
392 Bleecker Street bet. West 11th and Perry Street
212-647-1700
Return Policy: Store credit only; no returns on sale items.
All clothes have the Bonpoint label and are imported from Paris—but so are the prices! Shelves are full of dressy girls' blouses and skirts, as well as formal blazers and slacks for the boys. Sizes go from newborn to size eight. While this isn't the place to stock up on everyday basics, if you're looking for the perfect outfit for a special occasion, Bonpoint can help carry your baby through childhood in timeless Parisian style. Styles range from casual to dressy, with fabrics from cotton to silk. The atmosphere is formal, but if you (or Grandma)

are looking for only the best, its beautifully tailored French clothing is perfect.

Bu & The Duck

106 Franklin Street bet. Church Street and
West Broadway
212-431-9226
316 East 84th Street bet. First and
Second avenues
212-794-0721
www.buandtheduck.com
Return Policy: Store credit only.

These shops carry clothing for newborn to eight years old. Susan Lane, the owner, designs and sews most of the clothing herself—beautiful rayon sundresses with lace trim, striped leggings, flowery knit cardigans, and much more. The prices range from moderate to expensive. Along with clothing, Bu offers imported children's shoes as well as a special selection of accessories, toys, and gift items. Brands Carried: Lalalou, Quincy, Melagrano, Boofoowoo, Pom D'Api, Naturino, and Magnolia.

Buddha Belly NYC

917-620-6578
email: info@buddhabellynyc.com
www.buddhabellynyc.com
Return Policy: Store credit only.

Julie Garcés's sense of style is defined by her spirituality with a hint of rock-and-roll influence, which are both infused into her clothing designs. T-shirts are 100 percent cotton jersey with blind stitching, nontoxic dyed, and washed, with no shrinkage and excellent stretch.

Bundle

128 Thomson Street
bet. Prince and Houston streets
212-982-9465
email: stylebabe@bundlenyc.com
www.bundlenyc.com
Return Policy: Store credit or exchange within thirty days.

The concept for Bundle was born after owner Allison MacCullough became frustrated with the overpriced and underwhelming selection of unique baby gifts in New York City. In this small yet lovingly merchandised store, you will find beautiful clothing and gifts at acceptable prices for ages newborn to six years old. There's a hamper filled with toys for little ones to play with and prominently displayed on the wall behind the register are photographs of children wearing Bundle's clothing that appreciative moms have sent in. Bundle carries brands like Baby Bonkie, Splendid Littles, Neige, Jellycat, Kissy Kissy, Tea, and Feather Baby.

Catimini

1125 Madison Avenue at 84th Street
212-987-0688
www.catimini.com
Return Policy: Store credit within ten days; exchanges okay all season.

Catamini's stylish French clothing is bright and colorful and available in sizes ranging from newborn to age ten for boys and twelve for girls.

Century 21 Department Store

22 Cortlandt Street bet. Broadway and
Church Street
212-227-9092
www.c21stores.com
Return Policy: Refund within thirty days with
receipt and price tag attached.

Century 21, the discount department store,
has a large children's department. It's not difficult to find a bargain, with prices that hover
around 25 percent below retail. Accessories
include diaper bags, cloth diapers, and bibs.
It's crowded, especially on weekends, so it's
best to shop here without your baby. Brands
carried: Carter's, Little Me, Ralph Lauren, Ger-
ber, Absorba, and more.

The Children's Place*

See website for locations throughout NYC.
212-529-2201
www.childrensplace.com
Return Policy: Returns within six months
with receipt.

This growing chain with shops in Manhattan and
many across the tristate area is a real find. The
store is clean, its return policy is flexible, and the
clothing is comfortable, high quality, stylish, and
affordable. The collections are basic and come
in bright and traditional colors, with some fashion sense. We've seen beautiful fall/winter cor-
duroys in rich, royal colors—deep blue, ruby
red, and emerald green—as well as bright,
multi-colored summer clothing and bathing
suits. You can also find socks, hats, headbands,
scrunchies, and adorable sunglasses.

Crembebè

68 Second Avenue bet. 3rd and 4th streets
212-979-6848
www.crembebe.com
Return Policy: Store credit only within
fifteen days.

This store is funky and cheerful, with a wide selection of colorful American and Italian clothes in
sizes ranging from ages newborn to twelve years.
The owner creates some of the items herself,
scanning bright designs of apples, trains, and the
Crembebè logo onto T-shirts. She carries European imports such as Jean Bourget, IKKS, Pure
Pensee, and Nolita, as well as "The Rock Star"
collection that include pieces from local designers
such as Claude, Granny Takes the Strip, and
Trunk. Prices for T-shirts and onesies are under
$20 and jackets are $300. There are sales all year
round where you can find a great selection for
30–60 percent off. A selection of toys, stuffed animals, and accessories complete the mix. Crembebè carries brands like Malina and Shortcake.

Daffy's

See website for locations throughout Manhattan.
212-529-4477
Return Policy: Refund within fourteen days, otherwise store credit only.

Daffy's is a discount store for the whole family.
Its children's department is particularly good,
and our bargain-hunting friends swear by
Daffy's for some of the best deals in town. Like
Loehmann's, be prepared to pick through racks
and hunt for infant clothes that were misplaced
in the toddler section. Pamela picked up Flap-
doodle leggings here for $5.99. Daffy's carries

brands like Anavini, Flapdoodles, Sister Sam, Kashten, Marimekko, and Ike Behar.

Dig Og Mig

150 Seventh Avenue South at Charles Street
212-675-6112
www.digogmignyc.com
Return Policy: Refund or store credit within fourteen days, but they are very lenient.
This unique children's boutique offers products for boys and girls from newborn to age six and specializes in Danish-designed clothing, toys, accessories, and shoes. The owner, who designs some of the clothing herself, has a strict no-baby-colors policy. So while you won't find any pale pinks and light blues, the selection of rich and sophisticated adult colors is sure to keep both moms and kids happy. Dig Og Mig carries brands like Poppy Rose, Ver de Terre outerwear, Essencia, and Petit by Sofie shoes.

Estella

493 Sixth Avenue
bet. 12th and 13th streets
212-255-3553
www.estella-nyc.com
Return Policy: Return or exchange within seven days.
This deceptively large store has everything for children from newborn to age six, including clothing, accessories, high chairs, strollers, and diaper bags. Many items are moderately priced and the biannual sales in January and July are worth checking out. Estella carries brands like Bon Bon, Max & Lola, Salvor, Kit + Lili, Caramel Baby & Child, Claesens, and Lotus Springs.

Best Places for Sale Items Under $10

The Children's Place
Talbots Kids
Old Navy

Finn's Finds

917-755-7842
email: info@finnsfinds.com
www.finnsfinds.com
Return Policy: Store credit with receipt.
An eclectic kid's clothing line with designs from all over the world including Denmark, Holland, France, Australia, and the U.S. All of the clothing at Finn's Finds is manufactured by environmentally and ethically responsible partners.

Flora and henri

1023 Lexington Avenue
bet. 73rd and 74th streets
212-249-1695
www.florahenri.com
Return Policy: Store credit with receipt.
Flora and henri offers a unique line of vintage-inspired children's clothing, for sizes newborn to twelve years. The clothing is simple and classic and uses cotton fabrics in soft, natural colors that are "never too precious for climbing, digging, swimming, and running." Prices are moderate to high, with most pieces between $50 and $200.

Green Depot

222 Bowery
bet. Prince and Spring streets
212-226-0444
www.greendepot.com
Return Policy: Refund within thirty days with receipt.

While clothing isn't the focus of the newly expanding Green Depot, we feel that the entire concept deserves some attention. The Green Depot baby department has everything you need to create a healthy and safe environment for your child, including no-VOC paint, organic layette merchandise, cribs made from responsibly harvested wood, cork flooring, and BPA-free bottles and toys. They carry organic cotton T-shirts and leggings from EGG by Susan Lazar, adorable hooded towels from 3 Sprouts, and Klean Kanteen sippy cups.

Greenstones

442 Columbus Avenue
bet. 81st and 82nd streets
212-580-4322
1410 Second Avenue
bet. 73rd and 74th streets
212-794-0539
Greenstones, Too
1184 Madison Avenue
bet. 86th and 87th streets
212-427-1665
Return Policy: Store credit only; no returns on sale items.

These family-owned-and-operated stores contain a wide selection of European-imported clothing for boys and girls from newborn to age fourteen, with an especially good selection of outerwear. Prices are moderate for sportswear and more expensive for dressier designer items. Watch for their unbeatable 50-percent-off sales that take place in January and June. (When Rebecca and Benjamin were little, we got their winter coats here every year.) Greenstones carries brands like Catamini, I.K.K.S., and Petit Bateau.

Gymboree

1332 Third Avenue at 76th Street
212-517-5548
1120 Madison Avenue at 83rd Street
212-717-6702
2271 Broadway at 81st Street
212-595-9071
www.gymboree.com
Return Policy: Lenient.

The large, roomy Gymboree stores specialize in play clothes and active wear for boys and girls from newborn to eight years. The moderately priced clothes are 100 percent cotton and come in brightly colored designs, with new collections arriving every six to eight weeks. Kelly shopped the 83rd Street location for years and loved it.

H&M

558 Broadway at Prince Street
212-343-2722
515 Broadway bet. Spring and Broome streets
212-965-8975
www.hm.com
Return Policy: Full refund within thirty days with receipt.

H&M, the Swedish sensation, has many stores around Manhattan now, but only the Broadway store offers clothing for babies and kids. New Yorkers have fallen in love with H&M for its appealing range of products and reasonable prices.

✤ Hippopotamus

451 Amsterdam Avenue
bet. 81st and 82nd streets
212-787-1029
1163 Madison Avenue
bet. 85th and 86th streets
212-249-6182
30 Rockefeller Center, Concourse Level
212-246-0480
www.hippotots.com
Return Policy: Refund within fourteen days, with receipts; sale items are final.

Hippopotamus, which now carries only its in-house designs, is a great place to find basic preppy clothing at reasonable prices for children ages newborn to six years old. They have a large selection of solid polo shirts, dresses with fine embroidery details, roll-neck sweaters, and cashmere accessories. Prices begin around $20 for tops and can range up to $85 for wool jackets.

✤ Ibiza Kidz

46 University Place
bet. 9th and 10th streets
212-505-9907
Return Policy: Store credit within seven days.
This is the shop for cool downtown kids. Located within the Ibiza women's store, it offers a great selection of colorful print clothes for newborn children to size twelve. Ibiza carries the Malina line of beautiful silk suits and jackets, for age newborn to eighteen months, not to mention elaborate tutus with matching wings and wands, funky suitcases, hats, and a good selection of shoes. Prices are moderate to expensive. Ibiza Kidz carries brands like Luna Luna, Lili Gaufrette, CityThreads, Petit Bateau, Cotton Caboodle, Splendid Littles, Okkies, Zutano, and One Kid reversible coats.

✤ Io E Tu

1582 First Avenue
bet. 82nd and 83rd streets
212-794-1260
Return Policy: Store credit within fourteen days. This tiny Upper East Side shop is heavily stocked with beautiful and unique clothing for children ages newborn to six. You will find a charming mix of European-designed layette pieces and clothing that features vintage styles and fun prints. Little girls will love Io E Tu's selection of hair accessories! Io E Tu carries brands like Neige, Comme Si Comme Ca, Cashmerino, Charabia, Valeria, Judith Lacroix, Miss Sixty, Malina, and Tocca.

✤ J.Crew Crewcuts for Kids

99 Prince Street
bet. Mercer and Greene streets
212-966-2739
1200 Madison Avenue at 87th Street
212-348-9803
www.jcrew.com
Return Policy: Refund within sixty days with receipt; store credit after sixty days.

Crewcuts are adorable and are miniversions of J. Crew classics, ranging in size from two to twelve. You will find the same casual, beachy vibe as the grown-up clothing, including shirts, pants, shorts, sweaters, dresses, outerwear, and swimwear. An adorable line of children's accessories makes great gifts. You can find oxford shirts for $29.50, cable-knit cashmere sweaters for $115, and cotton dresses starting at $34.

Jacadi
1841 Broadway
bet. 60th and 61st streets
212-246-2753
1242 Madison Avenue
bet. 89th and 90th streets
212-369-1616
1260 Third Avenue at 72nd Street
212-717-9292
www.jacadiusa.com
Return Policy: Refund within seven days with receipt.
The Jacadi stores in New York (more in outlying suburbs) is independently owned and operated. The merchandise is imported from France and is mostly the Jacadi label. Both dressy and play clothes are available for newborns to twelve-year-olds, as well as towels, nursery furniture (by Pali, Periculture, and Peg Perego), and wallpaper. Be discriminating about what you buy because returns are next to impossible. Watch for sales popping up nearly every two months.

Julian & Sara
103 Mercer Street
bet. Spring and Prince streets

212-226-1989
Return Policy: Exchanges within ten days; within twenty days for gifts.
This tiny boutique imports most of its clothing from Europe and features an incredible selection for girls, with everything from party dresses to play clothes in sizes for newborns to fourteen-year-olds. There are also shoes and accessories, plus a beautiful line of pajamas by Arthur. Brands Carried: Lili Gaufrette, Jean Bourget, Trois Pommes, and the store's private label, Julsar.

Kico Kids
See website for pop-up locations throughout Manhattan.
212-675-5426
www.kicokids.com
Return Policy: Returns within fourteen days.
This innovative store located within Chelsea Market offers an array of products for boys and girls sizes two to twelve. You will find Kico's private-label knits, shirts, pants, skirts, dresses, and accessories, in addition to beautifully hand-knit dolls.

Kisan Concept Store
125 Greene Street
bet. Prince and Houston streets
212-475-2470
www.kisanstore.com
Return Policy: Store credit with receipt.
This charming Soho boutique is beloved by Europeans living in New York and looking for the feeling of home. The children's section is in the back of the store, and filled with classic French and Belgian clothing. Prices can be a little high, but

the quality and style are so perfect you won't think twice. Kisan also carries children's shoes, boots, toys, books and DVDs in both French and English, and Steiff stuffed animals. Kisan carries brands like Muchacha, Bon Bon, Pepe Shoes, Makie, Petit Bateau, Quincy, and Caramel Baby.

Koh's Kids

311 Greenwich Street
bet. Chambers and Reade streets
212-791-6915
Return Policy: Store credit only.
This intimate little store has served the Tribeca area for over fifteen years. With funky clothes for children ages newborn to twelve years old, Koh's Kids clothing goes from dressy to casual. Grace stocks sparkly sequined shoes, adorable knit hats, colorful bathing suits, diaper bags, toys, and accessories galore. Prices are moderate to expensive, stretching up to $200 for cashmere sweaters and jackets. Sales happen all year round. The store carries more than thirty brands including Ella Moss, Splendid Littles, Petit Bateau, and Kenzo.

La Layette . . . Et Plus Ltd.*

170 East 61st Street
bet. Third and Lexington avenues
212-688-7072
Return Policy: Store credit only.
This tiny boutique near Bloomingdale's specializes in personalized service (an appointment is recommended) and layettes. Almost everything is made especially for La Layette, and the selection is exquisite. These layettes can be rather expensive, however: from $500 to $5,000, with an average price of $800. Go see their beautiful (many one-of-a-kind) bris and christening outfits and custom clothing, bassinettes, and great gift items. Everything is exquisite!

Les Petits Chapelais

82 Thompson Street
bet. Prince and Spring streets
212-625-1023
www.lespetitschapelais.com
Return Policy: Store credit within ten days.
This adorable boutique is charming and fun. It offers its own brand, Les Petits Chapelais, and all of the clothes are designed by the owner. The style is high-end, brightly colored French clothing from newborn sizes to size ten.

Lester's*

1534 Second Avenue at 80th Street
212-734-9292
www.lestersnyc.com
Return Policy: Refund in seven days; store credit in fourteen.
Lester's has a wide variety of play clothes, accessories, and shoes for newborns to teens. Lester's enjoys putting layettes together, and appointments are preferred. With clothing ranging from trendy to classic, Lester's is a popular place to shop for uptown parents. Lester's carries brands like Juicy Couture, So Low, Splendid Littles, True Religion, Rock Candy, Quicksilver Kids, Junk Food, Ralph Lauren, and The North Face.

Lilliput SoHo Kids

240 Lafayette Street

bet. Prince and Spring streets
212-965-9201
www.lilliputsoho.com
Return Policy: Exchange or store credit within ten days.
The larger of the two Lilliputs (the smaller store is across the street and slightly north) is a charming small boutique featuring fanciful clothing, shoes, and accessories for children newborn to age eight.

Lucky Kid

127 Prince Street at Wooster Street
212-466-0849
Return Policy: Refund within fourteen days.
In the only Lucky store devoted solely to the little ones, you're sure to find great casual clothing. The mostly cotton styles feature fun colors, interesting prints, and funky embroideries. Lucky Kid clothing ranges from size six months to size twelve. Prices are moderate.

Lord & Taylor

424 Fifth Avenue
bet. 38th and 39th streets
212-391-3344
www.lordandtaylor.com
Return Policy: Lenient.
Spacious and inviting, the children's department at this grand old department store is filled with a wide variety of quality layette items and clothing. There's also a wonderful selection of stuffed animals, diaper bags, backpacks, bedding sets, and christening outfits. The staff at Lord & Taylor always seems to be exceptionally helpful. Lord & Taylor stocks brands like Polo

Ralph Lauren, Lilly Pulitzer, Little Me, Knitworks, Guess, and Lacoste.

Macy's

Herald Square, 151 West 34th Street
bet. Broadway and Seventh avenues
212-695-4400
www.macys.com
Return Policy: Lenient.
The largest kids' floor in the world sells everything from snuggly stuffed animals to Vera Wang teething rings, and offers a changing room for your baby in the public restroom. Macy's carries a huge variety of clothing for newborns and older children. The prices are generally moderate, and you can always find something on sale. Macy's stocks brands like Carter's, Ed Hardy, Polo Ralph Lauren, Nanette, Laura Ashley, Flapdoodles, Nautica, and Lacoste.

Magic Windows*

1186 Madison Avenue
bet. 86th and 87th streets
212-289-0028
www.magicwindowskids.com
Return Policy: Store credit within fourteen days.
Magic Windows specializes in unique children's clothing style mixed with a traditional, very Upper East Side flair. Kissy Kissy is a large part of its layette business, along with other truly special lines. This is the place to find baby clothes with handmade smocking as well as luxurious changing tables and bureaus. You can also find children's clothing from newborn to teen (the teen shop has its own entrance). Magic Windows carries Anavini, L'Arc-en-Ciel, Burberry, Lilly Pulitzer,

Ralph Lauren, Tartine et Chocolat, Vineyard Vines, Papo d'Anjo, and E-land Kids.

Oilily

820 Madison Avenue
bet. 68th and 69th streets
212-772-8686
465 West Broadway
bet. Prince and Houston streets
212-871-0201
www.oililyusa.com
Return Policy: Refund within fourteen days.
Exclusively carrying its own design, this Dutch store's trademark is bright colors and eye-catching patterns. Children's sizes start at three months. It sells sportswear, play clothes, and shoes. It also sells women's clothing if you desire that "mother/daughter" matching look. Prices are comparable to other Madison Avenue and SoHo European clothing stores.

Obaibi

1296 Madison Avenue at 92nd Street
212-369-8125
www.obaibi.com
Return Policy: Store credit within fourteen days.
Part of the Jacadi family, this French newcomer is a nice addition to the Upper East Side. It is pricey, but fashionable for dressing newborns to toddlers.

Old Navy*

610 Sixth Avenue at 18th Street
212-645-0663
150 West 34th Street at Seventh Avenue
212-594-0049

503 Broadway bet. Broome and Spring streets
212-226-0838
300 West 125th Street bet. Eighth Avenue and Frederick Douglass Boulevard
212-531-1544
www.oldnavy.com
Return Policy: Refund within ninety days with receipt, otherwise store credit.
Old Navy is owned by Gap and is a lower-priced alternative. These warehouse-like stores are great to visit, even if you don't need kiddie clothes. At all of the locations, you will find reasonably priced, 100 percent cotton items for newborns to adults. There are twill pea coats for $24.50, tons of dresses for under $20, and colorful onesies for under $10, in addition to sunglasses, socks, hats, bathing suits, and whatever else is currently fashionable. A word of warning: Old Navy is a mob scene on weekends.

Original Penguin

103 Greene Street bet. Prince and
Spring streets
212-219-3811
1077 Sixth Avenue bet. West 41st and
42nd streets
646-443-3520
www.originalpenguin.com

Best Stores for Value

Little Folks
Macy's
Baby Depot
The Children's Place

Return Policy: Full refund within thirty days with all tags and receipts.

Supercute and trendy clothing for infants to boys size twenty. A penguin-print hoodie for a twelve-month-old costs about $40, and prices range from moderate to expensive.

❖ Patagonia

426 Columbus Avenue
bet. 80th and 81st streets
917-441-0011
101 Wooster Street
bet. Prince and Spring streets
212-343-1776
www.patagonia.com
Return Policy: Lenient.

Patagonia has some great cold-weather gear for infants and kids: sturdy and warm outerwear, plus thermals that our little ones can wear close to their bodies to keep them extra toasty. It also carries warm hats and mittens.

❖ Paul Frank

195 Mulberry Street at Kenmare Street
212-965-5079
www.paulfrank.com
Return Policy: Refund within fourteen days; no cash back.

What kid doesn't love Paul Frank's bright prints and designs? This is the brand's only store on the East Coast, and it carries everything for newborns all the way to adults. Small Paul products include onesies and bibs, as well as dresses, jeans, blankets, and adorable sweatshirts with snap-on mittens.

❖ PB & Caviar

88 Thomas Street
bet. Hudson Street and West Broadway
212-608-1112
Return Policy: Exchange within fourteen days; sale items final.

Based on the idea that mothers and children should enjoy shopping together, this trendy Tribeca shop offers coed clothing from newborn to age eight, and women's styles of all sizes. You can find fun and casual clothing, with children's prices from $20 for a basic T-shirt up to $700 for a rabbit-fur jacket. Styles are shipped in from Mexico, Spain, England, and France.

❖ Petit Bateau

1094 Madison Avenue at 82nd Street
212-988-8884
www.petit-bateau.com
Return Policy: Store credit or exchance with receipt within ninety days.

The ubiquitous Petit Bateau onesie is seen on many of the Upper East Side's best dressed babies! This shop offers a complete layette, baby, and children's selection with a French flair. The T-shirts are great (you'll love them yourself), as are the beautifully designed pajamas and outfits.

❖ Pink Olive

439 East 9th Street
bet. First Avenue and Avenue A
212-780-0036
email: grace@pinkoliveboutique.com
www.pinkoliveboutique.com
Return Policy: Refund within seven days with receipt.

This tiny East Village shop is a haven for baby gifts. You'll find clothing from many local designers such as Brooklyn-based Atsuyo et Akiko. In addition to adorable Trumpet socks, Skipping Hippo ponchos, and Bla Bla hand-knit hats and dolls, they also have a selection of books, candles, lotions, and stationery. Clothing prices generally range from $20 to $50, including $38 for onesies and $38 for jeans.

Planet Kids

191 Amsterdam Avenue
bet. 68th and 69th streets
212-362-3931
2688 Broadway
bet. 102nd and 103rd streets
212-864-8705
247 East 86th Street
bet. Second and Third avenues
212-426-2040
www.planetkidsny.com
Return Policy: Refund with receipt within seven days; store credit after seven days.
Uptown moms swear by Planet Kids as the only place in the neighborhood to pick up baby supplies and quality clothing. The store carries clothes from sizes newborn to fourteen and sixteen. It also sells furniture and accessories for babies. Planet Kids carries brands like Zutano, Columbia, Baby Step, Sage Green, and I Play swimwear.

Prince & Princess

41 East 78th Street at Madison Avenue
212-879-8989
www.princeandprincess.com

Return Policy: Store credit only.
With prices such as $275 for a knit onesie, this European children's boutique is truly for princes and princesses or just the place to find a special holiday suit or dress. It also sells high-end sportswear and accessories such as headbands, bags, and hats. The store carries clothing for newborns to children age fourteen but will take special orders for women up to age twenty. Be prepared to browse on your own.

Ralph Lauren Baby

872 Madison Avenue at 72nd Street
212-434-8083
www.ralphlauren.com
Return Policy: Store credit with receipt.
Ralph Lauren's separate shop on Madison Avenue showcases clothing for kids from size newborn to size sixteen for girls and twenty for boys. His classic, traditional clothing is a must for preppy moms and dads. If you're looking for an unbelievable baby gift (and don't have a budget), check out the cashmere sweaters and pants for newborns!

Saks Fifth Avenue*

611 Fifth Avenue at 50th Street
212-753-4000
www.saksfifthavenue.com
Return Policy: Lenient.
This top-notch department store has an excellent infant and toddler department and carries a variety of brands, including a number of designers not found elsewhere. The department is wonderfully laid out and extremely easy to shop, and the salespeople are very accom-

modating. Saks carries Burberry, Il Baule D'Elainne, Juicy Couture, Lili Gaufrette, Lilly Pulitzer, Tea Collection, Isabel Garreton, Gold Rush Outfitters, and Diesel.

❄ Small Change

1196 Lexington Avenue at 81st Street

212-772-6455

Return Policy: Exchange and store credit within two weeks.

This small store has a diverse selection of European clothing in sizes newborn to sixteen years. The merchandise runs the gamut from the classic to the more avant-garde. Small Change also sells shoes, socks, tights, hair accessories, hats, gloves, and more. Small Change carries I.K.K.S., Petit Bateau, Magil, Lili Gaufrette, and Mini Man.

❄ Space Kiddets*

26 East 22nd Street bet. Park Avenue and Broadway

212-420-9879

Return Policy: Store credit only.

Most of the clothing here is funky but moderately priced. Space Kiddets has a little of everything, including toys, table and chair sets, fantasy play clothes, even Elvis memorabilia!

❄ Spring Flowers*

538 Madison Avenue bet. 54th and 55th streets

212-207-4606

907 Madison Avenue bet. 72nd and

73rd streets

212-717-8182

1050 Third Avenue bet. 62nd and 63rd streets

212-758-2669

www.springflowerschildren.com

Return Policy: Exchange or store credit within seven days.

Spring Flowers is especially known for its extensive collection of top-quality French and Italian clothes for children newborn to ten years old. The shop carries play clothes and an outstanding selection of party and holiday clothes for boys and girls. Dresses are sold with matching hats, tights, purses, and accessories. Boys' navy blazers and flannel pants are beautifully tailored. Spring Flowers also has a wide selection of European shoes, including the Sonnet brand from England—popular first walkers. Prices are high, as you'd expect, and the service is excellent. Spring Flowers carries brands like Leon, Eddie Pen, Mona Lisa, and Simonetta.

❄ Tribeca Girls

171 Duane Street bet. Greenwich and

Hudson streets

212-925-0049

www.tribecagirls.com

Return Policy: Refund within fourteen days; store credit only for cash purchases.

This small but well-stocked store features trendy yet age-appropriate gear for girls from twelve months to age fourteen. Here you will find a well-edited selection of cotton dresses, colorful silk-screened T-shirts, and designer jeans galore. The prices are befitting of the neighborhood, but you're sure to find a sale at the end of every season. Tribeca Girls carries brands like Tractor, I.K.K.S., Miss Me Jeans, and Small Paul.

❄ Tutti Bambini

1480 First Avenue at 77th Street

212-472-4238

Return Policy: Store credit only, but flexible with the timing of returns.

Tutti Bambini is a small boutique that carries a full line of clothing and accessories for newborns to preteens. You will find great deals during end-of-season sales. Tutti Bambini carries Petit Boy, I.K.K.S., Les Tout Petits, Catamini, Cotton Caboodle, Lili Gaufrette, Sister Sam, and Quiksilver.

❄ Z'Baby Company*

996 Lexington Avenue at 70th Street

212-472-BABY

100 West 72nd Street at Columbus Avenue

212-579-BABY

www.zbabycompany.com

Return Policy: Store credit within fourteen days of purchase with receipt; no returns on sale items.

At Z'Baby Company, you'll find a particularly good layette department—and the store's buyer and head layette specialist, a mom herself, will work with you to put together the layette of your dreams. It's best to make an appointment! Z'Baby carries a wide range of clothing, shoes, and accessories from France, Italy, and New York—for boys from newborn to eight and girls to age sixteen. Store services include phone orders, a baby shower registry, personal shopping, and layette by appointment. Z'Baby carries brands like Grain de Lune, Bienvenue sur Terre, Kenzo, Petit Industrie, Sonya Rykiel, Charabia, Cacharel, Aster, Pom Dapi, Buckle My Shoe, Primigi, Lili Gaufrette, and the company's own label.

trunk shows and private boutiques

This section includes makers of high-quality children's clothing that is either not readily available in stores, new to the U.S., or sold at trunk shows two to three times a year as well as in stores. At some shows you will have to custom-order pieces; others display racks of clothing you can buy that day. Get on these designers' mailing lists to be invited.

❄ Bodyscapes, Inc.

115 West 30th Street, Suite 1202

bet. Sixth and Seventh avenues

212-243-2414

www.bodyscapeskids.com

Henrietta Drewes has been designing clothes for over thirty years and, for the last fifteen, bright, whimsical clothing for children ages six months through eight years. Henrietta has a unique and loyal following of people she's worked with for years; she's dressed many of the daughters of her original clients, and just recently dressed one of their granddaughters! Most of her pieces are reversible and made of 100 percent cotton, corduroy, flannel, or any combination of the above. She has a huge array of prints to choose from. In fact, whatever you could imagine to interest a child, she's got. You might find a black corduroy pant that reverses into plaid flannel, a colorful farm print, or any number of other fun combinations. Parents are welcome to visit Henrietta's Chelsea loft (be sure to make an appointment) to pick out their own fabrics.

Little Follies

12 East 86th Street at Fifth Avenue
800-242-7881
email: info@littlefollies.com
www.littlefollies.com

Known for its pretty, classic hand-smocked rompers, dresses, and shortalls, Little Follies has recently expanded its line to include pants, shorts, shirts, and hand-knit sweaters. Almost all of the clothing is machine washable, and made of either 100-percent cotton or a cotton/polyester blend. Sizes start at three months and go up to size eight (shortalls stop at five), and prices average between $65 and $85 for cotton outfits, $100 for velvet shortalls, and $125 and up for velvet dresses. Little Follies holds trunk shows on the Upper East Side two to three times a year; call the 800 number for catalogs and show dates.

Nikki Kule

120 East 87th Street, #P10F
bet. Park and Lexington avenues
212-813-9182
email: info@kuleshop.com
www.kule.com

Created by Nikki Kule and inspired by her two children, Kule has a uniquely modern, eclectic vision of what the classics should be. Her recipe for the collection is part Bazooka bubble gum, part root beer, a little bit of Nantucket, and a dab of everything that was cool in prep school twenty years ago. The clothes are crafted to the highest standards and made from the most luxurious fabrics.

Papa d' Anjo

888-660-6111
Praça Luis de Camões n.36 3° Esq.
1200-243 Lisbon, Portugal
tel.: 011 351 21 865-0290
fax: 011 351 21 868-0172
e-mail: papodanjo@papodanjo.com
www.papodanjo.com

Portugal-based designer Catherine Connor travels all over Europe selecting fine, unusual fabrics for this high-end children's clothing line. Her clothes are all handmade, and the style is classic European. Sizes range from ages six months to twelve years; prices start at $49 for an oxford long-sleeved shirt, and go up to $300 for a traditional wool tweed coat. These clothes are sold in stores such as Saks, Small Change, Magic Windows, and other fine children's clothing boutiques, as well as in twice-yearly trunk shows at various locations in New York. Email for trunk-show information.

resale shops

On the other end of the scale, here's where you'll find real bargains—the big names, hardly worn, at prices way below those of the boutiques.

Clementine

39 ½ Washington Square South
bet. MacDougal Street and Sixth Avenue
212-228-9333
www.clementineconsignment.com
Return Policy: All items are final sale.
This hidden gem (the entrance is downstairs) is the brainchild of Cara Wall, who opened

Clementine after she found it nearly impossible to find quality maternity consignment when she was pregnant. Her goal was to create a shop that felt like a high-end boutique, and with the neatly merchandised shelves and a surprisingly spacious store, she has certainly succeeded. The store, complete with dressing room and child-friendly restrooms, carries designer consignment from maternity to toddler clothes through size 4T. No item is priced over $110. Among many, you will find brands such as Bonpoint, Christian Dior, Ralph Lauren, and Banana Cabana, some items with original tags still attached.

❊ *Jane's Exchange*

191 East 3rd Street
bet. Avenues A and B
212-677-0380
Return Policy: Generally no returns, but can be flexible.

This Alphabet City consignment shop is brimming with gently used, top-quality clothing and accessories for children ages newborn to twelve years old. Casual and colorful clothing fills the store, along with children's books, toys, games, strollers, and furniture. You'll find everything from simple Gap basics to hip European styles, including a growing selection of new clothing that features rock-and-roll-themed T-shirts and bright prints and patterns. The store has also put an emphasis on building its maternity wear section. Prices can go up to $100 for a single outfit, but most items are under $25. Don't forget to check out the 25¢ bin right by the front door!

malls

Consider the possibility of leaving town from time to time to do your children's clothes shopping—find bargains, skip the sales tax (in New Jersey), or enjoy strolling your baby around an air-conditioned mall on a hot and sticky New York day. Mall shopping makes for a good outing, and the food courts will keep the kids happy. We list malls in the tristate area that have several children's stores and are within an hour of the city. All driving directions are from New York City.

Many of the mall stores have been described throughout this chapter. Most, if not all, of these malls have large department stores with wonderful children's departments. Make a day of it. Pop into Toys "R" Us or the Disney Store to start the day off right, and then feed the kids an early lunch at the food court. (And while they nap in the stroller, you can shop for yourself!) Call or view the mall's website for a complete store directory.

Northern New Jersey

❊ *Fashion Center*

Route 17 and Ridgewood Avenue
Paramus, NJ
201-444-9050
Directions: Take the George Washington Bridge to Route 4 West. Take Route 4 to Route 17N and Ridgewood Avenue.
Stores: Lord & Taylor • T.J. Maxx • Toys "R" Us (adjacent)

Best Department Stores for Style and Selection

Lord & Taylor
Saks Fifth Avenue
Bloomingdale's
Macy's

The Mall at Short Hills

1200 Morris Turnpike
Short Hills, NJ
973-376-7350
www.shopshorthills.com
Directions: Take the George Washington Bridge to the Garden State Parkway and continue to exit 142, Interstate 78. Then take 78 West to Route 24 West and exit at 7C—JFK Parkway. Follow signs to the Mall at Short Hills. The mall will be on your right-hand side.
Stores: Bra Smyth • United Colors of Benetton Kids • The Children's Place • GapKids • Gymboree • Janie & Jack • Talbots • Oilily

Paramus Park Mall

Route 17 North
700 Paramus Park
Paramus, NJ
201-261-6108
Directions: Take the George Washington Bridge to Route 80 West, stay on Route 80 until you reach the Garden State Parkway North (Exit 163). Take the Garden State to Route 17N. Go half a mile, and you will see two entrances to the mall in the northbound lane.
Stores: babyGap • Build-A-Bear Workshop • Disney Store • GapKids • Gymboree • Stride Rite • The Children's Place • Toys "R" Us

Garden State Plaza

Route 17 South
One Garden State Plaza
Paramus, NJ
201-843-2121
www.westfield.com/gardenstateplaza
Directions: Take the George Washington Bridge to Route 4 West. Take Route 4 to Route 17 South, go 100 yards past the Route 4 interchange, and make a right into the mall entrance.
Stores: Abercrombie Kids • Build-A-Bear Workshop • The Children's Place • GapKids • babyGap • Gymboree • Jacadi • Janie & Jack • JCPenney • Lord & Taylor • Lululemon Macy's • Nordstrom • Old Navy • Talbots • Toys '"R" Us

Riverside Square Mall

Route 4 West
390 Hackensack Avenue
Hackensack, NJ
201-489-2212
www.shopriverside.com
Directions: Take the George Washington Bridge to Route 4. The mall is on the right-hand side of the street, past the Hackensack exit.
Stores: babycottons • Brooks Brothers Women • Bloomingdale's • GapKids • Gymboree • Janie and Jack • La Petite Gaminerie • Pottery Barn Kids • Saks Fifth Avenue • Vera Bradley

Westchester/Rockland

❄ Palisades Center

1000 Palisades Center Drive

West Nyack, NY

845-348-1005

www.palisadescenter.com

Directions: Take the George Washington Bridge to the Palisades Interstate Parkway North. Exit 9E to the New York State Thruway. Take 87 South to 287 East, then take Exit 12, West Nyack Palisades Center.

Stores: babyGap • Barnes & Noble • Disney Store • GapKids • Gymboree • JCPenney Kids Footlocker • Lord & Taylor • Macy's • Old Navy • The Children's Place • Target • Waldenbooks

❄ The Westchester

125 Westchester Avenue

White Plains, NY

914-683-8600

www.simon.com

Directions: Take the Hutchinson River Parkway or I-95 North to 287 West. Take 287 to Westchester Avenue (Exit 8). Make a left onto Bloomingdale Road for parking at The Westchester.

Stores: babycottons • babyGap • Build-A-Bear Workshop • Burberry Children • The Children's Place • Gymboree • Hannah Andersson • Janie and Jack • KB Toys • Lucky Kid • Neiman Marcus • Nordstrom • Pottery Barn Kids

❄ Woodbury Common Premium Outlet

498 Red Apple Court

Central Valley, NY

(Harriman, NY)

845-928-7467

www.premiumoutlets.com

Directions: Take the upper level of the George Washington Bridge heading west; make a right onto the Palisades Parkway North. Take the Palisades to Exit 9 West. Follow thruway for 30 minutes, exit at Harriman (Exit 16). First right after the tollbooth.

Stores: *All stores here are discount stores and/or outlets. Carter's Childrenswear • The Children's Place • Disney Store • Gymboree • J.Crew / crewcuts • NauticaKids • OshKosh B'Gosh • Polo Ralph Lauren Children • Stride Rite, Keds, Sperry • Tommy Kids • World of Fun

Long Island

❄ Roosevelt Field Shopping Center

630 Old Country Road

Garden City, NY

516-742-8000

www.simon.com

Directions: Take the Long Island Expressway to the Northern State Parkway (Exit 38). Take the Northern State to the Meadowbrook Parkway, and get off at Exit M2, Mall Exit. The mall will be directly in front of you.

Stores: Bloomingdale's • The Children's Place • Disney Store • Gap Kids • Geox • Gymboree • Janie and Jack • JCPenney • Kids Footlocker • Limited Too • Macy's • Nordstrom • Stride Rite • United Colors of Benetton

※ *Sunrise Mall*

Sunrise Highway

One Sunrise Mall

Massapequa, NY

516-795-3550

www.westfield.com/sunrise

Directions: Take the Long Island Expressway to Route 110 South. Get off at Sunrise Highway (Exit 27 West). Go down two streetlights and make a right. The mall is on Sunrise Highway.

Stores: The Children's Place • Disney Store • JCPenney • Kids Footlocker • Kidz Kutz • Lobel's • Sears • Stride Rite • Macy's • Tinkerbell • Walmart

※ *Walt Whitman Mall*

160 Walt Whitman Road, Suite 1101

Huntington Station, NY

(Dix Hills)

631-271-1741

Directions: Take the Long Island Expressway to Route 110 (Exit 49 North). Take Route 110 north five miles; the mall is on the right-hand side of Route 110.

Stores: Ann Taylor • Bloomingdale's • Brooks Brothers • The Children's Place • Gap • Gymboree • J.Crew • The Limited • Lord & Taylor • Macy's • Saks Fifth Avenue

Connecticut

※ *Stamford Town Center*

Tresser Boulevard

100 Greyrock Place

Stamford, CT

203-324-0935

www.shopstamfordtowncenter.com

Directions: Take I-95 North to Exit 8. Make a left at the first light, Atlantic Street. Go to the third traffic light and make a right onto Tresser Boulevard. From Tresser Boulevard, make a left into the mall entrance.

Stores: Barnes & Noble • Brooks Brothers • The Children's Place • GapKids • Gymboree • Justice • Motherhood Maternity • Macy's • Motherhood Maternity • Stride Rite • Saks Fifth Avenue

And for an indoor shopping experience a little closer to home, try the following centers:

Manhattan

※ *The Shops at Columbus Circle*

10 Columbus Circle at 59th Street

212-823-6300

www.shopsatcolumbuscircle.com

Stores: Aveda • Borders Books & Music • Cache • Dean & Deluca • Eileen Fisher • Equinox Pilates • Esprit • J.Crew • Kee-Ka • Montmartre • United Colors of Benetton Kids • Whole Foods

※ *Manhattan Mall*

100 West 33rd Street at Sixth Avenue (Herald Square)

212-465-0500

www.manhattanmallny.com

Stores: JCPenney • Gourmet Coffee • Toys "R"
Us • Footlocker

South Street Seaport

19 Fulton Street at Front Street

212-732-7678

www.southstreetseaport.com

Stores: J.Crew • Ann Taylor • Magic • Cartoon
World • Crocs • Steps • Footlocker • GapKids

Queens

Queens Center Mall

9015 Queens Boulevard

Flushing, NY

718-592-3901

www.shopqueenscenter.com

By Subway: R, V, or G* to Woodhaven Boulevard station. *The G train runs on a limited
schedule during weekends.

By Bus: The Q60 Bus stops at the north side of
Queens Boulevard (main entrance of Queens
Center) and directly across Queens Center on
the south side of Queens Boulevard.

Stores: Aldo • Children's Play Area • Disney
Store • Easy Spirit • GapKids • JCPenney • Jus-
tice • Kids Club • Kids Foot Locker • Macy's •
Motherhood Maternity • Starbucks •
Stride Rite • The Children's Place

Brooklyn

Atlantic Center

625 Atlantic Avenue at Fifth Avenue

Brooklyn

718-622-7893

Trains: Q, 2, 3, 4, 5, D, M, N, or R to Atlantic
Avenue

Stores: Burlington Coat Factory • Carol's
Daughter • The Children's Place • Chuck E.
Cheese • Daffy's • Marshalls • Payless Shoe-
Source • Starbucks • Target

toys, toys, toys...

You're about to rediscover the magic of toys, because you're going to be playing with them more than you can imagine. Having a baby is a great excuse to act like a kid again, and New York's toy stores, from the venerable FAO Schwarz to the tiniest neighborhood specialty shop, will help you remember what it was like when a toy store was the greatest place in the world. Of course, the world of toys has changed since you were a kid, so here are some tips to get you started picking the right toys, including where to find them.

Alice and Leslie Bergman from West Side Kids (see page 258), one of our favorite toy stores, believe that play is a child's version of work. Healthy, happy, imaginative play is crucial to a growing child's development. The more creative playtime a child has, the more likely she or he will become a creative, well-rounded adult. Creative thinking is important whether you are a doctor, an accountant, an actor, or a painter. Be creative with your child, play with abandon . . . but remember: no toy can replace you, and you can only enhance the toy.

❋ Toys must be safe, durable, and age-appropriate; that means no buttons, long strings, ribbons, or small parts for children under three years old. If a toy or toy part can fit through the cardboard center of a toilet paper roll, then it's too small.

❋ If you're looking for a specific item, call ahead. Some stores will gift wrap and deliver nearby, so you might be able to shop over the phone.

❋ There are many websites that are excellent for ordering toys. Once you know what you want, check the Web for the best prices.

❋ Pay attention to return policies and store credits. Some stores, like FAO Schwarz and Toys "R" Us, have an "anything, anytime" return policy, which can be useful if your youngster, as Alexander did on his first birthday, receives three Barney dolls.

There is no longer as much emphasis on black-and-white-colored toys because it has been discovered that babies can actually see contrasts in colors.

New research says that children under two years old should not watch videos, and that even the so-called educational videos are not educational at all. That being said, a thirty-minute video here and there while you are cleaning up dinner won't hurt, and might even allow that little bit of downtime that will help keep mommy sane even if it won't teach baby how to spell!

age-specific toys

Leslie Bergman suggests these toys for the specific age groups, but remember, more does not equal better. Stick to one or two toys that your child enjoys for each stage:

1st Month

At this age, babies are just beginning to focus on the face, and they can see high-contrast images. So you might want to consider boldly patterned toys for a newborn.

❋ Stim-Mobile (Wimmer Ferguson)
❋ Taggies
❋ Cloth books
❋ Pull-down musical toys (Kaloo, Luckson)

- ❋ Skwish (Manhattan Toy)
- ❋ Infant Mirror
- ❋ IQ Baby (Small World Toys)
- ❋ On-the-Go Musical Mobile (Tiny Love)
- ❋ Foam alphabet and number puzzle mat (it's a great gift, too!)

2nd Month

Baby can now grasp a rattle, and will begin to lift her head and roll over. Continue with above toys and introduce:
- ❋ Pat Mat (we recommend a pat mat with bright colors rather than pastels.)
- ❋ Gymini (Tiny Love)
- ❋ Small Rattles (Haba, Sassy, etc.) Place the rattle in the palm of the baby's hand and watch him or her grasp it.
- ❋ Whoozit (Manhattan Toy)
- ❋ Oball

3rd Month

As your baby begins to turn in the direction of voices or other sounds, it is a great time to introduce musical toys.
- ❋ Wiggly Giggler Rattle (Hands On Toys)
- ❋ Whoozit Pull Musical (Manhattan Toy)
- ❋ Musical keys (Parents)
- ❋ Music CDs

4th Month

Now the baby is beginning to raise her chest, and is reaching and teething.
- ❋ Soft blocks
- ❋ Teethers
- ❋ Activity Arch (Tiny Love)
- ❋ Musical Shape Sorter (Tolo)
- ❋ Small Bead Maze (Educo)
- ❋ WaterMat (Early Years)

5th Month

Your baby can now hold her head steady, roll over, reach for objects, grasp a rattle, raise herself up on her arms, and sit. And put everything in her mouth, as well. Your baby should be able to focus on more detail. In addition to the above toys, introduce more manipulative toys, such as:
- ❋ Pretend Cell Phone (Parents)
- ❋ Sensory Balls (Edushape)
- ❋ Curiosity Cube (Early Years)
- ❋ Spinning Tops (Chicco)

6th–7th Month

Now your child can sit, bear his own weight when held up, and comprehend cause and effect. He may pass object from hand to hand or look for objects dropped on the floor. To help with separation anxiety, play lots of hide-and-seek games using cups, puppets, jack-in-the-box, boxes, and your hands. Your baby will begin to understand that if the toy always comes back, so will you.
- ❋ Stacking Cups (Small World Toys, Sassy, Galt)
- ❋ Fascination Station (Sassy)
- ❋ Bath toys: squirts, cups, floating toys, bath

books, boats, and rubber duckies
- Sand toys: small shovel, sieve, and bucket
- Neobaby Pick 'n' Pull (Tomy)
- Cloth and Vinyl Books

8th–9th Month

Now your baby can bear weight on her legs. She'll work to get a toy out of reach, look for a dropped object, pull herself up to standing position, play patty-cake, and nest.
- Push-and-go toys
- Put-in-and-take-out play
- Lift-the-Flap books

10th–11th month

Your baby's becoming aware of his environment and is beginning to interact with toys as well as become more independent. He may be pulling himself up, cruising, and making a razzing sound.
- Mozart Magic Cube
- Activity Cube (Educo)
- Drums
- Pianophone (Small World Toys)

1 Year

Your baby may be walking, responding to your voice, cruising, making razzing sounds, and trying to nest, stack, and sort. It may be time to introduce:
- Simple Peg Puzzles
- Pull Toys (PlanToys, Guidecraft)
- Push Toys
- Pounding Bench (either plastic or wood) or Pound a Ball (many versions)

- First Dolls (Corolle, Mon Premier Calin, bath babies, Raggedy Ann, etc.)
- Stacking Rings (Sassy)
- Pop-up Friends (many versions; creature pops up when correct manipulation is done)
- Umbrella Stroller
- Sound Puzzle Box (Battat)
- Bubbles
- Shape Sorter

18 months

Your baby is gaining more control of fine motor skills, and is beginning to follow your direction.
- Lock Box (Tag Toys)
- Shape Sorter
- Pegboard (Lauri)
- Magic Sound Blocks (Small World)
- Mr. Potato Head (Hasbro)
- Locks & Latches Box (Melissa & Doug)
- Learn To Dress Monkey (Alex Toys)

2 Years

At two years of age, your child is beginning to build and create, and is interested in how things work. She's becoming verbal, learning to recite her ABCs and 123s.
- Magic Sound Blocks (Small World)
- Tricycle (Kettler)
- Figure 8 wooden train set (Thomas & Friends, Nuchi)
- Object recognition puzzles
- Bop Bag
- Trucks of all sizes
- Beginning phonics toys like Leapfrog's Phonics Bus

- Play pretend toys
- Art supplies
- I Spy Preschool Game

3 Years

Can you believe it? Your child's a preschooler! His construction and manipulative skills are increasing, and he's learning to play well with others. He is beginning to understand the concept of counting and reciting the ABCs. His fantasy world is expanding, and he's able to make associations.

- Tangrams (Mr. Mighty Mind)
- Marble Maze (Quercetti)
- Pretend & Play Cash Register
- Gearations (Tomy)
- Flashlight (Playskool)
- Think 'n' Go phonics (Leap Frog)
- Bingo Bears
- Floor puzzles (approx. 12 to 25 pieces)
- Games: Hi-Ho Cherri-o, Kids on Stage, Color-forms Silly Faces, Four First Games, Snail's Pace, Lotto
- Sequencing games: Tell-a-Story (Ravensburger), Magnetic Letters and Numbers
- Art Supplies
- Lacing aids: Lacing cards, beads, shoes
- Magna-tiles (Valtech)
- Zoomorphs
- Scooter (Micro Mini)

the stores

Boomerang Toys

173 West Broadway at Worth Street
212-226-7650
www.boomerangtoys.com
Return Policy: Store credit only.
This cozy Tribeca shop offers fun and educational toys and games for children from newborn to thirteen. You will find everything from rattles and building blocks to bath toys, stickers, books, dolls, puzzles, toy trains (including NYC subway cars), and art supplies. This colorful store carries many favorite brands including Melissa & Doug, Kid Galaxy, Alex Toys, Brio, Lego, and I Play, just to name a few.

Build-A-Bear Workshop

565 Fifth Avenue at 46th Street
212-871-7080
www.buildabear.com/NYC
Return Policy: Full refund on bears that are damaged.
At the biggest Build-A-Bear Workshop in the world, your children can let their imaginations run wild as they create one-of-a-kind toys. Do they want their teddy bears to be firefighters, Olympic medalists, or ballerinas? They've got every conceivable accessory here to choose from and the customization ensures that kids get exactly what they want. Private rooms are available for parties.

The Children's General Store

168 East 91st Street
bet. Third and Lexington avenues

212-426-4479

Return Policy: Store credit only.

This shop carries an appealing selection of toys that kids will love, from puppets to puzzles, stickers, cards, books, tutus, and train sets. For older children there are musical instruments, how-to kits, Plantoys, and Alex creativity kits. You can also find tons of great party favors here. It offers free gift wrapping for last minute gifts.

❊ Cozy's Cuts for Kids*

1125 Madison Avenue at 84th Street

212-744-1716

1416 Second Avenue at 74th Street

212-585-2699

448 Amsterdam Avenue at 81st Street

212-579-2600

www.cozyscutsforkids.com

Besides haircuts, Cozy's also sells toys and party favors, such as mini-Play-Doh kits, toy cars, barrettes, beach balls, pencils, stickers, and egg slime, as well as more educational material like books and puzzles. You can also find children's videos, handmade costumes, board games, and artist aprons—Pamela has found many party favors here for Rebecca and Benjamin's birthdays.

❊ The Craft Studio

1657 Third Avenue

bet. 92nd and 93rd streets

212-831-6626

www.craftstudionyc.com

Return Policy: Store credit or exchange.

At this adorable toy shop and craft party haven, you'll find everything needed to spark your child's creativity. The toy shop is right in front

and filled with a wonderful selection of toys and gifts relating to arts, crafts, hobbies, and imaginative play. Brands include Alex, Creativity for Kids, Melissa & Doug, Fashion Angels, and Corolle dolls.

❊ Cute Toonz

372 Fifth Avenue at 34th Street

212-967-6942

Return Policy: Store credit and exchange only within three weeks.

Lots of great Disney, Sesame Street, and other cartoon characters in all shapes and forms. Shop here for T-shirts, backpacks, cups, stuffed animals, watches, and Hello Kitty accessories. A great place for small gifts and party favors.

❊ Dinosaur Hill

306 East 9th Street

bet. First and Second avenues

212-473-5850

www.dinosaurhill.com

Return Policy: Lenient.

This specialty toy and clothing store has quality marbles, marionettes, mobiles, T. C. Timber and PlanToys wooden toys, and handcrafted toys. It also carries clothing, including an extraordinary selection of hats, games, and puzzles, mostly for children ages newborn to six. You can even find some grown-up toys, and a nice selection of adult jewelry. It offers free gift wrapping as well.

❊ E.A.T. Gifts

1062 Madison Avenue at 80th Street

212-861-2544

Return Policy: Store credit, or exchange only with receipt for item in original packaging.

This Upper East Side store is full of fantastic things, including all sorts of stuffed animals, toy cars, bath toys, puzzles, puppets, and an excellent selection of children's books. Beware—this is not a spot for bargain-hunters! There are also gift items for older children—from funky jewelry to activity kits and journals. This store is excellent for party planning, offering paper goods and balloons. There are tons of little toys, ideal for filling party bags, and a great selection of piñatas in shapes ranging from ballet slippers to basketballs. Kelly loves its selection of hard plastic bowls and plates featuring Arthur, Classic Pooh, Curious George, Madeline, and many other favorite characters. The famous E.A.T. restaurant is just next door.

✲ FAO Schwarz*

767 Fifth Avenue bet. 58th and 59th streets
212-644-9400
www.fao.com
Return Policy: Lenient.

FAO Schwarz is a city landmark and major tourist attraction. But that is because it has the best and largest range of toys in the world: from wonderful dolls (see the Barbie Boutique), board games, a jungle of stuffed animals, and an endless selection of arts and crafts. Whether you are looking for classic toys or modern favorites, you will find it here. All the hottest fads and rages are generally in stock. This is an exciting place for children. They will love it, and so will Grandma. Yes, it's expensive, but you can find many gift items for $50 or less, and

don't forget to check out the clearance section on the second floor, where you can find sales of up to 50 percent off. Gift wrapping is free. During the holiday season, the lines of people waiting to get in circle the block!

✲ Hom Boms

1500 First Avenue bet. 78th and 79th streets
212-717-5300
Return Policy: Refund within thirty days with original packaging and receipt.

Among other things, Hom Boms carries soft, plush toys for infants, wooden pull-along toys for toddlers, and activity kits for older children up to age thirteen, and features major brands like Playmobil, Brio, and Fisher-Price. Of course, no toy store is truly complete without an art-supply section. You will find everything from basic Crayola crayons to glitter pens and stickers here. Hom Boms offers free gift wrapping and free delivery from 70th to 86th streets.

✲ Homefront Kids

202 East 29th Street 3rd Floor
bet. Second and Third avenues
212-381-1966

This incredible store is located on the third floor of the Homefront Hardware store. You will find educational and developmental toys, crafts, and books for children ages newborn to six. The store also stocks giant stuffed animals, a selection of cars and trains, and adorable clothing and costumes. They also have some great accessories for mom, including colorful diaper bags. Homefront Kids offers free gift wrapping, and has recently added a "Kids Cuts" hair salon inside the store.

Kidding Around*

60 West 15th Street bet. Fifth and Sixth
avenues
212-645-6337
Return Policy: Store credit only.
Kidding Around has a nice infant section with rattles, mobiles, and squishy toys, and a larger selection of toys for one- to eight-year-olds. The store also carries many games to entertain kids and parents alike. There are unique puppet theaters, musical instruments, Native American and African-American dolls, a nice French doll line, and an extensive selection of wooden toys. You'll find Brio, Ambi, Battat, Playmobil, Haba, and Alex toys here, as well as beach balls and books. The store supplies personalized party bags and offers free gift-wrapping, too.

Kid O

123 West 10th Street at Greenwich Avenue
212-366-5436
www.kidonyc.com
Return Policy: Store credit only.
This spacious children's boutique features modernist toys, books, and even furniture for kids ages newborn to six and over. Much of the merchandise is imported from Europe and is artist-inspired. (A Calder-like mobile is one example.) The furniture is quite unique and expensive—but it will make for a beautiful and one-of-a-kind baby's room. There isn't always a huge selection in-store, but salespeople will gladly place a special order for you. Be sure to check out Kid O's own line of products, including wooden blocks, games, and puzzles.

Kidrobot

126 Prince Street bet. Wooster and
Greene streets
212-966-6688
www.kidrobot.com
Return Policy: Store credit only.
This tiny store in the heart of Soho is quite busy on the weekends with kids (and adults!) looking to add to their action-figure collections. Kidrobot specializes in collectible vinyl toys, twelve-inch action figures, mini figures, mini remote-controlled cars, and more! Pamela even spotted some cute party favor items here.

Mary Arnold Toys

1010 Lexington Avenue
bet. 72nd and 73rd streets
212-744-8510
Return Policy: Refunds with a receipt within thirty days; otherwise store credit only.
A neighborhood favorite for decades, here you'll find the fine brands from Fisher-Price to Haba and Madame Alexander, as well as videos, games, dolls, puppets, and arts and crafts galore. The staff can create party-favor bags or a special gift basket. Free gift-wrapping and local delivery.

New York Doll Hospital

787 Lexington Avenue bet. 61st and
62nd streets
212-838-7527
Return Policy: All sales final.
This Doll Hospital has been in New York City since 1900. It will repair any broken, damaged, and worn stuffed animals and dolls. It also car-

ries a nice selection of dolls and is popular with collectors of antique dolls. You will find original Shirley Temple dolls, as well as Howdy Doody, Patty Play, and themed dolls from every decade.

❋ NY Firestore

17 Greenwich Avenue bet. Christopher and West 10th streets
212-226-3142
www.nyfirestore.com
Return Policy: Store credit or exchange with receipt within seven days.

Formerly known as NY Firefighter's Friend, this store offers all the things an aspiring little firefighter might need. You can find books and toys like fire trucks, stuffed fire bears, and fire helmets. This store also offers clothing items such as rain boots, raincoats, and baseball caps—all in firefighter fashion. No gift-wrapping here, but it will ship anything via UPS or priority mail.

❋ Promises Fulfilled

1592 Second Avenue
bet. 82nd and 83rd streets
212-472-1600
Return Policy: Store credit only.

You'll find a varied selection for babies and lots of choices when you need a birthday present for an older child (from costumes to construction kits). You can also buy personalized and coordinated accessories for your child's room: toy chests, benches, frames, bookends, clocks, coat racks, mirrors, and lamps. The most popular items are the hand-painted rocking chairs, and personal-

ized birthday party favors. Cute baby books and photo albums are a specialty. You'll also find fun seasonal items, including winter sleds and summer beach chairs, all of which can be personalized. They also offer free gift-wrapping.

❋ The Scholastic Store

557 Broadway bet. Prince and Spring streets
212-343-6100
www.scholastic.com
Return Policy: Refund with a receipt; otherwise store credit only.

The Scholastic Store is located on the street level of the company's corporate office. As expected, it offers an incredible selection of books for ages newborn to thirteen and up, but the store also offers great toys for children, too. You will find stuffed animals, puzzles, costumes, DVDs, and beautiful toys from Nuchi.

❋ Toys "R" Us

1514 Broadway at 44th Street
646-366-8858
Babies "R" Us
24-30 Union Square East
bet. 15th and 16th streets
212-798-9905
www.toysrus.com
Return Policy: Refund with a receipt; otherwise store credit only.

Toys "R" Us discounts every well-known brand-name toy. It carries a lot of Fisher-Price, Safety 1st, Playskool, and Mattel; it also has all the latest toys, and the prices and selection on books, videos, and the Barbie dolls are usually the best in town.

Toy Tokyo

121 Second Avenue, 2F

bet. St. Marks and 7th Street

212-673-5450

www.toytokyo.com

Return Policy: Store credit only.

Located on the second floor, Toy Tokyo is diffi-cult to find but the most eclectic store you've ever seen. The enormous selection includes treats for kids of all ages, but some toys are inappropriate so don't let the kids wander! For children, you'll find everything from Uglydolls, wind-up robots, and hand puppets to Disney paraphernalia, bobble heads, and backpacks.

West Side Kids*

498 Amsterdam Avenue at 84th Street

212-496-7282

Return Policy: Store credit only.

This is a terrific neighborhood store, with excel-lent service and a varied selection of educa-tional toys, quality books, and "imagination" items for playing pretend, such as miniature brooms, pretend food, and kitchen utensils. There is also a selection of puzzles, games, musical instruments, and art supplies, plus a great assortment of small toys for party favors. All products in the store adhere to the most recently implemented safety regulations, and many are made from eco-friendly materials. Check out the array of Halloween and dress-up costumes, too. It offers free gift-wrapping.

Zittles*

969 Madison Avenue bet. 75th and 76th streets

3rd floor of Zitomer

212-737-2040

Return Policy: Refund with receipt within ten days; otherwise store credit only.

Zittles is a pharmacy/cosmetics emporium downstairs, yet upstairs it is a treasure trove of children's commercial, educational, and specialty toys. You'll find dolls, puzzles, books, arts and crafts, videos, games, computer games, "dress up" items, and toys from brands like Battat, Ambi, Brio, Fisher-Price, Leap Frog, Chicco, Melissa & Doug, and Papo. The sales staff in knowledgeable and will steer you in the right direction when shopping for toys and gifts. Zit-tles will ship to the U.S. and Canada and will deliver locally. They also offer free gift-wrapping.

Costumes

At least once a year (more if you have a child like Benjamin who loved to dress up like a superhero), you will need to pick up a costume for your little one. You can easily find selections at your regular toy stores, clothing stores, and department stores. The following specialty stores, however, are the authorities when it comes to Halloween and cos-tume parties. These are great stores to check out:

Abracadabra Superstore

19 West 21st Street

bet. Fifth and Sixth avenues

212-627-5194

www.abracadabrasuperstore.com

This is truly a superstore of all things scary—monsters, skeletons, ghosts, and ghouls. Also, you can find clown supplies, makeup, horror props, masks, and costumes. Children's costumes for sale include superheroes, characters from Disney classics, Star Wars, and much more. For infants, it has costumes like bunnies, angels, and pumpkins. This store is not for the weak of heart. If your child is easily frightened, we suggest leaving your little trick-or-treater at home. Abracadabra has excellent magic shows every Sunday.

❋ Gordon Novelty

52 West 29th Street bet. Broadway and Sixth Avenue

212-254-8616

Gordon Novelty is a warehouse of props and costumes. It carries over a thousand different hats, wigs, and masks portraying celebrities like Einstein, Elvis, and Michael Jackson, as well as monsters and other characters like Spiderman, Superman, Cinderella, Snow White, and Disney Channel favorites.

❋ Halloween Adventure

104 Fourth Avenue bet. 11th and 12th streets

212-673-4546

www.halloweenadventure.com

Open year-round, Halloween Adventure has recently expanded and is crammed with even more beautiful costumes, novelties, and accessories. It has a magic department (with a professional magician to give demonstrations at 1 p.m. every day) and a professional makeup department. Children's costumes range from Disney and Star Wars characters to knights, wizards, angels, fairies, and princesses.

books, dvds, cds, catalogs, and magazines

No doubt about it: city babies—and their moms—love city bookstores! Together they can listen to stories, pick out videos and CDs, and, best of all, discover the joys of children's books. This multimedia universe is one of the most exciting aspects of baby culture today. In every case, talented writers, artists, and musicians are creating lasting treasures for your children.

This section lists the best children's bookstores in New York and all they hold, from the classic must-haves, like *Goodnight Moon* or *Where the Wild Things Are*, to useful adult titles such as *Practical Parenting Tips*. We have recommended our favorite CDs (essential for those long car rides) and videos, not only to entertain the kids but to provide you with a few moments of peace. We have also listed some of the best parenting magazines, along with a selection of catalogs and websites to assist you with at-home shopping.

Of course, the web has totally changed and enriched the way we get our parenting information. Be sure to scope out the NYC Mom Blogs section at the end of this chapter.

Best Reading Tip We've Ever Heard

Carry a book (or your Kindle) with you and read to your child whenever and wherever you can:

* ❋ over breakfast in the morning
* ❋ on a bus
* ❋ in the pediatrician's office

best bookstores for children

❋ **Bank Street Bookstore***
610 West 112th Street at Broadway
212-678-1654
email: books@bankstreet.edu
www.bankstreetbooks.com
Return Policy: Store credit only.
With more than 40,000 titles for children, parents, and educators, Bank Street Bookstore is perhaps the best resource in the city for children's books. The knowledgeable staff can help you find age-appropriate books.

❋ **Barnes & Noble Discount Store**
105 Fifth Avenue at 18th Street
212-807-0999
www.bn.com
Return Policy: Generous.
The second floor of this discount branch has a nice selection of children's books. It's a good destination for party-favor books for children's birthdays. Kelly likes to give a small book as a party favor instead of those plastic bags filled with lots of silly items. The many traditional Barnes & Noble stores also offer great selections of children's books.

❋ **Bookberries**
983 Lexington Avenue at 71st Street
212-794-9400
Return Policy: Store credit or exchange within two weeks.
This intimate bookstore has a great selection of

books for all ages, with a darling elevated section for kids in the back. The area is carpeted with plenty of space to sit down and read. The selection includes all of the classics, from Curious George to Eloise, and everything is clearly marked by age group. The staff is very friendly.

❊ Books of Wonder

18 West 18th Street bet. Fifth and Sixth avenues
212-989-3270
www.booksofwonder.com
Return Policy: Store credit only.
This is a very special children's bookstore carrying new, out-of-print, vintage, and rare books, with an entire section devoted to the Wizard of Oz—not to mention a great selection of illustrated books. No television or movie tie-ins here, (meaning no Barney- or Sesame Street–type books). Call for information on story hours.

❊ Borders Books & Music

576 Second Avenue bet. 32nd and 33rd streets
212-685-3938
461 Park Avenue at 57th Street
212-980-6785
100 Broadway at Wall Street
212-964-1988
10 Columbus Circle
212-823-9775
www.borders.com
Return Policy: Refund or exchange with receipt within thirty days.
Borders has a lovely children's department with small tables to sit at as you peruse you and your child's favorite books. Like Barnes & Noble,

Borders has everything; a coffee bar, the latest magazines, and a newspaper rack make this store complete. Call ahead for the monthly children's calendar.

❊ Corner Bookstore

1313 Madison Avenue at 93rd Street
212-831-3554
Return Policy: Store credit or exchange only.
This is Pamela's neighborhood bookstore and she loves it! It is a charming spot where you truly want to sit and browse. It has a terrific selection of books for children and parents, and a very knowledgeable and friendly staff who are always willing and happy to provide recommendations.

❊ Integral Yoga Bookstore

227 West 13th Street at Greenwich Avenue
212-929-0586
Return Policy: Store credit or exchange only.
Don't let the name fool you—this bookstore has books on prenatal and postpartum care, many parenting titles, and health-related child nonfiction books. Instructional videos and audio tapes as well as lullaby music are also available. It has everything you could need for doing yoga too!

❊ The Shops at the New York Public Library

476 Fifth Avenue at 42nd Street
www.nypl.org
212-930-0641
Return Policy: Store credit or exchange only.
Located within the library, the Library Shop is a

place where classic storybook characters come to life. In addition to kids' favorite stories, you will find great gifts such as Curious George alarm clocks, Wild Things dolls, and Madeline bookends.

Logos Bookstore

1575 York Avenue bet. 83rd and 84th streets
212-517-7292
www.logosbookstorenyc.com
Return Policy: Store credit only.

Logos is a very neighborhood-oriented little bookstore, and a popular place to take your kids. There is a wide selection of books for children of all ages, on topics including religion, poetry, science, nature, and history. Logos also offers special events for children, including birthday parties and reading groups. Be sure to check out story time with Lily Nass every Monday at 3 p.m. The owner, Harris Healy, is very knowledgeable and hands-on.

Rizzoli Bookstore

31 West 57th Street bet. Fifth and
Sixth avenues
212-759-2424
Return Policy: Refund with receipt within thirty days; store credit thereafter.

Rizzoli bookstore is very upscale and is a great place to buy gifts. It also boasts a nice selection of children's and parenting books, as well as some educational toys and gift items.

The Scholastic Store

557 Broadway bet. Prince and Spring streets
212-343-6166

www.scholastic.com
Return Policy: Refund with receipt.

This is a store that makes us uptown parents jealous! It is huge, with plenty of space to maneuver around with your stroller and toddler. It has special events often on weekends and holidays featuring costumed characters like Clifford—even story hours for parents and babies. It carries the entire line of Scholastic products including books, toys, stuffed animals, puzzles, CDs and more. There are lots of things to play with around the store ,too.

Shakespeare and Company

939 Lexington Avenue
bet. 68th and 69th streets
212-570-5148
716 Broadway at Washington Place
212-529-1330
137 East 23rd Street (be advised that this location only carries course books and textbooks)
212-220-5199
www.shakeandco.com
Return Policy: Store credit only.

These homey bookstores offer a nice selection of books for babies and children, as well as some parenting books. The staff is always willing to lend a hand in choosing quality books for your child.

The Strand Bookstore

828 Broadway at 12th Street
212-473-1452
www.strandbooks.com
Return Policy: Refund within three days with receipt.

This family-owned bookstore is famous for its "eighteen miles of books," and has been since 1927. There is a huge selection of discounted books, mainly used and out-of-print, but also some publishers' overstock and reviewers' copies—all at fabulous prices. The children's department is mostly in the basement, where kids can lose themselves in the nooks and crannies with shelves crammed with books. On the third floor you'll also find a nice selection of rare children's books.

choosing a book for your child

There are so many benefits to reading with your child: it will familiarize him with speaking patterns, increase his vocabulary, develop his attention span, introduce him to new concepts, and most importantly, help him learn to enjoy reading. Books provide influences that will be key in forming his personality. As a New York parent, you have an abundance of resources available to help you find the newest in children's literature and give you an opportunity to rediscover old classics. Sometimes all of this information can be overwhelming, but there are a few pointers we can give you to make the process of choosing a book for you and your child to share as smooth as possible. We have searched high and low throughout the city, visiting bookstores and libraries, and speaking with the experts. Here is what we've come up with:

❈ Don't be afraid to ask for help from the children's department at your favorite bookstore or from the children's librarian at your local New York

Public Library branch. That's what the staff is there for and they will be more than happy to help you!

❈ Especially for very small children, pick books that are durable (cloth books and board books are very popular) and with pages that little fingers will be able to turn. Bright, simple illustrations are always great!

❈ For slightly older children, be sure to follow your child's interests. If he likes sports or history, choose books with simple story lines in these areas. Children especially enjoy books about kids their own age in different historical periods. (The American Girl series was a favorite of Rebecca's.)

❈ Books should be challenging and stimulating—they should give children a chance to ask questions, think about possible solutions, use their imaginations, and have fun!

❈ Read your child the books that you read as a child. It will be more enjoyable for both of you if you like what you are reading ,too.

❈ Most important, let your child be active in choosing the books she wants to read. She might feel ready to start exploring simple chapter books (like *Winnie-the-Pooh*, *Pippi Long-stocking*, or the Ramona series from Beverly Cleary) when she is about five or six years old and first learning how to read. Take turns reading aloud (you'll probably have to do most of the reading at first). Your child will grow into the book and enjoy the challenge.

❈ Many suppliers and carriers of children's books maintain websites. You can go to these to find new releases, locate places to borrow or purchase a specific book, and order books online. Of course, Amazon.com is one of the most expedient ways to order books online, and they offer suggestions for books broken down by age.

* Barnes & Noble publishes a great book for choosing reading material for your child: The Barnes & Noble Guide to Children's Books. It can be purchased in the children's section of any Barnes & Noble store.

Making the Most of Reading with Your Child

When reading aloud with your child, set aside a certain time each day and make it part of his daily routine. Snuggle up together and make it a time that you share. We suggest reading a story at night right before bedtime. This is an easy habit to develop, helps your child wind down at the end of the day, and can become a lifelong love. Let him be active in the reading process: encourage him to point out and describe pictures, suggest possible endings, and ask questions. Older babies can participate by pointing and helping to turn the pages. Use silly voices for the characters—it will make storytelling more enjoyable for all involved. Introduce your child to the reading process early on, and tell short, simple stories to your newborn. A parent's voice evokes special responses from a child, and it is never too early to take advantage of this. Also, don't be afraid to read just one or two words per page and skip the rest. This is how a one- or two-year-old reads. Toddlers like to jump around a lot, and the constant stimulation is good for them. Turn those pages quickly!

best books for young children

There are so many great books out there for children of all ages! For newborn babies to children ages five or six, there are three main categories to use as guidelines. Baby books (infant–2 years) are simple and repetitive with lots of pictures. These books are bright and colorful, and connected to the baby's surroundings in some way. They should be sturdy and are rounded at the corners for safety. The most popular forms: bath books (great in the tub), cloth books (perfect for the crib), board books, and touch and feel books.

Once your child is around two, you can introduce her to preschool books. These books are concept-based and should be helpful in developing a sense of humor. They also begin to teach children about social interaction and the difference between right and wrong. They should be easy, fun, and colorfully illustrated. Preschool books are especially popular in pop-up form.

Finally, picture books should have slightly more complex story lines and illustrations. They often address a key life issue: siblings, sharing, potty training, starting school, and so on. These come in hardcover and paperback and some have plush figures as well. Classic books have been kept in a separate category—they're great for all ages. We've also included some special needs books that explain issues like divorce or adoption to young children.

It is important to remember that reading levels are just recommended ages and that what may be right for one three-year-old may be too advanced or too simple for another. Your child will let you know when she is ready to move on by showing interest in more difficult concepts and reading material. The age ranges given for the following books are generally appropriate for most children in that age group. Use your judgment and enjoy.

Learning How To Read

The LeapFrog Tag system features an amazing touch-and-talk device that brings stories to life. It is designed to encourage a child's love of reading with talking words, singing pictures, and interactive games. Funny voice-overs and cool sound effects add to the fun. Children learn reading skills such as word recognition, reading comprehension, and phonics. Tag Junior is recommended for children ages two to four, and the original Tag system is for children ages four to eight. The books range from classic stories (*The Little Engine That Could* by Watty Piper) to Disney movies, Nickelodeon shows, and parent favorites such as *Star Wars*.

We worked with the incomparable Beth Puffer at the Bank Street Bookstore (www.bankstreetbooks.com) to assemble our list of recommended books for babies and toddlers.

baby books
Board Books

❊ Anne Geddes board book series
(*Garden Friends, Colors, Dress-ups, Faces*)
There's nothing babies love more than looking at other babies, and photographer Anne Geddes shows them in a whole new light. There are baby mushrooms, baby flowers, and baby animals.

❊ Architecture board book series
by Michael J. Crosbie
These colorful books introduce the built environment to preschoolers through beautiful photographs and corresponding rhymes. The books feature animals, colors, shapes, and numbers.

❊ Big Little
by Leslie Patricelli
Bold and colorful illustrations humorously introduce different concepts to very young children. Be sure to check out *Yummy Yucky, Quiet Loud,* and *No No Yes Yes,* too!

❊ Click, Clack, Moo: Cows That Type
by Doreen Cronin and Betsy Lewin
Farmer Brown has a problem—his cows like to type! A *New York Times* best-seller.

❊ Counting Kisses
by Karen Katz
This book is all about how many kisses you can give your baby.

❊ The Finger Puppet board book series
by Lenz Mulligan
A brightly colored finger puppet is attached to each book and peeks out from every page. The series includes children's favorite animals such as ladybugs, puppies, and penguins.

❊ Helen Oxenbury Board Books
(*Working, Dressing, Friends*)
These great books teach little ones about the basics with simple illustrations and single words.

Just Like You
by Jan Fearnley

This book is all about how a little mouse and his mother see the animals in the forest getting ready to go to sleep for the night.

Little Spot board book series
by Eric Hill

(Spot's First Words, Spot at Home, Spot in the Garden, Spot's Toy Box)

These books tell simple stories that are easy for small children to follow. Spot helps children learn to associate words and images.

Neil Ricklen board book series
(Daddy and Me, Mommy and Me, Baby's Clothes, Baby's Colors)

These books use one word per picture to describe familiar situations. They are adorable and use real baby photographs rather than illustrations.

Sandra Boynton board book series
(Snoozers; A to Z; Moo, BAA, La La La!; Doggies)

Kids love the rhyming sentences with cute cartoon pictures. Pamela's kids loved these books and came back to them time and time again.

Sesame Street board book series
(Elmo's Guessing Game about Colors, Ernie and Bert Can . . . Can You?, Ernie Follows His Nose, Hide and Seek With Big Bird)

Sesame Street has been entertaining and educating children for years and these books help even the youngest children learn useful concepts. Hide and Seek with Big Bird was one of Benjamin's favorites.

Thomas and the Freight Train
by Rev. W. Awdry

This is an early introduction to the beloved little tank engine named Thomas.

Touchy Feely board book series
by Fiona Watt

(That's Not My Truck, That's Not My Car, That's Not My Tractor)

Babies love the variety of textures they can feel with these books.

Cloth Books

Baby Tales series by Roger Priddy
(Dotty Dog and Kitty Cat)

This cute plush series of books conveniently attach to a baby's high chair, stroller, or crib.

Spot Cloth book series
by Eric Hill

(Animals, Clothes, Home)

These charming books by the creator of Spot are perfect for little ones.

Thomas the Tank Engine Says Good Night
by Owain Bell

This cute book is perfect for reading by the crib.

Bath Books

Babar's Bath Book
by Laurent de Brunhoff
This elephant makes a great companion in the tub.

Spot bath book series
by Eric Hill
(Spot Goes Splash, Spot's Friends, Spot's Toys)
Make a splash with Spot, the adorable puppy!

Bath books
by Beatrix Potter
(The Tale of Benjamin Bunny, The Tale of Jemima Puddle-Duck, The Tale of Mr. Jeremy Fisher, The Tale of Mrs. Tiggy-Winkle, Peter Rabbit)
Looking at these classic characters will make baths more enjoyable for your little one.

Bath Party!
by Simms Taback
This gift set comes with a bath-time book and puppets—everything you need for bath time fun!

Curious Baby: My Little Boat
by H.A. Rey
From the popular Curious George series of books, this bath time favorite visits the beach with George, his boat, and some fishy friends.

The Rainbow Fish Bath Book
by Marcus Pfister
A softer version of everybody's favorite book about sharing.

Sesame Street bath book series
(Elmo Wants a Bath, Ernie's Bath Book)
No one knows bath time like the experts, Ernie and his rubber ducky.

Preschool Books

The Arthur books
by Marc Brown
(Arthur's Really Helpful Word Book, Arthur Goes to School, Arthur's Neighborhood)
Starring the adorable aardvark Arthur, these books help small children learn about word association and social interaction.

The Clifford the Big Red Dog book series
by Norman Bridwell
(Clifford the Big Red Dog, Clifford and the Big Storm, Clifford and the Grouchy Neighbors, Clifford Goes to Hollywood, Clifford the Small Red Puppy, Clifford's Big Book of Stories)
Everybody loves the big red dog! Follow him and Emily Elizabeth through their adventures in this popular series by Norman Bridwell.

The Curious Garden by Peter Brown
This is a magical story that explains how the efforts of one small person can help change the world in a way that children can understand.

Everyone Poops by Taro Gomi
This book uses simple illustrations and explanations to show a kid that going to the bathroom is perfectly natural. (You will love this book as well.)

Going to the Potty

by Fred Rogers

Mr. Rogers patiently and supportively explains potty training to parents and children.

Grandfather Twilight

by Ben Berger

This lovely story of Grandfather Twilight walking through the woods is thoroughly enchanting.

Kiss Good Night

by Hest/Jeram

A teddy bear reads a story to a little boy at bedtime.

Knuffle Bunny: A Cautionary Tale

by Mo Willems

A cautionary tale that teaches children to keep an eye on their favorite toy! Colorful illustrations combined with great Brooklyn photos are an added plus for New York parents.

Little Blue Truck

by Alice Schertle

This book teaches children kindness and cooperation through the story of animals helping a friendly truck that is stuck in the mud.

Lost and Found

by Oliver Jeffers

Beautifully illustrated and simply told, this heartwarming story explores the importance of friendship and companionship.

My Very First Mother Goose

by Iona Opie

This is a great rhyming book for the very young.

On The Night You Were Born

by Nancy Tillman

This is a beautifully illustrated book that reminds every child how special he or she is.

The Paper Bag Princess

by Robert Munsch

This is a wonderful twist on the classic Disney princess story. It's sure to bring out the feminist in even the youngest little girls!

The Peter Rabbit book series

by Beatrix Potter

(Peter Rabbit and Friends: A Stand-Up Story Book, Peter Rabbit: A Lift-the-Flap Rebus Story Book, Peter Rabbit's A B C and 1 2 3)

These books make learning interactive and fun.

Sesame Street Preschool Books

(The Sesame Street Word Book, Elmo's Lift-and-Peek Around the Corner Book, Tickle Me My Name is Elmo, Sesame Street Lift-and-Peek Party!, Lift and EEEEK! Monster Tales: There's a Monster in the Closet, The Monster at the End of This Book)

Kids love reading about characters from their favorite show—and everyone loves Elmo!

Spot Books

by Eric Hill

(Where's Spot?, Spot Goes to a Party, Spot Goes to School, Spot Goes to the Beach, Spot

Goes to the Farm, Spot Sleeps Over, Spot's Birthday Party, Spot's First Christmas, Spot's First Walk)
These books are great for every preschooler. Kids can lift the flaps to accompany Spot as he makes his way through many of his big firsts.

❊ Time for Bed
by Mem Fox and Jane Dyer
This new bedtime story is a great hit with simple text and great illustrations.

Classics

❊ Beatrix Potter books
(The Complete Tales, The Tale of Benjamin Bunny, The Tale of Peter Rabbit, The Tale of Squirrel Nutkin, The Tale of Tom Kitten, The Tale of Two Bad Mice)
For generations, children have enjoyed the cute, troublemaking little animals in Beatrix Potter's stories.

❊ Bread and Jam For Frances
by Russell and Lillian Hoban
Your picky eaters will learn the importance of trying new foods when they read about what happens when Frances's parents grant her wish to eat bread and jam at every meal.

❊ The Curious George book series
by H. A. Rey
(The Adventures of Curious George, Curious George Gets a Medal, Curious George Learns the Alphabet, Curious George Rides a Bike, Curious George Takes a Job, Curious George Flies a

Kite, Curious George Goes to the Hospital)
Curious George loves life in the city with the man in the yellow hat, but his curiosity for new things can get him into trouble!

❊ Dr. Seuss Books
(One Fish, Two Fish, Red Fish, Blue Fish, etc.)
These are silly, rhyming stories with amusing drawings and creative characters with the power to bring you back to your own childhood as well.

❊ George and Martha
by James Marshall
This classic series (originally published in the 1970s) shares the everyday experiences of two hippopotamuses who are best friends. It teaches children the importance of trust, privacy, positive thinking, and kindness—just to name a few.

❊ The Giving Tree
by Shel Silverstein
(Giraffe and a Half, The Missing Piece, The Missing Piece Meets the Big O)
This is the story of the lifelong friendship between a little boy and a very generous tree.

❊ Goodnight Moon*
by Margaret Wise Brown
Everyone loves this timeless, charming picture book about a little rabbit who says goodnight to everything, including the moon outside his window.

Guess How Much I Love You

by Sam McBratney and Anita Jeram

The story of a mommy and baby hare that has become a classic. We have read this to our children many times.

Harold and the Purple Crayon

by Crockett Johnson

(Harold's ABC, etc.)

Join Harold as he draws his way through adventures.

The Little Engine That Could*

by Watty Piper

This inspiring tale about the brave little engine has been popular for over seventy years for good reason.

Madeline

by Ludwig Bemelmans

(Madeline and the Bad Hat, Madeline and the Gypsies, Madeline in London, Madeline's Rescue, Mad About Madeline)

Follow Madeline and her friends on their adventures in Paris.

Make Way for Ducklings

by Robert McCloskey

(Blueberries for Sal, One Morning in Maine, Time of Wonder)

This classic book tells the tale of Mrs. Mallard and her eight ducklings crossing a busy Boston street.

Olivia

by Ian Falconer

(Olivia Saves the Circus, Olivia and the Missing Toy, Olivia Counts)

This little pig has lots of adventures.

Pat the . . . book series

by Dorothy Kunhardt

(Pat the Bunny, Pat the Cat, Pat the Puppy)

Your child will love touching the soft bunny and Daddy's scratchy face.

The Very Hungry Caterpillar*

by Eric Carle

(The Grouchy Ladybug, The Very Busy Spider, The Very Lonely Firefly)

This is a beautiful, interactive picture book about a caterpillar, which eats and eats until eventually turning into a butterfly.

Where the Wild Things Are

by Maurice Sendak

(Alligators All Around: An Alphabet, Chicken Soup With Rice: A Book of Months—one of Rebecca's favorites, One Was Johnny: A Counting Book, Pierre: A Cautionary Tale in Five Chapters and a Prologue, In the Night Kitchen)

When Max gets sent to his room without dinner, he sails off to the land of the wild things, where he can misbehave as much as he wants. But is this as great as it sounds? Also, check out Chicken Soup with Rice. This is how Rebecca and Benjamin learned the months of the year.

Other great reading recommendations

* *Ten, Nine, Eight*
  by Molly Bang

* *Brown Bear, Brown Bear, What Do You See?*
  by Bill Martin, Jr., and Eric Carle.
  Also *Polar Bear, Polar Bear, What Do You Hear?*

* *Jamberry*
  by Bruce Degan

* *Time for Bed*
  by Mem Fox and Jane Dyer

* *Bus Stops*
  by Taro Gomi

* *Diary of a Worm*
  by Doreen Cronin

* *Eating the Alphabet: Fruits and Vegetables from A to Z*
  by Lois Ehlert

* *Goodnight, Gorilla*
  by Peggy Rathmann

* *Happy Birthday, Moon*
  by Frank Asch

* *Jesse Bear, What Will You Wear?*
  by Nancy White Carlstrom

* *The Lady with the Alligator Purse*
  by Nadine Bernard Westcott

* *Library Lion*
  by Michelle Knudsen

* *The Line Up Book*
  by Marisabina Russo

* *The Paper Princess*
  by Elisa Kleven

* *Peek-A-Boo!*
  by Jan Ormerod

* *Sammy & Sue*
  by Suzanne Corso and Samantha Corso
  This book series is based on a mother-daughter team that seeks to educate children about the environment, the planet, nutrition, and how to lead to an eco-friendly or "green" life.

* *Silly Sally*
  by Audrey Wood

* *The Snowy Day*
  by Ezra Jack Keats

* *Toy Boat*
  by Randall de Seve and Loren Long

Special Needs Books

❋ *Adoption Is for Always*
by Linda Walvoord Girard and Judith Friedman

❋ *At Daddy's on Saturdays*
by Linda Walvoord Girard and Judith Friedman

❋ *The Day We Met You*
by Phoebe Koehler
A mother and father remember the exciting day they adopted their baby.

❋ *Dinosaurs Divorce: A Guide for Changing Families*
by Laurence Krasny Brown and Laurene Krensky

❋ *I Love You Like Crazy Cakes*
by Rose A. Lewis and Jane Dyer
The author recounts her own experiences while traveling to China to adopt a baby girl.

❋ *I'd Rather Laugh: How to Be Happy Even When Life Has Other Plans for You*
by Linda Richman
An inspirational look at how one mother survived losing a child.

❋ *Julius, Baby of the World*
by Kevin Henkes

❋ *Let's Talk About It: Divorce*
by Fred Rogers

❋ *Lifetimes: The Beautiful Way to Explain Death to Children*
by Bryan Mellonie

❋ *Over the Moon: An Adoption Tale*
by Karen Katz

❋ *Tell Me Again About the Night I Was Born*
by Jamie Lee Curtis and Laura Cornell

❋ *The Tenth Good Thing about Barney*
by Judith Viorst and Erik Blegvad
This classic book follows a young boy as he deals with his first experience of death.

❋ *We Adopted You, Benjamin Koo*
by Linda Walvoord Girard and Linda Shute

❋ *What's Heaven?*
by Maria Shriver and Sandra Speidel

❋ *When a Pet Dies*
by Fred Rogers

❋ *When Dinosaurs Die: A Guide to Understanding Death*
by Laurie Krasny Brown and Marc Brown

best books for parents

As a new mother, you'll want to stock your shelves with books by experts such as Penelope Leach, Dr. Spock, and T. Berry Brazelton. Here are a few more titles. You can get these books at any of the major bookstores or order them online. Also, don't forget to take advantage of your local library!

General

※ *The Baby Book: Everything You Need to Know About Your Baby from Birth to Age Two*
by William Sears, MD, and Martha Sears, RN

※ *The Best Children's Books of the Year*
by the Children's Book Committee of the Bank Street College of Education
A comprehensive annotated book list for newborns through age fourteen. The Children's Book Committee reviews over four thousand titles each year for accuracy and literary quality, as well as emotional impact on children and picks the best six hundred books for their list.

※ *Games Babies Play**
by Julie Hagstrom and Joan Morrill

※ *How to Calm and Soothe Your Baby*
by Harvey Karp, MD

※ *The Mother's Almanac**
by Marguerite Kelly and Elia S. Parsons

※ *The Parent's Guide to Baby and Child Medical Care*
by Terril H. Hart, MD

※ *The Pediatrician's Best Baby Planner for the First Year of Life*
by Daniel W. Dubner, MD and D. Gregory Felch, MD

※ *Practical Parenting for the 21st Century**
by Julie A. Ross

※ *Practical Parenting Tips*
by Vicki Lansky

※ *Solve Your Children's Sleep Problems**
by Richard Ferber
Pamela couldn't have survived the last seven years without this book! It's not for everyone, but it's definitely worth a close look.

※ *25 Things Every New Mother Should Know**
by Martha Sears, RN, and William Sears, MD

※ *What to Expect the First Year**
by Arlene Eisenberg, Heidi E. Murkoff, and Sandee E. Hathaway
This is referred to as the bible—as it should be. This is the month-by-month guide to your baby's first year.

※ *Your Amazing Newborn*
by M. Klaus and J. Kennell

* *Your Baby's First Three Years*
  by Dr. Paula Kelly

Breastfeeding

* *Breastfeeding: The Nursing Mother's Problem Solver*
  by Claire Martin, Nancy Funnemark Krebs, ed.

* *The Breastfeeding Book: Everything You Need to Know About Nursing Your Child From Birth to Weaning*
  by Martha Sears, RN

* *The Complete Book of Breastfeeding*
  by Marvin S. Eiger, MD and Sally Wendkos Olds

* *The Girlfriends' Guide to Toddlers*
  by Vicki Iovine
  The Vicki Iovine books are hilarious! Written for mothers by a mother who has seen it all with her four children.

* *How to Take Great Trips with Your Kids*
  by Sanford and Joan Portnoy

* *Kid's Book to Welcome a New Baby*
  by Barbara J. Collman

* *The Smart Parents' Guide to Kids T.V.*
  by Milton Chen, PhD

* *Successful Breastfeeding*
  by Nancy Dana and Anne Price

* *The Womanly Art of Breastfeeding**
  by La Leche League International

* *Your One-Year-Old to Your Four-Year-Old series*
  by Louise Bates Ames, PhD, and Frances L. Ilg, MD
  A series of books for each year of a child's life that highlights growth, development, and what to expect. Both of the series authors have taught and lectured at the Yale Child Study Center in New Haven.

Special Interests

* *In Praise of Single Parents*
  by Shoshana Alexander

* *The Manhattan Family Guide to Private Schools and Selective Public Schools*
  by Victoria Goldman and Catherine Hausman

* *Overachieving Parents and Under-achieving Children*
  by Dorothy Bodenburg, MFCC
  Particularly relevant to NYC moms who find they have their baby in five or six classes a week during the first year of life.

* *New York City's Best Public Elementary Schools: A Parent's Guide*
  by Clara Hemphill

The 7 O'Clock Bedtime
by Inda Schaenen
Discover the benefits of an early bedtime for the whole family!

The Single Mother's Book: A Practical Guide to Managing Your Children, Career, Home, Finances, and Everything Else
by Joan Anderson

Skinny Bitch Bun in the Oven: A Gutsy Guide to Becoming One Hot (and Healthy) Mother!
By Rory Freedman & Kim Barnouin
The newest book from Skinny Bitch authors highlighting the health benefits of a vegan pregnancy.

Twins from Conception to Five Years
by Averil Clegg and Anne Woolett

dvds

Almost all the superstores and many toy stores carry both children's entertainment and grown-up DVDs, covering a range of topics concerning new parents—breastfeeding, child development, and baby proofing. Also, don't forget your local library video store, Barnes & Noble, Borders, and Netflix for more video options.

In this day and age, everything can be found online. But because of how accessible video footage is, it has grown increasingly difficult to prescreen what your kids watch. With the help of an incredibly useful site called Kideos.com, you can now safely watch almost every child-friendly video that exists…on your computer! Developed by two parents whose daughter was seeking entertainment while being hospitalized, Kideos is the premier destination for kids to safely watch videos online. Each video on Kideos has been prescreened by their Video Advisory Council with the goal of empowering parents to feel comfortable allowing their child to spend time on Kideos, while also making sure children have a thoroughly entertaining experience. (www.kideos.com)

Best DVDs for Children

During your child's first two or three years, he is going to fall madly in love with Barney, Dora, Backyardigans, Big Bird, Winnie-the-Pooh, or some character that hasn't even been invented yet. You'll be renting or buying any number of videos featuring these lovable creatures, even if, like Kelly, you once swore no child of yours would ever watch a purple dinosaur sing.

Here's a listing of DVDs based on popular television series (the titles give you an idea of what each is about). All the DVDs listed here offer either fun and/or instruction:

Barney
(Best for nine months and up)
Children love sharing adventures with Barney and Baby Bop. Your child will love the sing-along songs, even if they drive you crazy.
Barney's Alphabet Zoo
Barney's Birthday*
Let's Pretend with Barney*

Riding in Barney's Car
Barney and Mother Goose*
And more . . .

✳ Backyardigans

(Ages two to five)
The show's five friends—Pablo, Tyrone, Uniqua, Tasha, and Austin—rely on their vivid imaginations to transform their backyard into completely different worlds in which they explore new stories and adventures.
Robot Repairman
Singing Sensation
Robin Hood the Clean
And more…

✳ Disney Spot Series

(Best for newborns to nine months)
The Spot series is just as charming as Eric Hill's books.
Spot Goes to the Farm
Spot Goes to School*
Spot Goes to a Party
Where's Spot?*
Sweet Dreams Spot

✳ Disney Classics

(Best for ages two or three and up)
Everybody loves the Disney classics, even Mom and Dad. The animation is enjoyable for all ages and the tales are timeless.
A Bug's Life
Aladdin
A Goofy Movie
Bambi
Cars

Cinderella and Cinderella 2
The Fox and the Hound
The Great Mouse Detective
The Lion King
Mulan
Up
Pocahontas
Sleeping Beauty
Snow White and the Seven Dwarfs
The Three Musketeers starring Mickey Mouse
Toy Story and Toy Story 2
Wall-E
One-Hundred-and-One Dalmatians
One-Hundred-and-Two Dalmatians
The Aristocats
And more...

✳ Disney's Winnie-the-Pooh Series

(Best for eighteen months and up)
Follow Winnie, Piglet, Tigger, and the others as they make their way from adventure to adventure. These are great because, aside from being fun, they teach valuable lessons.
Pooh Party
Pooh Learning
Cowboy Pooh
Sharing and Caring
Making Friends*
Winnie-the-Pooh and the Blustery Day
Winnie-the-Pooh and a Day for Eeyore
Winnie-the-Pooh and Tigger Too*
Winnie-the-Pooh and the Honey Tree

Julie Angier–Clark's Baby Series

(Best for newborn to age two)

What's better than cultural enrichment that's fun, too? This series was not around when our kids were newborns, but our new mommy friends swear by them as the only videos/DVDs their newborns will focus on.

Baby Bach

Baby Einstein

Baby Mozart

Baby Shakespeare

Richard Scarry

(Best for toddlers ages two to four)

Join the little worm Lowly and his friends in their animated adventures.

Richard Scarry's Learning Songs

Best Sing-along Mother Goose Video Ever!

Best Busy People Video Ever!

Best Counting Video Ever!

Best ABC Video Ever!

Best Silly Stories and Songs Ever!

Best Birthday Party Ever!

Sesame Street

(Best for twelve months and up)

Sesame Street DVDs are as educational as the television show. Elmo, Bert, Ernie, Big Bird, and other beloved characters will help teach your little one how to sing, spell, and say his or her ABCs.

My Sesame Street Home Video

Play-Along

Sesame Street Sing Along

Big Bird Sings

The Best of Bert and Ernie

Do the Alphabet

The Best of Elmo

Sing, Hoot & Howl with the Sesame Street Animals

Sesame Street's 25th Birthday Celebration

Thomas & Friends

Children learn important life lessons as they embark on exciting adventures with Thomas the tank engine and all of his friends.

Calling All Engines

Carnival Capers

Engines and Escapades

High Speed Adventures

Percy and the Bandstand

Railway Friends

Team Up With Thomas

Thomas' Trusty Friends

The Great Discovery

The Wiggles

The Wiggles are Australian children's entertainers who have rewritten the book about how children can be entertained with song and dance. Educational, fun, and addicting!

Cold Spaghetti Western

Dorothy Meets Santa Claus

Dorothy Memory Book

Dorothy the Dinosaur Party

Feel Like Dancing

Here Comes the BRC

Hoop Dee Doo

Hot Poppin' Popcorn

KOP Favourite Fairytales

Live Hot Potatoes

Make Me Feel Like Dancing

Pop Goes the Wiggles

Racing to the Rainbow
Sailing Around the World
Santa's Rockin' DVD
Sing a Song of Wiggles
Space Dancing
Splish Splash B R Boat
The Kingdom of Paramithi
Toot Toot
Top of the Tots
The Wiggles Big Big Show
The Wiggles Go Bananas
The Wiggles Movie
And more…!

❉ *WordWorld*

(Preschool ages)

In WordWorld (PBS Kids) words come alive, words save the day, and words become a child's best friend.

Bear's Masterpiece
Boppin' with the Bug Band
Castles in the Sea
Dancing Dog
Flying Ant
Happy Birthday WordFriends!
Happy Holidays WordFriends!
A Kooky Spooky Halloween
Lots of Letters Box Set
Lucky Duck
Meet the Letters
Meet the Sights Words 1 and 2
My Fuzzy Valentine
The Race to Mystery Island
Rocket to the Moon
Sheep's A Star
Welcome to WordWorld

Miscellaneous

(Eighteen months and up)
Here are some additional favorites of ours:
Baby Songs
Shari Lewis's Don't Wake Your Mom!
Wee Sing Grandpa's Magical Toys
Bedknobs and Broomsticks
Leap Frog—Letter Factory, Talking Words Factory
Rugrats in Paris, the Movie
The SpongeBob SquarePants Movie
The Wild Thornberrys Movie

DVDs for Parents

DVDs are an easy, convenient way to pick up parenting tips and gain some know-how. They will save you precious time by allowing you to stay at home with your little one. The Lifetime cable channel also offers some interesting parenting programming. Check your local listings.

Baby's Early Growth, Care, and Development

❉ *Baby's First Months "What Do We Do Now?"*

Developed by twelve pediatricians, it leads parents from birth through their baby's first few months. New parents are instructed on the daily care of a newborn.

❉ *The First Two Years: A Comprehensive Guide To Enhancing Your Child's Physical and Mental Development*

This award-winning video observes babies involved in everyday activities. The developmental periods are divided by age: one day to three months, three to six months, six to twelve months, and twelve to twenty-four months. Other topics include breastfeeding, early child care, infant nutrition, physical growth, and mobility/motor skills.

❋ *Dr. Jane Morton's Guide to Successful Breastfeeding*

Using a case study and graphics, this video shows the critical steps to comfortable, effective breastfeeding, including how to avoid common problems.

❋ *Touchpoints: The Definitive Video Series on Parenting, Volume 1: Pregnancy, Birth, and the First Weeks of Life**

This practical guide to child development defines Touchpoints as periods preceding rapid growth in learning, which are significant to future development. Points covered include pregnancy, delivery, preparation for birth, and the first weeks of your baby's life to three months.

❋ *Your Baby—A Video Guide to Care and Understanding with Penelope Leach*

A comprehensive and practical guide to newborn baby care and development, this video demonstrates techniques of everyday care in a variety of situations.

❋ *What Every Baby Knows— A Guide To Pregnancy*

An instructive DVD with sensible information concerning the development of children from birth to three months. It also explores a father's emotional involvement during pregnancy, gives a detailed profile of one couple's delivery, and

looks at typical issues that arise in the early months after birth.

Exercise/Well-Being

❋ *Jane Fonda's Pregnancy, Birth, and Recovery*

This exercise program demonstrates pregnancy and recovery workouts, baby massage, and infant care, and skills to physically prepare for birth.

❋ *Kathy Smith's Pregnancy Workout**

Both mothers-to-be and three different childbirth experts instruct mothers on how to maintain their energy and strength. Divided into prenatal and postnatal sections, the ninety-minute tape covers exercise for the new mothers up to six weeks after giving birth. Pamela used this tape to exercise at home, and found it challenging.

❋ *The Nursing Mothers Companion by Kathleen Hugging*

A how-to guide to nursing available on video and DVD.

Safety Videos

❋ *Barney Safety*

Barney and friends instruct little ones on safety with cars, traffic, and in the home.

❋ *Fire Safety for Kids with Beasel the Easel*

Endorsed by educators and firefighters, it teaches basic fire safety to children ages two and up. Children will enjoy the cast of characters and an original soundtrack.

CPR To Save Your Child or Baby*

This award-winning video carefully explains the step-by-step procedures of CPR, including instructions on the Heimlich maneuver and choking rescue. If you haven't had a chance to take a CPR-instruction class, this is the next best thing.

Infant and Toddler Emergency First Aid

(Volume 1: Accidents, Volume 2: Illnesses) These are endorsed by the American Academy of Pediatrics. They explain emergency medical services including the proper procedures and actions to take when giving CPR or dealing with choking or poisoning.

Metrobaby Manhattan: City Sights, Street Safety

Mr. Baby Proofer

Designed to teach parents how to make their home a baby-safe environment, this hands-on guide also describes key safety products.

Choosing Quality Child Care

It answers questions such as how to recognize quality child care, how to make sure a child is safe, and what to ask during an interview.

cds for children

Just because you have a baby doesn't mean you have to spend the next few years listening to terrible, sappy music. There's some great music being written for children these days; don't be amazed when you find yourself humming the tunes to yourself (even in the company of other adults). In fact, you can find a lot of the adult music you like recorded for children. Much of the music recommended here is in Baby's Best by Susan Silver, or the Music for Little People catalog (800-409-2757). Also, don't hesitate to listen to your own music in the car. Pamela's friend Elizabeth only listened to classical music on car rides with her son, and he not only became accustomed to it, but he enjoys it, even now as a seven-year-old!

Raffi

Baby Beluga
Bananaphone*
Grocery Corner Store and Others
Singable Songs for the Very Young

Joanie Bartel

Joanie Bartel's award-winning sound really appeals!
Lullaby Magic*
Bathtime Magic
Dancin' Magic*
Morning Magic
Sillytime Magic

Sesame Street

The Best of Elmo
Ernie's Side by Side
Family and Friends

Sesame Street Silly Songs
Sing-Along Travels
Sing the Alphabet

Other Suggestions

* A Child's Gift of Lullabies
  by Someday Baby
* Brett Band for Kids
  by Brett Rothenhaus
* Dance on a Moonbeam
  by David Grover
* G'Night Wolfgang by Ric Louchard
* Hap Palmer's Follow Along Songs*
* Hush-A-Bye Dreamsongs
* Little Mo' McCoury—an all-bluegrass
  all-kids album
  by Ronnie McCoury
* Lullabies of Broadway by Mimi Bessette
* Lullaby Berceuse by XYZ
* Peter, Paul, and Mommy
  by Peter, Paul, and Mary*
* Shakin' It by Parachute Express
* Sleep, Baby, Sleep by Nicolette Larson*
* The Lullaby and Goodnight Sleep Kit
* Sugar Beats* The Car Tunes is
  especially popular
* Toddlers Sing Storytime by Jerry Butler
* The Beatles for Kids
* Music by Laurie Berkner and David Grover is
  popular right now.

children's catalogs

Shopping by catalog can be the world's greatest convenience; there are loads of them, all filled with great things for babies and children, and all of these great things can be delivered right to your doorstep. Most of these catalogs also have websites, which makes shopping online easier than ever. Here are a few of our favorites offering one-of-a-kind accessories, toys, and practical imported clothing not available in stores.

* ## Chinaberry Book Service*
  2780 Via Orange Way, Suite B
  Spring Valley, CA 91978
  800-776-2242
  www.chinaberry.com
  Chinaberry has wonderful books for children, with the most detailed descriptions we've ever come across!

* ## Constructive Playthings*
  13201 Arrington Road
  Grandview, MO 64030
  800-832-0572
  www.ustoy.com
  An array of colorful, entertaining toys for young boys and girls, with a section called "First Playthings" that's especially good for newborns to one-year-olds.

* ## crewcuts
  800-562-0258
  JCrew.com
  I only wish my kids were young enough to fit into these adorable and stylish clothes. We have always loved J. Crew, and the clothing for the youngest set won't disappoint.

The Disney Catalog

of Children's Clothing

800-328-0612

www.disneydirect.com

All of the merchandise from your child's favorite Disney characters and movies.

Ecobaby Organics, Inc.

332 Coogan Way

El Cajon, CA 92020

888-ECO-BABY

www.ecobaby.com

This catalog has more than organic baby accessories—it also has nontoxic furniture, and a selection of breast pumps. It augments the Natural Baby Catalog very nicely.

Hanna Andersson*

1010 NW Flanders Street

Portland, OR 97209

800-222-0544

www.hannaandersson.com

Hanna Andersson carries moderately priced, superior quality cotton play clothes for young children, including swimwear and hats, plus some matching outfits for parents. These clothes last forever!

L.L. Bean Inc.

Freeport, ME 04033-0001

800-441-5713

www.llbean.com

Casual clothes for rugged kids. Great for outerwear. L.L. Bean is one of the few companies to offer clothing for larger body types.

Lilly's Kids

Lillian Vernon Corp.

Virginia Beach, VA 23479-0002

800-285-5555

www.lillianvernon.com

From Lillian Vernon, a catalog with well priced toys, games, and costumes.

The Natural Baby Catalog

7835 Freedom Avenue

North Canton, OH 44720

www.kidsstuff.com

The Natural Baby Catalog carries natural, ecological, and health-minded products, including cloth diaper covers, bedroom furniture, many beautifully crafted wooden toys, and books.

One Step Ahead*

75 Albrecht Drive

Lake Bluff, IL 60044

800-274-8440

www.onestepahead.com

One Step Ahead is good for baby products, including carriers/strollers, car seats, cribs, bottle holders, and some toys and clothing. Safety, travel, and mealtime helpers are also available.

OshKosh B'Gosh

1112 Seventh Avenue, P.O. Box 2222

Monroe, WI 53566-8222

800-692-4674

www.oshkoshbgosh.com

OshKosh is simple, all-American kids' wear, including classic denim overalls and jeans for your toddler or young child, in both boys' and girls' sizes.

Parenting and Family Life

P.O. Box 2153, Dept. PA7
Charleston, WV 25328
800-468-4227
www.cambridgeeducational.com
Extensive selection of videos on parenting, discipline, and health-and-safety issues.

Patagonia Mail Order

P.O. Box 8900
Bozeman, MT 59715
800-336-9090
www.patagonia.com
Patagonia is known for its own brand of rugged everyday clothing and parkas, as well as its cozy fleece jackets.

Perfectly Safe*

7245 Whipple Avenue, NW
North Canton, OH 44720
800-837-5437
www.kidsstuff.com
Safety gates, bathtub spout covers, and other items to child-proof a home.

Play Fair Toys

1690 28th Street
Boulder, CO 80302
800-824-7255
www.playfairtoys.com
Games, blocks, nesting animals, videos, and many other play items that just may help your little one learn to play fair.

Talbots for Kids

One Lakeville, MA 02348
800-543-7123
www.talbotskids.com
This is Kelly's favorite children's catalog and she buys lots of Angela's clothing from it. Amazing sales at the end of each season. The basics are as good as Gap if not better.

Toys to Grow On

P.O. Box 17
Long Beach, CA 90801
800-542-8338
www.ttgo.com
Every kind of toy you can think of, for newborns to preteens.

Troll's Learn & Play

100 Corporate Drive
Mahwah, NJ 07430
800-247-6106
www.magiccabin.com
Creative toys, costumes, activity books, videos, art supplies, and counting toys, mostly for ages two and up.

magazines for parents

There's always something to do with children in New York. Check these publications for monthly calendars plus services and helpful articles just for New York parents. Many are free at local shops. Here are some of the better ones.

New York Parents

❊ Big Apple Parent

www.parentsknow.com

This monthly publication features topical articles on parenting and kids. It has been around for over ten years and is an invaluable resource for Manhattan parents.

❊ The bump

www.thebump.com/new-york

Thebump.com is an informative website that offers everything from baby registries to top baby names. Their publication, the bump, has a New York edition that is super helpful for New York City parents.

❊ New York Family

www.newyorkfamily.com

This monthly magazine offers useful event calendars as well as features on everything from children's health to traveling with kids.

❊ Observer Playground

(*The New York Observer's* monthly magazine)
www.observer.com/playground

Dynamo Lyss Stern is the editor in chief of this upscale and informative magazine for New York City parents.

❊ Parent Guide

212-213-8840
www.parentguidenews.com

This monthly magazine is for New York families with young children offering information on schools, camps, entertainment, and more.

National Magazines

Two of our favorite magazines are *Parents* and *Child*, but all of the magazines listed offer practical advice and information on parenting and child development.

❊ American Baby

www.americanbaby.com

A monthly magazine for expectant parents and parents of children one and under.

❊ Baby Talk

www.babytalk.com

A monthly magazine for expectant parents and parents of children two and under.

❊ Child*

www.childmagazine.com

A popular, authoritative magazine full of information for parents of newborns through teens.

Parents*

www.parents.com

The most popular and informative magazine out there for parents. A favorite of Kelly's! The website is super, too.

Twins Magazine

www.twinsmagazine.com

The only bimonthly national magazine for parents of twins.

Working Mother

www.workingmother.com

A monthly magazine for parents of infants through teens.

Best Mom Blogs

Baby Gizmo

www.babygizmo.com

Dedicated exclusively to baby products, news, reviews, and price comparison.

Dooce

www.dooce.com

Heather B. Armstrong's humorous and painfully blunt take on all the ins and outs of being a woman, a mother of two, and everything else in between.

MYOB Moms*

www.myobmoms.com

Mind Your Own Business Moms founders Pamela Weinberg and Barri Waltcher created MYOB Moms to help women discover their personal passions and use them as a guide as

they consider re-entering the workforce.

Mom Prep

www.momprepnyc.com

Online resource for new moms including info, classes, tips, seminars, and events!

Moms Like Me

www.momslikeme.com

"Where local moms meet." Talk with other local moms, share advice and photos, organize events and groups, and find other moms just like you.

My Baby Radio*

www.mybabyradio.com

An around-the-clock website and radio station for families and new parents; includes interviews with all types of parents, including celebrities who have children as well as experts on parenting.

My Baby To Do

www.mybabytodo.com

A comprehensive parenting community online.

NYC Moms Blog

www.nycmomsblog.com

Part of the larger silicon Valley moms blog, this is a place for mom bloggers. Pamela is a contributor.

Role Mommy, LLC

www.rolemommy.com

Role Mommy is an online community and events company created to inspire, entertain, and inform today's busy moms.

❊ Stroller Traffic NY*

www.strollertraffic.com/new-york
Published by a former *New York* magazine editor, Tara Mandy, StrollerTraffic is a free weekly email and website for city moms with kids under three, designed to keep you posted on the latest inventions, developments, and trends in the world of babies and toddlers.

❊ Urbanbaby.com

A resourceful website with a blog component and the hottest message board in New York City.

❊ Woman Around Town*

www.womanaroundtown.com
Woman Around Town will help you find what you are looking for—a new restaurant, spa, apartment, or weekend getaway. Pamela has been a frequent writer here.

index

About the Authors

PAMELA WEINBERG is a NYC mom is a contributor to the Nycmomsblog.com and the E.L.F. Cosmetics blog where she writes on parenting and mom related topics. Pamela is a frequent speaker on baby-related topics in the Tri-state area. Pamela's latest venture, Mind Your Own Business Moms, is dedicated to helping moms return to the workplace (www.myobmoms.com).

KELLY ASHTON writes and speaks on child-related topics. She holds a B.A. from Yale University and an M.B.A. from Harvard.